Accepting Ourselves & Others

*A Journey into Recovery
from Addictive and Compulsive Behaviors
for Gays, Lesbians & Bisexuals*

Sheppard B. Kominars, Ph.D.
Kathryn D. Kominars, Ph.D.

 HAZELDEN®

Hazelden
Center City, Minnesota 55012-0176
1-800-328-9000 (Toll Free U.S., Canada, and the Virgin Islands)
1-612-257-4010 (Outside the U.S. and Canada)
1-612-257-1331 (24-hour FAX)
http://www.hazelden.org (World Wide Web site on Internet)

Library of Congress Cataloging-in-Publication Data
Kominars, Sheppard B.
    Accepting ourselves and others : a journey into recovery from addictive and compulsive
behaviors for gays, lesbians,and bisexuals / Sheppard B. Kominars, Kathryn D. Kominars.
— 2nd ed.
        p.   cm.
    Rev. ed. of: Accepting ourselves. New York : HarperCollins, © 1989.
    Includes bibliographical references and index.
    ISBN 1-56838-120-4
    1. Gays—Alcohol use—United States. 2. Gays—Substance use—United States.
3. Alcoholics—Rehabilitation—United States. 4. Addicts—Rehabilitation—United States.
5. Alcoholism counseling—United States. 6. Twelve-step programs—United States.
7. Compulsive behavior—United States. I. Kominars, Kathryn D. II. Kominars, Sheppard B.
Accepting ourselves.
III. Title.
HV5139.K65   1996
362.29'2'08664—dc20

                                                                        96-25095
                                                                        CIP

                00 99 98 97 96   6 5 4 3 2 1

                Book design by Ginger McCauley
                Cover design by David Spohn
        Typesetting by Universal Press and Link, Minneapolis, Minnesota

Editor's note
    Hazelden offers a variety of information on chemical dependency and related areas. Our
publications do not necessarily represent Hazelden's programs, nor do they officially speak
for any Twelve Step organization.
    The Twelve Steps are reprinted with permission of Alcoholics Anonymous World
Services, Inc. Permission to reprint the Twelve Steps does not mean that AA has reviewed or
approved the contents of this publication, nor that AA agrees with the views expressed
herein. AA is a program of recovery from alcoholism *only*—use of the Twelve Steps in connection with programs and activities that are patterned after AA, but that address other
problems, does not imply otherwise.

In loving memory:

Mary Kominars, Alma Granoff,
and Harold Kominars

And to all the others who have helped us along the way

A survivor's testimony is more important than anything that can be written about survivors. It's important for them, important for the world. And for me, that is the most rewarding thing—to free, to open up the survivors. They live clandestinely. What made their being most unique was something they hid. That is most tragic—to suffer and then to suffer for having suffered.

—ELIE WIESEL

◁ CONTENTS ▷

The greatest gifts of recovery are the people who have touched our lives with love and friendship. Their insights and understanding and support have made us richer, by far, than we can ever account. We are grateful for the sense of family, connection, these loving individuals have shared with us. Many are no longer with us and we acknowledge our deep indebtedness to their memory.

To those who remain, Kathryn would like to thank Portia Hunt, James Mallon, Stiles Seay, Cynthia Thompson, and Linda Wood. I wish to thank David Azzolina, Allen Burke, John Bush, Ben Gardiner, K Kaufman, Lionel Kranitz, Lani Lange, Vivien Larsen, Tom Moon, Elmer Olhaber, Michael Picucci, Anne Prescott, Tillie R., Jerry Rehm, Kenneth L. Schmidt, and Andy Street.

Both Kathryn and I are deeply grateful for all the care and patience in editing that Marvin D. Appelbaum, my friend and partner for the past ten years, spent in helping us develop this second edition. We also wish to thank Dan Odegard and Steve Lehman at Hazelden Publications for their invaluable support for this project. We could not have done it without all of you and all of your gifts. Our lives are changed by those who love us, and we are grateful.

To the reader:

I have heard some people glibbly say that "Recovery is simple, but not easy." I dis-agree with the first part and agree with the second. Recovery is difficult, and it's not easy. And addiction is even more difficult. Recovery is difficult, and it is possible! Recovery is difficult and it is worth it! Do not lose hope. If you have picked up this book because you are wondering whether you need to start a "recovery process," be assured that there is help waiting for you. Lots of help, in fact! Do not despair. Help comes in lots of forms. It is important to be open to the ways in which help can appear. Getting help is not as difficult as being open to receiving that help when it arrives in a different form than expected.

It is essential to be open to the many types of help available. One of the things that has been in the foreground of my mind while writing this book is to provide a wide array of information about the many varieties of help available. With this overview of what is available, I hope that you will be encouraged to explore the helping approach that seems inviting to you at this time. Help that works for you at one point in your life may not help at some other point in time. That does not mean that help is not there. It means that you must seek help from a different source.

KATE KOMINARS, PH.D., C.A.C.
Ft. Lauderdale, Florida
July 1996

"Think, Think, Think!" NOT "Dwell, Dwell, Dwell!" People recovering from addictive/compulsive behavior often remain stuck in the past instead of creating a new history. Shying away from tales of old horror stories told at Twelve Step meetings, many lesbians, gay men, and bisexuals seek support in exploring the road into the new lives they are struggling to create.

Because recovery from any form of addiction is different for gays, lesbians, and bisexuals, it requires special attention and sensitivity. Individualized, personalized approaches that maintain privacy, support one-on-one and group counseling, and provide exercises that lay the groundwork for changes are essential for anyone struggling with addictive/compulsive behavior. *Accepting Ourselves and Others: A Journey into Recovery from Addictive and Compulsive Behavior for Gays, Lesbians, and Bisexuals,* is an expanded edition of *Accepting Ourselves* (Harper & Row 1989). The revised text consists of three sections: part I, "Understanding and Navigating the Issues"; part II, "Exercising the Twelve Steps in Your Life" (including workbook sections for each chapter); part III, "For Therapists."

Accepting Ourselves and Others is written for beginners and "old-timers" in and outside all Twelve Step programs, and is for both clients and the psychotherapists or addiction specialists to whom they have come for help. Internalized homophobia—a basic cause of individual and societal denial and neglect—is dealt with head-on so that it no longer inhibits the healing process of gays, lesbians, and bisexuals who suffer from addictive/compulsive behavior.

Accepting Ourselves and Others also reflects the changes that have occurred over the past years in the recovery field. It provides new and insightful hands-on material to meet the needs of gay men, lesbians, bisexuals, psychotherapists, parents and friends of gays, as well as Twelve Step groups across the entire spectrum of addictive/compulsive behavior.

Accepting Ourselves and Others offers a broad range of materials with a positive, intimate, gay/lesbian user-friendly perspective. It addresses major recovery issues, such as an analysis of alternative models of addiction, the use of professional therapists, the use of medication, switching addictions, and HIV-positive and HIV-negative concerns. Part II presents the Twelve Steps in a unique modular workbook approach that has been field-tested over the past six years.

Each chapter of part II contains left brain and right brain exercises: creating lists, identifying alternatives, creating affirmations, visualizing changes, guided meditations, developing new skills, journal keeping, making connections with both helpful and hindering behavior, exploring previous relationships, considering dreams and fantasies in terms of wishes, reading selections, etc. These exercises help readers to explore themselves exactly as they are and to acknowledge what they discover as the basis on which they can take an active role in the process of accepting themselves—and others.

Why Is This Book Needed?

In the United States, at least one person in ten suffers from some form of dependency on addictive/compulsive behavior. In the gay and lesbian community, it appears that this ratio leaps to one in three! Individuals, as well as their communities, continue to be in deep denial of these appalling statistics.

In spite of this denial, over 20,000 copies of the first edition of *Accepting Ourselves* were sold from 1989 to 1994. *Accepting Ourselves* was nominated for a Lambda Literary Award in Nonfiction, and has been on the Hazelden list of educational materials since it first appeared. The need for cogent information about therapy and the Twelve Steps that will reach out to gay men, lesbians, and bisexuals has been amply demonstrated by the use of this book by individuals and groups all over the United States and abroad.

The need continues to grow for more current information that will speed the recovery progress of gay men, lesbians, and bisexuals. In spite of all of the other titles in the field of addiction, the audience for *Accepting Ourselves and Others* is very large: gay/nongay/bisexual men and women and groups in all of the Twelve Step programs, individuals not in any program or even in recovery, psychotherapists or other clinical specialists working with clients with compulsive behavior issues, school counselors, and parents, family, clergy, and friends of lesbians and gays.

Accepting Ourselves and Others presents a useful reference list/bibliography for the entire field of recovery. Valuable appendices are also identified.

Accepting Ourselves and Others provides everyone with a deeper understanding of certain conditions that many gay men and lesbians, for most of their lives, have denied or minimized. To accept ourselves without any intellectual understanding of what we are accepting keeps us always off balance, always at the mercy of the next assault. This is a road map written *for* gays, lesbians, and bisexuals to provide an important dimension, as well as an experience-based context and perspective, for the process of healing that is necessary in recovery from addictive/compulsive behavior.

In a normal, healthy growth process, the individual searches for knowledge and understanding. Wanting to belong, to be part of society, many homosexuals deny their homosexuality to the world (and often to themselves); wanting to recover, they need intellectual as well as emotional supports to enhance the process of acceptance of their sexuality. Those who have already begun the recovery process from addictive/compulsive behavior are constantly looking for insightful material to provide them with a sense of safety and self-identification in the midst of their struggle.

For gays, lesbians, and bisexuals who live in large cities with specifically identified Twelve Step meetings in each of the recovery programs, along with other kinds of support groups, there are extensive resources to encourage the process. For those who live far from these centers, and for those whose lives are painfully closeted, there is a significant need for additional perspective and support. This book provides an understanding and understandable companion for those who need one in times of discouragement and stress.

Many parents, spouses, and children and friends of gays, lesbians, and bisexuals; those in other Twelve Step programs like Al-Anon and Adult Children of Alcoholics; and those who do not participate in Alcoholics Anonymous, Narcotics Anonymous, Overeaters Anonymous, or any other support system often suffer from some form of "alcohomophobia"—fear of the gay or lesbian substance abuser. For their own recovery, they need to better understand the predicament of their loved ones, as well as the efforts they themselves can make to focus on their own well-being. We have written *Accepting Ourselves and Others* to provide a perspective in which they can participate positively in the recovery process instead of continuing to suffer from either guilt over the past or fear of the future.

Psychotherapists who work with gays, lesbians, and bisexuals will also find this book useful because it provides specific details about the steps of the healing process, along with information about the experience and perspective of those who have come to them for help.

Nongay men and women who are concerned with addictive/compulsive behavior and the process of recovery may also find useful insights and workbook exercises to assist their understanding of this journey. *Accepting Ourselves and Others* explores the learning process in which individuals become active participants in their own recovery and find freedom from addictive/compulsive behavior.

Over fifteen years have passed since my daughter, Kathryn, and I began our journey in recovery. This book that we have written together is a record of our own experience encountering the obstacles and challenges of recovery in our lives and in the lives of those we have had the privilege of working with, individually or in groups. Motivating us to develop this new edition has been our personal commitment to help others who, like us, are still finding the way. We hope you will find it a useful companion for your journey.

After it was published in 1989, many readers wrote and shared their insights and experience using *Accepting Ourselves*. With this new publication, we are looking forward to receiving comments from everyone who wishes to write to us. We know that your comments will be invaluable for future editions. Please let us hear from you either through our publisher or on the Website we have created for this purpose. The address of this Web page is **http://sibyllineofbooks.com/acceptingourselves.html**.

PART I

Understanding and Navigating the Issues

CHAPTER 1

Alternative Models of Addiction

Many different approaches are used to explain the causes and treatment of addictive/compulsive behavior. A brief overview of four representative models developed over the years will help us to understand the issues this book will explore. Both the models and their implications complicate the problems of gays, lesbians, and bisexuals in recovery.

The *Moral Model* considers individuals with addictive/compulsive behavior to be weak and morally deficient. If relapse (i.e., a return to obsessive/compulsive behavior) occurs, it is the result of moral deficiency.

The second model, the *Medical Model,* widely endorsed by treatment programs around the country, sees addiction as being caused by an underlying disease from which individuals can recover with medical intervention. In this approach, physicians and other trained individuals assist individuals in their recovery.

The *Spiritual,* or *Enlightenment Model,* on which Alcoholics Anonymous (AA) and other Twelve Step programs are based, is a third approach. This model assumes that individuals with addictive/compulsive behavior are powerless over the development of their addiction—and of their recovery, as well. Reliance on a power greater than the individual self—God or Higher Power—and the Twelve Steps brings about recovery.

Model four is the *Social Learning Model.* According to this approach, individuals have learned addictive/compulsive behaviors as strategies to cope with problems. The learned strategies are the problem, not the individual. Individuals are helped to make active changes with the implementation of a new learning process, called "relapse-prevention therapy." It uses a variety of techniques, such as helping individuals identify situations that may have a high risk for relapse. Treatment focuses on helping individuals develop new strategies and coping skills to prevent relapses.

It is important to note that even though these models have been implemented in treatment programs across the country, research has been unable to prove that any one approach is more successful than another.[1] Frequently, aspects of one model have been integrated into another, creating a multimodal treatment approach.

Research on the treatment of addictive/compulsive behavior has focused on comparing outpatient programs with inpatient programs. In many clinical settings, alcohol and drug users are treated together, along with individuals with different histories of substance abuse and substance dependence. The results of these studies are therefore inconclusive. Even though modified drinking has been explored, the predominant treatment models stress complete abstinence from all forms of alcohol and all self-prescribed medications, regardless of the diagnosis of substance abuse or substance dependence. (See chapter 26 for a more in-depth exploration of the models.)

Implications for Gays, Lesbians, and Bisexuals

Moral Model

Because of their sexual orientation, gays and lesbians are already vulnerable to feeling less-than, not-as-good-as, or second-rate. Adding moral impairment to this attitude further erodes self-esteem.

The Moral Model is based on the belief that some people are constitutionally incapable, because of moral deficiency, of dealing with life. Such persons lack a backbone and consequently must rely on alcohol or drugs or compulsive behavior as a crutch in order to survive.

The morals of gays, lesbians, and bisexuals have been a traditional focus of condemnation by heterosexuals. Whether heterosexuals are less promiscuous than homosexuals or bisexuals is moot. Gays, lesbians, and bisexuals are already the focus of societal disapproval that results in feelings of shame and guilt. The Moral Model adds further weight to this already crushing load.

Medical Model

In the Medical Model, addictive/compulsive behavior is treated as a medical condition requiring the advice and treatment of a medical professional. If the doctor is already biased about homosexuality—that it is a "disease" in need of "curing"—this raises additional concerns about revealing sexual orientation.[2] Sexual minorities already have difficulty confiding and trusting in anyone in positions of authority. Giving power to any authority inhibits reliance on our own internal strengths and values that are essential for maintaining positive self-identity in a homophobic, heterosexist society.

Seeking treatment poses other risks. In addition to being gay, lesbian, or bisexual, the person may obtain still another label, such as "alcoholic" or "addict." (The extensive variation in the meaning of these terms in different parts of the country is itself the source of confusion for everyone.) Being "diseased" does not enhance the self-image of any gay, lesbian, or bisexual, nor does the possibility of risking identification through insurance reimbursement appeal to those who wish to *and need to* maintain a low profile on the job.

Spiritual Model

Some implications of the Spiritual Model for gays and lesbians relate to concerns about religious authority. Despite focusing on a Higher Power or a personal God "of our own understanding," this model, in its pure form, is really about *God*. Because most people come from cultures and organized religions (the Judeo-Christian tradition) in which God is a male figure, issues of patriarchy and male chauvinism can become a dominating force in this modality.

Many sexual minorities, regardless of gender, have difficulty thinking about any male spiritual figure as a benevolent entity that would interact in a positive manner to help them. They may have already suffered the effects of spiritual abuse from religion's staunchest proponents, having been condemned for who they are. Given such life experiences, why would sexual minorities seek help from a deity that damns them? As a result, AA and other Twelve Step self-help programs may seem to espouse a kind of religious dogmatism to the extent that they require members to take the program *on faith*. This may feel like simply more oppression!

The impression of needing to believe in a Higher Power to belong in AA can, therefore, be quite an obstacle for many sexual minorities.[3] In particular, many women have been taught to think of themselves as less-than-men. The need for an external male power to "fix" oneself seems like more male chauvinism, just in a different form. The past several hundred years of spiritual abuse of gays and lesbians and bisexuals can leave them with doubt that they can experience much comfort or confidence in a spiritual-treatment approach.

Social Learning Model

According to the Social Learning, or Biopsychosocial, Model, people learn from and are conditioned by their environment to respond to problems by drinking or by using other substances to take away pain, or to get needs met. This viewpoint, in itself, is particularly important for gays and lesbians who may not have had needs met in formative years. Without appropriate reinforcement from other sources, we have taken matters into our own hands and learned, in a culture that supports the use of substances, to use these substances to cope with problems.

The Social Learning perspective fails to account for extensive research indicating that family history and heredity are important components in compulsive/addictive behavior. Also, individuals can misconstrue the implications of the Social Learning Model and focus on blaming themselves for what they have learned. While taking personal responsibility for change is an important dimension of recovery, people gain nothing useful by blaming themselves for biological, genetic preconditions or for learning behaviors that once appeared effective and adaptive.

Alternatives in Treatment

Most chemical dependency treatment programs in the United States stress complete abstinence from all forms of alcohol and all self-prescribed medications, regardless of the diagnosis of substance abuse or substance dependence.[4] There has been an intentional association between treatment programs and Twelve Step programs, with the latter seen as a source of social support for individuals. In practice, some chemical dependency treatment programs based on the Medical Model have adapted concepts and intervention strategies (relapse-prevention approaches, coping-skills training, and relaxation and visualization procedures) from *outside* the theoretical orientation of the Medical Model, or even the Spiritual Model. However, these strategies are frequently modified and incorporated into Medical Model programs without understanding that they are not necessarily part of treatment interventions that require individuals to select abstinence as the only possible (and acceptable) treatment goal.

Another treatment alternative is "Guided Self-Change," a motivational intervention premised on the idea that individuals "with alcohol problems can solve their problems on their own if they are sufficiently motivated and are provided with some guidance and support" (Sobell & Sobell 1993b, xi).

And still another alternative for individuals who feel that they have a drinking problem is "Moderation Management," a nine-step program aimed at helping people reduce their alcohol consumption.[5] This alternative, intended for individuals who have encountered mild-to-moderate degrees of alcohol-related problems, is connected with the Moderation Management Network, a support group network intended to help people reduce their drinking.[6]

The majority of individuals with drinking problems do not seek formal treatment (Imber et al. 1976; Narrow et al. 1993; Sobell et al. 1992), and many individuals who never receive professional treatment become stably abstinent or moderate drinkers. A great deal more research is needed on people with addictive/ compulsive behavior and the various treatment modalities before there is conclusive evidence for advocating one approach over any of the others.

Inpatient, Outpatient

A physician who has specialized in addiction medicine is an excellent resource to assess whether or not detoxification is medically necessary. Following detoxification, when needed, different treatment environments are available.

Outpatient counseling entails meeting with the therapist, one-on-one, at different intervals: once a week, twice a month, or over a period of months. The schedule can vary according to the practitioner, the circumstances, the client's needs, and other factors. Treatment might include group therapy, or it might not. There are different combinations.

A variety of *inpatient treatment* programs are offered around the country. These programs vary in intensity and duration. The recent emphasis on having people receive the least-restrictive treatment possible and on making treatment as cost-effective as possible has diminished considerably the number of people going for inpatient treatment, as well as the length of hospital stays. Essentially, inpatient treatment is currently reserved for those who are most severely impaired and who have the greatest need to be in a controlled environment.

Inpatient programs often require health insurance. Many gays and lesbians are underemployed for a variety of social reasons and therefore work at jobs that offer no health insurance for addiction treatment. Those who do have this coverage, if they need to be open about sexuality, may feel considerable anxiety over having employers pay for it. Signing the releases so the health care provider can receive insurance reimbursement can be a cause of deep concern. Frequently, the terms of the release are unclear, raising the fear that someone in the company may see case material. Another concern is that down the road, information will be revealed to someone who has no reason or right to know. Unless there is anonymity, there is risk that the record can be accessed.

Intensive outpatient treatment, as an alternative to inpatient programs, often spreads treatment out so that it doesn't interfere with a client's livelihood or remove a client from social supports. Clients can get treatment while in the midst of life, and receive the needed support to make the necessary changes. If problems arise in maintaining whatever treatment goal is set, the therapist can either alter the goal or arrange for more intensive treatment.

Unless clearly indicated otherwise, treatment should start with the least intensive method. Beginning with outpatient treatment can provide insight into the individual's problems and a basis for working them out. If that approach is not successful, intensive outpatient treatment can be initiated. If still unsuccessful, inpatient treatment can be recommended.

Choosing a Treatment Program

Inpatient programs designed to meet the needs of sexual minorities provide several benefits. In these treatment programs, gays, lesbians, and bisexuals can talk more openly and comfortably about sexual orientation issues. They can meet others who have been through the same experiences, and they do not have to come out to a group of presumed heterosexuals in order to address issues related to sexual orientation and addictive/compulsive behavior. In such a treatment program, individuals will not have to listen to homophobic comments or jokes or encounter other manifestations of homophobia. Alternatively, some wonderful healing happens when we learn we *can* take these risks in treatment programs with heterosexuals. We can be surprised that the experience differs from what we anticipated.

An environment that encourages openness and honesty is a critical factor for gays, lesbians, and bisexuals in every treatment program. During our treatment, it is essential for us to feel free enough to explore the complex issues we are facing now, along with those waiting for us in the future. If we can do this, we have much greater prospects for successfully changing addictive/compulsive behavior.

If an inpatient treatment program is necessary, the available options may be limited by insurance coverage reimbursement factors. For example, only certain facilities may be covered by a specific insurance plan.

There are some general differences between inpatient treatment programs. Some are hospital-based with all the advantages, disadvantages, and costs associated with hospitals. These programs are well suited for medical detoxification and emergency consultation with other medical providers. Other inpatient treatment programs are "freestanding" in the community, with varying degrees of medical intervention available. These facilities usually admit individuals who do not require medically supervised detoxification, or those who have received such services elsewhere.

Beyond these major distinctions there is little substantive difference in inpatient treatment programs. Although many programs will say they use a multimodal or biopsychosocial treatment approach, in the United States almost all chemical dependency inpatient treatment programs are based on a combination of the Medical and Spiritual models, with a treatment goal of complete abstinence.

Programs generally provide a majority of the clinical treatment in a group setting. This fact is particularly relevant for gays, lesbians, and bisexuals. As mentioned, it is essential that the treatment setting be a safe environment for sexual minorities. The staff providing the treatment should be capable of creating this environment and have an understanding of the issues and concerns of sexual minorities. Although the need is great for competence in this area, formal training is not currently required. Therefore, it is imperative for the gay, lesbian, or bisexual considering inpatient treatment to determine what type of environment the program is likely to promote.

In addition, the person considering inpatient treatment may be in crisis and a lengthy exploration and screening process, such as one might conduct in order to find a therapist, is not feasible. In such cases, it is advisable to seek the assistance of a family member, friend, or therapist who is capable of helping select an appropriate treatment program.

Just as there are treatment programs specially designed to meet the needs of certain groups (e.g., religious or medical professionals) there is an inpatient treatment program located in Minnesota called Pride Institute, the nation's only JCAHO accredited chemical dependency treatment center exclusively for lesbian, gay, and bisexual patients.[7]

❋   ❋   ❋

CHAPTER 2

Stages in Addiction; Stages in Recovery

The Progression of Addiction

Tracing the progression of addiction is very helpful in determining whether or not the individual is chemically dependent or has a drinking problem (and, if so, to what degree). An individual can go from social drinking to alcoholism, according to the National Institute on Alcohol Abuse and Alcoholism, in many ways. Jellinek's studies (1952, 1971) with individuals severely dependent on alcohol showed a progression of the effects of alcohol on the individual:

- First is the *prealcoholic stage,* where the person drinks socially and, on occasion, heavily, to relieve tension or to forget about problems. In times of crisis, the person drinks more and more heavily and resorts, more frequently, to the comforting effects of alcohol.

- The second stage is the *prodromal stage,* where drinking becomes secretive and may be accompanied by blackouts, when the person remains conscious and relatively coherent, but cannot remember later what happened. In this stage the person becomes more and more preoccupied and involved with drinking and feels guilty about it, and worries about when and where she or he will have the next drink.

- Then, there is the *crucial stage,* in which all control is lost. The person starts drinking and continues until stupor. Social adjustments deteriorate; there is morning drinking. Abstinence is still possible; individuals can go for several weeks without drinking, but once they take a drink, the whole pattern begins again. This is called the "crucial" stage because, unless individuals get help, there is danger of entering the fourth stage.

- The fourth stage is the *chronic stage:* drinking is continual. The individual lives only to drink; the body has become so accustomed to alcohol that the person suffers withdrawal symptoms without it. The person has lost all concern for physical appearance, self-esteem, family, friends, and social status. This is the stage of the "skid-row drunk."

One problem with this classification system is that it does not offer enough ways to categorize people. It does not identify people who binge-drink, and who experience great ability to control their drinking. There may be times between binges when they are drinking only socially; and then, suddenly, they binge. It also does not help to understand those individuals who would consider themselves as "problem drinkers" but who would not consider themselves as "prealcoholic."

Another classification system is Jellinek's (1960) alpha, beta, gamma, delta, epsilon typology. Jellinek asserted that there are five species of alcoholism, and he labeled them with Greek letters. The five species are as follows (Heather & Robertson 1983, 11):

> *Alpha alcoholism* is said to represent a purely psychological and continual dependence or reliance upon the effect of alcohol to relieve bodily or emotional pain. There is no pharmacological addiction. Drinking may be undisciplined and may contravene the rules of society but does not lead to loss of control. Some instances may simply be developmental forerunners of alcohol addiction, but in respect of pure alpha alcoholism there are no signs of a progressive process. The alpha alcoholic is clearly equivalent to Jellinek's (1952) "habitual, symptomatic excessive drinker."
>
> *Beta alcoholism* refers to the presence of physical complications from excessive drinking, such as polyneuropathy, gastritis and liver cirrhosis, but without any physical or psychological dependence. In this case, heavy drinking may reflect customs of a particular social group combined with poor nutritional habits. Beta alcoholism may also develop into alcohol addiction but the transition is less likely than with the alpha variety.
>
> *Gamma alcoholism* is the term used to refer to what Jellinek (1952) called "alcohol addiction" and is the species he describes as having been molded in the image of Alcoholics Anonymous. It is characterized by (i) acquired increased tissue tolerance to alcohol; (ii) adaptive cell metabolism; (iii) withdrawal symptoms and craving (i.e., physical dependence); and (iv) loss of control. In this species alone there is a definite progression from psychological to physical dependence, accompanied by the behavioral deterioration described in Jellinek (1952). The type of loss of control attributed to gamma alcoholics was termed by Marconi (1959) "inability to stop."
>
> *Delta alcoholism* shows the first three characteristics of gamma alcoholism just listed but instead of "inablility to stop" there is "inability to abstain." That is, the ability to control intake on any

given occasion remains unaffected but there is no capacity for abstention from alcohol even for a few days without the occurrence of withdrawal symptoms. This species is associated especially with the "inveterate drinking" found in France and other wine-drinking countries and, hence, there may be little pre-alcoholic psychologcial vulnerability.

Epsilon alcoholism describes the relatively rare and little known form of periodic alcoholism, previously called dipsomania.[1]

Unfortunately, many caregivers are still using this typology in treatment programs without realizing it is based on only a small segment of Jellinek's work (i.e., thinking that everyone is a "gamma alcoholic") (Willerman & Cohen 1990). Many people use addictive substances but only a fraction become addicted: only 8 to12 percent of regular drinkers are addicted to alcohol, and only 25 percent of heroin users are addicted (Jaffe 1980, 509).

Treatment providers usually assess the severity of addiction on the basis of four clinical features: 1. *preoccupation* with the drug; 2. *tolerance,* such that a larger dose is needed to produce the results achieved with the smaller, previous dose; 3. *dependency,* with psychological withdrawal symptoms, such as agitation and depression, and physiological withdrawal symptoms, such as seizures or cramps occurring after abrupt cessation of the drugs; 4. *debilitation* of social and physiological functions (Willerman & Cohen 1990, 509).

These criteria, however, are unsatisfactory for the so-called recovered addicts who must resist temptation to relapse. The sustained absence of urges in widely different settings, rather than the ability to resist the urges, signifies the end of dependency on the substance or behavior. There are several different theories on the causes of addiction. Some theories focus on the physiological properties of addictive substances, others on personality traits that promote addiction, and still others on newly acquired motivations after exposure to drugs. No single theory has been sufficient to account for all of the observations; it is very likely that different theories may not be applicable to different aspects of addictive behavior. In other words, one theory may not explain why everyone may develop an addictive disorder (Willerman & Cohen 1990, 511).

People who drink can also be classified as *social drinkers* and as *problem drinkers.* Social drinkers drink moderately on some occasions, and on other occasions, they drink heavily. But they are not preoccupied with alcohol, and they have no withdrawal symptoms when they stop using it. Their lives do not revolve around whether or not they are going to use this substance, and they experience no cravings.

Problem drinkers can often drink alone as well as with others. Some who drink in social situations may have more problems with their drinking than those who drink alone. There is not a hard and fast rule. Some problem drinkers are heavy drinkers, and they drink heavily all the time, or they may drink heavily only in spurts and fits. Problem drinkers are defined as those individuals who have "identifiable alcohol problems but who have not experienced severe consequences or serious alcohol withdrawal symptoms" (Sobell & Sobell 1993a, 138). Sobell and Sobell (1993b) assert that "problem drinkers" frequently respond favorably to interventions aimed at helping them assert control over their behavior (irrespective of the individual's chosen goal—abstinence or moderation).

There are also people who, because of other health conditions (e.g., diabetes), suffer ill effects from even a small amount of alcohol. If you have a problem with alcohol, whether psychological or physiological, then that is a problem *for you.* Using alcohol is just not a healthy thing for some people to do. Individuals must come to understand that they have a problem *because* they are drinking, and therefore they need to modify their alcohol consumption. They must then figure out the severity of their problem. Once they ascertain the level of severity, they can determine an appropriate goal for change (i.e., abstinence or moderation). Based on what individuals decide as the appropriate goal for themselves, then an appropriate intervention strategy to meet that goal can be selected.[2]

Primary and Secondary Alcoholism

Some professionals distinguish between primary and secondary alcoholism (Willerman & Cohen 1990, 521). Alcoholism is *primary* when there is no other diagnosable disorder present that is thought to cause the alcohol dependency; alcoholism is *secondary* if it arises as a consequence of some other disorder, such as psychopathy, or depression.

Different reasons are given to explain why some people are alcohol dependent and others are not. One theory is that dependency is a tension-reducing practice; people who have difficulty with tension and stress develop alcohol dependency to reduce the tension and stress that they are feeling. A second hypothesis is that dependency is a genetic propensity. "At least 31 percent of alcoholics have an alcoholic parent—usually the father" (Willerman & Cohen 1990, 525). Family studies alone cannot disentangle genetic and environmental factors; the research is mixed. There is also some empirical evidence that those who are tolerant (i.e., capable of ingesting more alcohol) are more likely to become alcohol dependent, because they do not suffer the negative side effects of overconsuming.

People can reach different stages of addiction at different times. Dependency advances in stages and plateaus. Part of being human is having plateaus. When things are on an even keel, when no crises rock the boat, individuals may become dissatisfied because they want more excitement. Or, perhaps, they find themselves in a regrouping phase: they may be consolidating the benefits of what they've already learned. Advancing to the next level of severity is never inevitable. Crises usually present challenges that offer a variety of responses; individuals may progress through more intense stages or retreat into more balanced behavior. No one can predict the direction individuals will take: toward dependency or away from it. It is up to individuals themselves; the substance does not determine the direction.

If we contrast chemical dependency with a diagnosis of cancer, we see there is no tissue mass on which to target the treatment with either radiation, surgery, or chemotherapy. Instead, any number of factors may be the cause of the problem, and the task in therapy is to discover each of the factors and the role they play. This process takes time and patience, and we return as many times as needed in order to discover more about these factors and our response to them. Therapy assists individuals to work at changing the effect of these factors.

Stages in the Recovery Process

It is helpful to see the recovery process as circular rather than as linear. With the growth and change that recovery introduces comes new understanding of old issues. Even though it may seem that problems are similar, the place we come to is never really the same as the first time we reached it. New and different dimensions present themselves, and we can remember things about ourselves in a new way. With this perspective, working the Twelve Steps of AA can be very useful over time rather than as fixed and static exercises that grow less and less meaningful for our lives. The circle, the spiral, of our experience in recovery is always opening beyond our original encounter with it.

Saying that the actual recovery process is circular simplifies what is very, very complex. As in all cases, the complexity depends on the individual's past experience, heredity, and behavior. When individuals develop a dependency on a substance or a behavior to solve or respond to needs, the problem is not *in* the substance but in the individual's behavior.

Substance abuse is a way of filling a void caused by unmet needs. People have unmet needs because their needs were much greater than the environment could respond to. They didn't get enough of what they required in order to experience a sense of safety and well-being. These individuals are struggling with a hunger to get such needs met and to have this void filled. The behaviors they utilize work to overcome the feeling of not having enough, of not being filled enough. Often, individuals who begin recovery think that their problem is the substance itself; when the substance is taken away, they discover, however, that the hunger is still there. Their pain remains.

The substance is not the problem. Chemical dependency is internal and not external. That is why it is so complicated: everyone responds to alcohol/drugs differently because everyone has grown up with different genes, environment, culture, and background. What individuals lack is inside them. Different theoretical therapeutic orientations offer different answers for these needs. These orientations are not only voluminous but also beyond the scope of this book.

"The Dynamic Model of Alcoholism Recovery"[3]

Brown (1985) has developed a model of the recovery process that identifies the complex interactions that occur within the individual. There are four stages in this model: (1) drinking; (2) transition; (3) early recovery; (4) ongoing recovery. In each stage, three components operate at the same time: (1) the alcoholic axis; (2) environmental concerns; (3) interpretation of the self and others. Individuals have their own unique recovery process through these stages, as well as their own unique interactions of the three components. Therapy needs to take into account this complex interplay in each individual.

The actual movement through the four stages passes from an individual's belief in control over using alcohol, acceptance of the fact of losing control over alcohol, conversion to abstinence because of the acceptance of the loss of control, emergence of new attitudes and values based on this conversion, and the integration of the individual's needs with external demands resulting in an entirely new way of dealing with life. Throughout each of these stages, participation in AA is important for many people both as a resource and a catalyst for finding their way into recovery.

Brown goes on to say,

> No one mode of treatment is sufficient to deal with the constantly changing complexities of the process of recovery. It is not a report of the outcome of "treatment." The experience of recovery may have included treatment for some—medical detoxification, inpatient alcohol program, psychotherapy before or after abstinence—but that treatment is a part of the process.[4]

Even though Brown's model deals specifically with recovery from alcohol dependency, it is also useful in understanding the recovery process for addictive/compulsive behavior in general.

Homophobia as an Impediment to the Recovery Process

When sexual minorities have significant unresolved issues about their sexual orientation, and also have a drinking problem, the issue of homophobia is very likely to emerge with unpredictable regularity. We may reasonably ask, who has ever dealt with their homophobia fully? Likely, no one; nevertheless, the recovery period teems with surprises that catch dormant, internalized homophobia off guard.

As the developmental process continues over their lifetime, gays and lesbians constantly have challenges that differ from those of nongays. Gays and lesbians in their early twenties who are not getting married, when most heterosexuals *are* getting married, must deal with the issue of being single in the midst of their peers. Later on in their thirties, when heterosexuals are creating a family with children, gays and lesbians experience certain developmental issues about being without this type of family. In their forties, gays and lesbians face additional issues that arise at the time when children are being sent off to college, or, when caring for elderly, infirm parents. Sexual minorities may start thinking about what their future may be like alone without a child to look after *them.* All these issues must be seen through layers of homophobia and heterosexism. Over and over, sexual minorities are presented with challenges that require them to struggle with the sense of not being good enough, of not being as good as, or of having lost out in life because of their sexual orientation.

Admittedly, all individuals face challenges throughout their lifespan because of specific life events that present developmental issues. As some of us become less encumbered by society's expectations, and how society sees us either as lesbians or as gays, we may think more about different possibilities we hadn't considered before. The present lesbian baby-boom is a good example of an alternative for women who want to be mothers but who are not heterosexual. These lesbians are redefining themselves as lesbians AND as mothers. Because of their stance, all of us can now understand that motherhood is no longer the exclusive province of heterosexuality. This is an example of innovating lesbians who are working through the impact of homosexuality and its dimensions.

Alcohol-dependent sexual minorities may suddenly discover that because of others' homophobia, or the internalized effects of homophobia on them, and their response to that by drinking, all of the issues have changed. For some women, one of the most significant of these issues is that it's too late to have children. This can be traumatic, and the more significant the trauma, the more significant the consequences.

People who have developed compulsive/dependent behavior have been put in a state of suspended animation as a result of using a substance or behavior to cope with the pain of living. They have not matured along the same time lines as the rest of their peers. When they enter recovery, these individuals are often devastated when they discover how much they have missed. They quickly discover that they cannot go through their adolescence at age forty. Some life events cannot be done again, and the pain of this can be intense. Working through this issue with the help of a therapist can be very beneficial to our recovery.

Getting in Touch with Our Lives

Many things can help us to become more aware of the significance of unhappy or homophobic experiences in our lives. Left unexamined, these experiences can often become a source of anxiety and discontent and impede our progress.

Perhaps we can be lucky enough to find an old photograph album that we hadn't glanced at in years. We can look at these old photos and recognize in the images of ourselves the painful discomfort we felt wearing those weird outfits and standing in those lifeless poses that captured our awkwardness and discomfort. The photos can help us to see where we have been, and help us to understand that there has been a change in the way we live in the world today.

Reading old journals can often provide us with unusual insights about ourselves. The documents can reveal what we were focused on, and what our priorities were at different times in our lives. For example, it can be helpful to appreciate that in the past all of our time and attention was focused on being in relationships, or disguising our sexual orientation, or defying authority. We can begin journaling now to help our memory, and this supports us in turning what might not seem very special or unusual into events of significance. Instead of losing good times to the "same ol' same ol,'" we can have them back again. Observing the new focus on our efforts at balance today is evidence of progress.

Depending on one's own disposition, journaling and dating things can be very beneficial. However, for people who don't find writing that easy or creative, it can be helpful to reflect on the different kinds of people we once had in our lives, and those who are in them now. We can take a second look at the kinds of relationships we had, how mutual, how intimate, how much of a give-and-take there was. Then, as we consider those presently in our lives today, we can understand how much we have changed.

We may look at progress in any number of different ways. We can step back and observe the way interaction occurs in our work life (some people keep their performance evaluations from work), our family life, our significant-other relationships. Many different kinds of milestones can be developed to assist us in gauging our progress in recovery.

For those of us who write and read, or are creative in some fashion (and this includes almost all of us), it is important not to take our talents for granted. We need to be able to look at our efforts over time in recovery. And *all* of us can feel creative, artistic in some way, about *how* we are living our lives whether or not we write, draw, dance, or take photographs. We can all view our lives artfully; we can all observe progress by looking at the ways we did things in the past and the ways we do them now.

Dangers in the Appearance of Progress

Real progress can be very deceptive. Abstaining from one substance but indulging immoderately in a different one is not progress. Progress means increasing moderation in the way we handle every aspect of our lives. If we are not able to do something in moderation, that is a good sign of its being a potential problem for us. When we find ourselves doing anything, anything at all, that we *cannot* do in moderation, and especially something that is "addictible," it is a very serious sign of a problem. Real recovery, the ideal of recovery, would be the ability to function well in social interactions, as well as in intimate interactions—on the job, with family of choice, if possible with family of origin (or be able to abstain from that if it were unhealthy). In all areas of life, real recovery means the ability to function with a balance between being able to take care of one's own needs and being helpful and useful in society—without getting out of balance.

It is quite natural for most people to have an occasional period when they eat too much turkey at Thanksgiving, or impulsively spend more money than they should have, or feel low and decide to do something extravagant for themselves. All people have an up or a down period when they do something that does not reflect moderation in all things at all times. However, by taking a step back and looking at these activities over the period of a week, they should be able to get a feel for how balanced this behavior is. If it remains out of balance for over a month, that should indeed be cause for concern. If it is for longer than a month, they need to find out what is going on internally. They need to discover what they are not coping with and why they are looking for something external as a solution. Some people, in addition to addictive/compulsive behavior, may have some other disorder. We will explore this in the next chapters.

※　　※　　※

CHAPTER 3

A New Look at the No-Nos

A great deal of advice about recovery that people in Twelve Step programs offer newcomers and old-timers alike is based on sound, common sense. Some advice, however, deserves careful scrutiny as well as reconsideration in looking at the recovery process of individuals who come from a broad spectrum of backgrounds. Not only are their backgrounds numerous and complex, so are the problems and crises that affect them. The "no-nos" is what we might call these problematic issues that people in Alcoholics Anonymous have passed along as if axiomatic for recovery in the Twelve Step program.

Using Medication

Many Twelve Step programs strongly caution members regarding the use of over-the-counter as well as prescription drugs for any reason. In a society in which the media vigorously market over-the-counter drugs, the practice of self-medication has wide approval. It is likely that behind the AA caution is the very real need to discourage the tendency of people in recovery to indulge in or condone self-medicating.

A serious problem arises when this caution is applied inappropriately as a proscription. People may actually need specific prescriptions to address certain disorders. It is absolutely essential to draw the distinction between self-medicating and receiving appropriate medical attention that calls for the use of certain drugs for psychiatric or physiological interventions. The sense of guilt that people experience over using appropriately prescribed medication needs to be eliminated.

Admittedly, in the past, physicians have treated problems of addiction as if they were "Valium deficiencies." In effect, these physicians switched alcohol dependency problems to Valium dependency problems—as if that and other barbiturates were the solution.

There is always an interaction between the culture, what we know at the time, and how people view problems. Understandably, in its early days, AA believed that the medical profession couldn't be useful in the treatment of alcoholism and, instead of helping, only contributed to the problem. Over the years, AA has continued to remain dubious of the kind of help that the medical profession could give the "alcoholic." Nevertheless, beginning in the 1980s, AA made efforts to increase physicians' awareness about the nature of alcoholism and the ways of treating it. AA has specifically reached out to introduce medical students and interns to the Twelve Step approach by inviting them to attend open meetings of the fellowship.

For people in recovery, there are any number of circumstances when a full-blown proscription about taking *any* medicine, or *any* mood-altering drug *under any circumstance,* is seriously harmful. For individuals who are having certain kinds of problems, prohibiting the use of medication can endanger life as well as inhibit recovery. It is well to remember that recovering from alcohol dependency does not inoculate anyone from other psychological problems, such as mood disorders (anxiety, depression, etc.), or from other organic problems. When these problems arise, people need to be encouraged to get responsible, appropriate treatment from professionals who have full awareness and understanding of chemical dependency.

For this reason, it is important to be clear about whether or not a dependency problem exists. Those in the problem stage may choose not to run the risk of developing a dependency, and therefore they may prefer not being treated with addictable or habit-forming substances. Optimally, they should be in the care of a professional who is aware of the properties of different medications and the risks involved. In every circumstance in which medication is suggested, it is important for the individual to weigh the risks and the benefits of taking any prescribed drug. Individuals, on the advice of their physicians, must make that decision for themselves.

For example, neither minor medication nor stress-reduction exercises will relieve chronic migraine once it sets in. Some people are able to reduce the incidence of migraine by using specific drugs; without these drugs, their lives are unbearable. Under these circumstances, it is inappropriate to endanger the well-being of the individual because of the perceived rule against taking any mood-altering, mind-altering substances. Taking the drug does not get the sufferer high; it takes the migraine away. Intervention, for migraine, is essential to stop the onslaught of the attack. Without the intervention, the migraine runs rampant.

Having surgery, and recovering from surgery, is another circumstance that requires an appropriate response involving medication. It is important for the patient preparing to have surgery to have a trusting relationship with the surgeon— and to be reasonably assured that the physician understands chemical dependence. With that trust, it is possible to have confidence that what has been prescribed should be taken—*as directed.* The problem is not *in* the medication itself.

People can medicate themselves with *anything*—aspirin, or exercise, or even orange juice—and a dependency on any of these can begin. Not the IT, but the process, the motivation, needs to be examined: are we trying to take away the anxiety because we cannot cope with it—or are we doing what is really responsible? Perhaps we may need someone else to give us some direction in this matter. That is why it is important to research the physician, and to monitor the support group with whom we choose to surround ourselves. Are they sensible, or not?

The Panacea for Everything

Another no-no is the conviction on the part of many Twelve Steppers that the Twelve Step program is the answer to any and all problems. For some individuals in AA, it is unthinkable that the program might be less than adequate to deal with every problem that arises in life. Simply because some individuals in recovery are not getting results through working the program does not mean something is wrong with what they are doing. They may, for example, have other medical or psychological problems. Anyone who insists on maintaining the contrary has a misconception about the tools of the Twelve Step program and how they can be used.

For the individual trying to cope with long-standing problems, such as childhood trauma or chronic depression, the inquiry, "Well, have you done the Third Step?" is meaningless, infuriating, and counterproductive. The Third Step is intended to help individuals work through problems dealing with alcohol or drugs, not the trauma of childhood sexual abuse! Anyone who suffers from deep-seated, trauma-fraught problems of this nature needs to understand that the AA program is not designed to deal with these other issues! The Twelve Steps of AA definitely help us understand how we have inappropriately coped with long-standing problems by using alcohol and drugs. But, AA doesn't give us all the tools or all the answers about how to cope with the problems underlying addictive/compulsive behavior—*nor does it claim to do so.* Professional intervention and other techniques from different orientations are needed. Only after the benefits of these other approaches have been incorporated in recovery can the benefits from using AA tools be fully experienced.

That is precisely the reason care providers in chemical dependency programs have adapted techniques from other models. We can only hope that care providers are theoretically grounded; nevertheless, many of them have adapted relevant techniques in order to facilitate the recovery process.

Relationships in the First Year

Let us consider another no-no that has become incorporated into the folklore of the program in some parts of the country: starting a new relationship in the first year. Let's face it, relationships are unavoidable. We all have relationships, and the new and open environment offered at Twelve Step meetings is the most immediate and accessible place to encounter new people. The question arises: is this no-no really about *sexual* relationships? If it is, then perhaps that should be added to the list of Steps up on the wall of the meeting room. Since it is missing from this list, we need to consider it in the context of our lives as sexual minorities.

Consider how discriminatory this is for those who do not have a permanent sex partner, such as a wife or a husband. Obviously, gays and lesbians who are not in committed relationships need to think of this no-no and its implications for recovery in a fundamental, personal way.

A great many people have problems with sex, in general, and some think that the simplest way to handle problems is to avoid dealing with them. If we reflect on the injunction for any length of time, the question arises: why is one year magical, why not five, or ten? These numbers, themselves, are arbitrary. What we must consider, instead, is what makes sense for us. Recognizing how stressful intimate relationships can be, we need to ask ourselves, how much strain can we handle? Can we keep the focus on our recovery instead of getting lost in complex entanglement, or rosy limerance, or old patterns? Can we risk the consequences of the relationship not working?

Instead of a moratorium on *all* relationships, the suggestion not to have sex for ninety days is certainly more manageable. You may indeed find it useful, as well. However, for some people who like to think that what they have heard in the program is the answer to everything, breaking any rule (whatever the rule is and wherever it may have really originated) then gives them permission to use a substance or act out in another fashion. This is an unfortunate use of a no-no to return to dependent/compulsive behavior.

Connections with Others

Another problematic no-no is the one against maintaining connections with others who are not in recovery and who may be using substances. If this is about avoiding those who are chemically dependent or who suffer from problems relating to alcohol and drug abuse, it is a very useful suggestion. On the other hand, most people who use substances don't have substance-abuse problems or a chemical dependency. These same individuals can be supportive to someone who wishes to make a change. A blanket dismissal of all the people in our lives who use substances can have devastating effects on our well-being.

And those who enforce this condition on themselves often end up espousing the extreme of this position: the Us-and-Them dichotomy. "The only people who understand us are those in the Twelve Step program; everyone not in the program doesn't and *can't* understand us." What a burden of isolation this creates! In addition to the harmful isolation this imposes, it also forces people to have an identity based exclusively on their chemical dependency—based only on an *illness-sense* of themselves. The effect of this is to diminish the individual and inhibit the recovery process. The core of anyone's identity is NOT alcohol (or any other substance) dependency, yet many in AA lose sight of this and begin to sound as if dependency is the only thing that makes them who they are!

For recovery to flourish, it is important to go beyond believing that being "alcoholic" is the prime focus of our identity. There is no question that it is absolutely vital to our lives not to forget that we have had a chemical dependency. Seducing ourselves into thinking that perhaps we really made a mistake, and we really weren't dependent on substances or behavior can be a real danger. Nevertheless, it is essential to see ourselves with all of our attributes, and as part of a larger perspective, instead of conceiving ourselves as only an alcoholic. Recovery must offer more freedom than that if we are going to live happy and fulfilled lives.

Not beginning or having relationships with others outside the program is another facet of this no-no. If you are going to have a relationship with someone who is chemically dependent, yes, it would be better to have someone who is in recovery rather than someone who isn't. Rather than any categorical injunctions, we need always take circumstances, as well as individuals into consideration.

It is likely that we will choose to relate to people who are on our same level of psychological health. If we are not feeling particularly healthy, we are not going to be in very healthy relationships. Here are some questions to consider: (1) Where are you in terms of your identity development? (2) Where are you in your recovery process? (3) Are you prepared to take on the anxieties and strains that will occur under the best of circumstances in relationships? Talking over your responses with someone you trust can help you make a meaningful decision.

Attendance at Meetings

Let us consider another rule that is, for some, almost sacred: in order to "get" the AA program, you've got to go to ninety Twelve Step meetings in ninety days. If you don't do this, *you're going to get drunk.* (Many individuals in Twelve Step programs extend this even further: you must go to meetings on a regular basis for the rest of your life. Anyone who does not do that is going to relapse.) There are even some people who go so far as to say that if you are not in regular attendance week by week, month by month, and year by year, then you are not in recovery.

The only AA requirement for membership "is the DESIRE to stop drinking." No one even has to stop! It is *the desire* that counts. It is up to the individual whether to be in recovery or not, and no one except the individual can make that decision. Other people are entitled to their judgments, and may live their lives in accordance with their ideas. But not someone else's life!

With regard to a prescribed number of meetings or the regularity of attendance, individuals have to determine for themselves what level of support they need. Many of us have come into Twelve Step programs without friends or any group that will support our efforts. Indeed, we may *need* to go to ninety meetings in ninety days in order to develop a whole new social network. We must decide that for ourselves. No one has the prerogative to make us feel unwelcome or uncomfortable about our decision. We belong in whatever room we choose to sit in, whenever we decide to sit in it. And no one may tell us that we won't make it in recovery unless we _____ (fill in the blank). What is perfectly clear is that we won't make it IF we decide we won't make it!

It is helpful to remember that danger lurks behind someone else's judgment: "You won't make it!" We may hear in this warning the invitation to believe that because we have failed to do this or that, then we don't have a solid program and may as well relapse. We need constantly to guard against planting seeds for future self-sabotage. The simple truth is that no matter how many changes we make, no matter how many high-risk situations we are in, we are still the only ones responsible whether or not we relapse.

All or Nothing

Another rule asks for our scrutiny: either accept the whole system implicitly, "believe in" AA, or else there is no help for you. Refusal means exclusion. The dogmatism that may grow up in particular AA meetings is so often taken for granted that unless someone articulates it clearly we do not realize how harsh and devastating it is. Having learned to mistrust authority figures, many gays, lesbians, and bisexuals with addictive/compulsive behavior are unable to make such a commitment without first experiencing some results in their lives. For this reason, because of feeling cut off from help, they have never known any of the benefits of recovery.

It is important for everyone in recovery to hear what is said as *suggestions* and not commandments handed down from on-AA-high. This is certainly AA's true position, no matter what you may be told to the contrary by individuals in groups. Every individual needs to decide what to take and what to leave. No one can give the stamp of authority to anything said at a Twelve Step meeting; what is shared are solutions that have worked for the person who offered them. Listeners need to take responsibility for what they embrace and what is left behind.

It is also important to remember that we need to experiment, to modify what we have heard in order to discover whether it works for us or not. And then, we need to be encouraged not to be ashamed of the way we have chosen to modify these suggestions.

All of us must be encouraged to look ourselves in the eye and take ownership for the positives and the negatives we have experienced using the Twelve Step programs. The Twelve Steps, as you will find as you work them in the exercises offered in part II, actually insist on this kind of ongoing reflection and evaluation. Instead of being clones, we need to become responsible for the choices we have made and accept the consequences for what we have done. This is always possible if we will consider ourselves to be in a learning mode, to be vulnerable and teachable. Achieving new levels of "teachability," rather than cloneship, needs to take the place of any meeting dogmatism that may have led some people to think of AA as a kind of cult. Along with themselves, people need to keep AA in perspective.

Frequently, people have transferred addiction to substances to addiction to Twelve Step programs: AA, Al-Anon, Overeaters Anonymous, Sex and Love Addicts Anonymous, Debtors Anonymous, and others. They have no other life; instead, attending Twelve Step meetings has become their life.

In *The Real Thirteenth Step,* Tessina (1991) suggests that in Twelve Step programs the ultimate goal of recovery should be to develop independence *from* Twelve Step programs. She believes that developing skills such as risk taking, problem solving, and coping with failure are central to developing autonomy. This autonomy will make it possible for individuals to move forward on their own. They will not need to attend Twelve Step meetings in order to maintain abstinence and live fulfilling, rewarding lives.

This concept may be heretical and frightening for many people to consider. But the idea—ultimately achieving freedom from dependency on Twelve Step programs— is an important one. Considering it dispassionately and examining its merits has potential benefits for many. For example, it might cause individuals who feel discouraged at the thought of a lifetime of AA meetings to reconsider their resistance to making a change in their substance use. Independence from Twelve Step meetings and development of autonomy may actually be happening; individuals are just not returning to Twelve Step meetings to tell of their experiences. Many of those attendees of Twelve Step meetings who do not come regularly after seven to fifteen years or more are not "out there" using and abusing. They are alive and well, and living in recovery that began in AA and continues to be nourished by things they learned there.

Higher Power

The issue of needing to believe in a Higher Power to really belong in AA is a major obstacle for many gays and lesbians. It is unclear whether this is more troublesome for men or women; however, it is certainly an issue for some with serious consequences.[1] This issue, in fact, helped to launch Women for Sobriety (Kirkpatrick 1978). The Thirteen Steps of Women for Sobriety address the problem head-on:

1. I have a drinking problem that once had me.
2. Negative emotions destroy only myself.
3. Happiness is a habit I can develop.

4. Problems bother me only to the degree that I permit them in.

5. I am what I think.

6. Life can be ordinary or it can be great.

7. Love can change the course of my world.

8. The fundamental object of life is emotional and spiritual growth.

9. The past is gone forever.

10. All love given returns two-fold.

11. Enthusiasm is my daily exercise.

12. I am a competent woman and have much to give others.

13. I am responsible for myself and my sisters.[2]

Another major issue arising from the same source is the insistence on having a conscious contact with a Higher Power. In fact, for some people in AA, without this conscious contact, the individual is not in recovery. This assessment provides another dangerous setup for self-sabotage!

Unless agnostics, atheists, or non-Gentiles are lucky enough to discover each other in the meetings, they often feel the AA program has nothing for them. Some even believe themselves beyond receiving help because of the appearance of God-centered beliefs. In spite of the words "God, *as we understood Him*," it is difficult to minimize the significance of this Christian idea that is central to the program.

For many sexual minorities who have suffered the spiritual abuse of certain religions, along with the sexist presumptions of these denominations, it is difficult to separate organized religion from spirituality in early recovery. Dodging other people's religious convictions, or even their spirituality, can greatly inhibit the recovery process of those who are not yet ready for spirituality in any formal organization.

Some people in AA are offended that some individuals do not wish to join in the common practice of holding hands at the end of the AA meeting to say the Serenity Prayer or the Lord's Prayer. But, after all, no one is required to hold hands either to say a prayer or to do anything else—including having a spiritual awakening. "The only requirement is the DESIRE to stop drinking."

※　　※　　※

The Twelve Steps and the Twelve Traditions are the basis of the AA program and the inspiration for all the other "anonymous" programs, as well. Over the past sixty years, people attending AA meetings have introduced many other precepts. These additions to the fundamental ideas of AA may create obstacles to the basic recovery process of individuals who wish to avail themselves of a sequence of truly valuable, workable *suggestions*.

It is fact and not speculation that these ideas can change people's lives—if they use them. All interventions aside, both divine and human, unless individuals with addictive/compulsive behavior take action to implement change in their lives, they will continue to suffer the effects of their condition. Individual choice is central to the recovery process.

❋   ❋   ❋

CHAPTER 4

Recovery Issues for Gays, Lesbians, and Bisexuals

Homosexuality and Therapy

U ncertainty about one's sexual orientation is a cause of anxiety for many people. Even those who are clear about being gay or lesbian or bisexual may feel inhibited from getting help because of their orientation, or they may not know how to get help.

Many communities in the United States do not advertise or provide gay and lesbian counseling services. The task for individuals seeking counseling or support in these communities is therefore difficult and even risky. Some people fear that a counselor might attempt to change them or manipulate their sexual orientation. They may even have had a treatment provider who subscribes to reorientation therapy, and they are naturally terrified of repeating this ordeal. (The American Psychological Association does not sanction such practice; nevertheless, there are still some care providers who use this approach.)

A therapist might easily manipulate men and women who are already vulnerable because of substance dependency to believe something is terribly wrong with being gay, lesbian, or bisexual. Accepting or making the best of abuse and misinformation is not part of recovery, and clients need to blow the whistle on this kind of treatment. For this reason, it is important to carefully investigate from the start the kind of care provided by anyone in recovery work. (See chapter 6 for information on choosing a therapist.)

Sexual minorities have other reasons for concern about the therapist they go to for problems with compulsive/dependent behavior. It is not at all unusual for anyone, no matter their sexual orientation, to have difficulty talking about sexual behavior. Often, people feel uncomfortable about being sexual, period. The added discomfort, embarrassment, or (for some) shame of talking about gay or lesbian sex with someone who is heterosexual can make the problem even more acute.

A great many of us have experienced the intimate connection between sex and alcohol/drugs. Some of us thought it was only possible to have sex under the influence. We suffered intense anxiety over our sexual behavior, and the substances either reduced that anxiety or allowed us to pretend someone or something else was acting sexually—it was the substance. In recovery, there is no substance to blame. We do what we do, and we need to take responsibility for doing it. Some of us need a great deal of support to get rid of the burden of shame and guilt that pursues us in recovery.

Gays, lesbians, and bisexuals need to work through their anxiety, discomfort, and whatever shame or guilt they may have about their sexuality. We need to be able to discuss how we feel about specific sex practices because often these same practices led to our drinking and using.

We have suffered in darkness and silence because of a long list of fears beginning from childhood, and we may be terrified of exposure and punishment by authority figures. Verbalizing our experience with someone we know we can trust is crucial to our recovery. The ability to talk with a therapist about sex is very freeing and helps us develop a new understanding of self-esteem. Being open with a heterosexual care provider can be a major issue for gays and lesbians in recovery.

To Come Out to Others or Not

Another area of concern is coming out. There are risks, as well as benefits, in revealing one's sexual orientation. In each individual case, we must weigh consequences. Regardless of the decision, we need to give ourselves permission to do what we decide. Fortunato's *Embracing the Exile* (1982) is a wonderful resource for anyone who is considering disclosing being gay, lesbian, or bisexual.

> *Disownment or rejection by family—often the norm for gay people—is different from family turmoil revolving around an adolescent's adjustment at puberty, or a daughter who, at twenty-two is trying to cut the umbilical cord, or a son who is about to marry a woman his parents don't like. It's different because, unlike these other situations, it's not how a son or daughter is acting that's being rejected, it's who they are constitutionally. They don't have a choice about being gay, there isn't anything inherently destructive in their sexual orientation, and yet, once found out, they are treated like lepers by the people who supposedly love them the most. How do you get closure when there's no way out?*[1]

Inventorying the risks of coming out is often very difficult to do on one's own, and counselors can assist in this process. In all circumstances, on the job/professional scene, with our parents and relatives, with our nongay friends, we face risks involving our economic and emotional security. Heterosexual counselors may need to be educated about this before they can assist in this decision.

In the workplace, there is always the fear—and possibly the reality—of lost job security, of reduced opportunity for advancement, of being pigeonholed, or of being discounted for our opinions. The possibility of harassment is also very real whether or not those around us articulate homophobia; its emergence may be triggered by a complex array of events on the local or the national scene. The feeling of safety is crucial to job performance, and coming out on the job is one of the most unsafe decisions we may make.

Both location and occupation are major factors in deciding to come out or not. Being out in New York City, or San Francisco, or Chicago can be quite different from being out in Salt Lake City or Normal, Illinois. For this reason, some of us choose to live in places where there is more freedom to be who we are. Additionally, some occupations pose less risk because the tolerance is greater. The risk of being out as a therapist may be perceived as different from the risk of being a chiropractor or massage therapist. (Police officers, or senators, or congressional representatives are all high-risk positions for the individual who is out.) However, being an openly gay therapist or an openly lesbian peace officer in Fairbanks is much riskier professionally than in Los Angeles. No matter how much our services may be needed in the work that we do, our ability to perform these services may be seriously affected if we are out in a community that discriminates in thought and deed against gays and lesbians.

Academics, for example, are frequently fearful of doing research on gay and lesbian issues because of what this will mean for them professionally—being pigeonholed, not getting tenure, or being actively or subtly discriminated against.[2] Admittedly, some of us are able to be freer, more confrontive, or even more "militant" than others. Handling the potential threat involved in self-disclosure may be easier on some of us than others.

Coming out to parents and relatives can present a major issue in recovery. Fear of harming loved ones may cause us to avoid disclosing our orientation. "If I come out it'll kill her; him; them; etc." The health and well-being of the people we love is, of course, a valid concern. In our recovery, we discover that we, too, are loved ones. We discover that we, too, are entitled to health and well-being, and that our deception *may* be killing US!

We may also risk losing our families by NOT telling them. By being out with parents and other family members, we may be able to interact with them in an entirely new and loving manner. Instead of all the secrecy and deception that has stood in the way of intimacy, self-disclosure may open the door to meaningful and supportive relationships that benefit us in our recovery and them in their aging and integrating process.

Before disclosure, we may be preoccupied with the decision whether or not to visit our families at holiday time. Shall we go or stay away? How should we behave when we get there? Should we come with our lover, life partner, significant other,[3] or alone? When family members visit us, do we "straighten up" or "de-dyke" the house? Behind these questions is the larger one: when will we stop living the way we were and start living a new way? The answer requires careful consideration. Working with someone who can help explore the options is very beneficial to recovery.

At the heart of coming-out decisions is the issue of honesty: how far do we go to disclose who we are? What will we lose, and what will we gain, by being honest about our sexual orientation? What kind of contact or relationship will we have if we pretend we are someone different from the person we are? When we play a role, what is the risk to ourselves? As in all situations, honesty always brings up risks.

There are also risks the other way—the risks of NOT coming out. We may lose a relationship if we are not honest; or we may maintain a relationship that is only semisatisfying. Disclosing orientation to the landlord might result in having to move out of the apartment. Sometimes, however, we may be surprised by others' reactions of affirmation and support. We can't know how they will respond until we have revealed ourselves.

Being Out in the Community

In the past few years, there has been intense controversy and backlash about gays and lesbians who come out in society. We are kept out of the military; lesbian or gay political appointments have been vetoed or stalled; national churches have expelled congregations that hired gay or lesbian ministers. How, then, can we feel safe about self-disclosure?

We need always hold up the positive and the negative. A rainbow bumper sticker on our car can provoke homophobic reactions. Is the threat of attack greater than the good feeling we have when we see others on the road with the same sticker? Where does our wish to honestly affirm ourselves end and safety begin?

Most importantly, we need to appreciate that knowing who we are and affirming our identity helps us make our way in the world. We can never escape ourselves. How we choose to label ourselves is a convenience. These labels can help to reduce anxiety, and we can use them to help us to cope better with the world in which we find ourselves.

For some people, because of all the practice they have had in their lifetime, being unauthentic with nongays is not difficult. They can separate and segment themselves without great cost. We don't know very many people who are tremendously successful with this, but perhaps they are so good at it we just don't know them.

There are always consequences, and all of us need to weigh these carefully.

When people are contemplating self-disclosure, it is very useful to have support to make these decisions.

The Lack of Support

Another issue sexual minorities face is the absence of family support in learning to deal with sexual orientation. We may need help from a therapist to deal with this absence of support and our therapists need to understand the issue. Heterosexuals in recovery often experience some sense of haven in the community. Not only friends but also families are usually kind, understanding, and helpful once the individual begins to change in recovery. Sexual minorities, however, have no guarantee that family or friends will provide this sense of haven.

Many families with alcoholic members struggle with issues of denial about substance dependency. However, this shame is nothing when compared with the shame and guilt and fear of parents, brothers, sisters, or children who find a gay or lesbian in their midst. If these revelations are combined, the lack of family support may be acute. Sometimes, when families have had a bad response to one revelation, we are unwilling to present them with the other. "Do I have to go through this again?" For some, it is much easier to reveal they are in recovery than it is to disclose their sexual orientation. This may, in part, be the result of society's willingness to say, "Oh, alcoholism is a disease." Disease is much easier for the family to deal with than the fear of homosexuality. Homosexuality has frequently been presented as a family's moral failure that, in turn, results in personal guilt and blame.

Struggling without the support of our families of origin, we may also feel especially bereft because of not having friends who are without substance-related problems. For most of us, before entering recovery, our circle of friends often narrowed to exclude anyone who did not use substances. Now, we may feel socially inept and awkward; we may even have endured the loss of a partner who is not yet ready or willing to enter recovery with us.

If we do find our way into gay and lesbian support groups, we may not experience a haven at all. As we look around at the people in the room, it is difficult not to wonder who will be gone next month or next year because of HIV. Often, some of us struggle with the question, why should we even go to the effort to develop a support group among gays and lesbians? How close should we let ourselves be to anyone around us because they could die, I could die, we could die? Support groups do not offer the same sense of permanence that families provide.

The gay and lesbian community frequently shows a general lack of support for the individual in recovery. Even in cities where Twelve Step groups are active, there is a prevailing reluctance on the part of other gays and lesbians to acknowledge the extent of compulsive/dependent behavior in our community. This is denial on a grand scale.

People in recovery need to pay attention to high-risk places, high risk people, and high-risk behavior. The fact that one's peers are actively abusing substances is not a reason to resume this behavior. If there are peer pressures to drink, we may have to stay away from these people until we can be with them without resuming old habits. Or, we may be able to clarify our need to be abstinent, and our friends will respect this and become supportive and not pressure us. Keeping our priorities in order and creating healthy relationships with gays and lesbians who do not have substance-dependency problems are of utmost importance. We can seek support for these issues from Twelve Step groups and from those individuals who truly care about us.

AIDS and Recovery

If gays and lesbians remain in recovery for any length of time, they will have to deal with the anxiety, the fear and the loss that AIDS leaves in its wake. Some may have acquired HIV disease prior to coming into recovery. They will then need to deal with the issue without the use of substances. If they are not HIV-positive, they may have to deal with survivor guilt, and the grief of losing friends and dear ones around them.

Some people's survivor guilt may be so intense that they feel compelled to contract the disease. For others, the thought of surviving the death of all these people may be so overwhelming that suicide seems like an option. One gay client, sharing his feelings about being HIV-negative, and coping with the continuing illness and death from HIV/AIDS of a large number of his friends, was fearful that he might never be able to find a life partner. "I am in my mid-thirties; I don't want to go out with someone barely twenty. That's not what I want. Who is going to be around here for me? I am losing my peer group! What will it be like for me in ten or twenty years?" It is of the utmost importance to speak to these fears and face these demons. And not to despair!

Recovery means becoming responsible. Some people engaged in unsafe behavior and did not become HIV-positive. The significance of this issue for them has, in some cities, resulted in the creation of support groups to help HIV-negative gay men cope with the tremendous guilt they feel over their negative status. Feeling discounted for being HIV-negative by others who are HIV-positive is difficult to deal with. Remembering all the friends who have already died, and anticipating the loss of friends in the immediate present, is cause enough to devastate anyone. Losses go hand in hand with being gay, with being lesbian, in this country, because of AIDS, because of hate crimes, and because of society's unwillingness to be open about homophobia and the devastation it creates. No one can remain naive about AIDS or homophobia. AIDS has forced awareness on everyone.

Medical Consultations

Sexual minorities' suspicion about the medical profession exists in general, and arranging any medical checkup, let alone a complete medical exam, is often put off for a longer time than is wise. The fact that a medical exam can be embarrassing is an additional element! If you are a lesbian, going to a physician may mean answering some intimate and sometimes embarrassing questions. The following scene occurred recently in a physician's office:

PHYSICIAN:
Are you using any birth control?

FEMALE PATIENT:
No.

PHYSICIAN:
Are you sexually active?

FEMALE PATIENT:
Yes.

PHYSICIAN
You should be using some birth control!

FEMALE PATIENT:
Doctor, listen, before you go any further, I'm lesbian. I wish I needed birth control!
(She wanted to have a child.)

The physician almost fell out of his chair apologizing, and then backed off from his customary interview routine of addressing the subject of sex.

For a man, complications arising from sexual relations may cause tremendous embarrassment and shame, as well. By and large, the medical profession relegates the issue of homosexual orientation to the closet. There is no place on medical forms to self-identify. (Whether or not such questions would be answered honestly is another issue. Some sexual minorities might respond yes openly if they had a sense that doing so would be safe.)

The fact that someone is lesbian or gay is frequently not acknowledged or accepted by physicians or hospitals. Because they are in charge, this form of homophobia prevails, even to the extent of denying significant others visitation rights during hospitalizations. This need not be the case. Both visitation rights and medical power of attorney can be secured by sexual minorities if they avail themselves of the necessary legal forms.[4]

Remembering the Past

Individuals in recovery may begin to remember past events. They may also see a new significance in the events they remember. In recovery, they may become traumatized by the reality of what they endured. Some may come to see that a relationship they thought was nurturing and loving is, in fact, a fantasy. Or they may come to see that an experience they appreciated was really exploitation.

A broad range of possibilities usually shows up whenever people begin to reexamine their experience without layers of denial. People will encounter and rethink experiences that haven't made sense, or they may reach a different understanding of the importance of things. Having siphoned off their feelings in the past left them believing not much had happened. Avoidance, denial and repression have prevented them from appreciating the true dimension of the events they lived through.

In recovery, we either have to continue those psychological defenses, using our energy to keep those things in place, or we must find other ways to feel whole and safe along with other things to protect us as we continue our process. The guidance of a professional therapist is crucial in undertaking, dealing with, and resolving these issues.

Career Counseling

In recovery, we may get back in touch with what we may have thought to do with our lives long ago. Many of us have remembered wanting to pursue careers that had been aborted because of dependency on substances. A light goes on: "Oh yes, that *is* what I wanted to do!" We may require more education and be faced with the question, "Am I worth it?" or "Can I afford it?" We may have felt that we could never make it because of being gay or lesbian. The number of gays and lesbians who are underemployed because of fear of being exposed in positions with high profiles is legion. Facing old aspirations is a serious challenge for many of us in recovery.

Close to our kernel of being is a big hole of feeling like second- class citizens without any hope of achieving success. Some of us who did succeed believed we were really impostors. And as impostors, few of us lived through a day in our lives when we didn't chide ourselves, "If they really knew me, I wouldn't be where I am!" The effect of this on self-esteem and the tremendous energy drain that results are massive.

Everyone in recovery, and especially sexual minorities, needs some assistance with career counseling from a therapist who can offer good testing and competent interpretation. Consultation of this nature may even be considered central to the change process.

❋   ❋   ❋

Dealing with Internalized Homophobia

Self-styled AA "fundamentalists" frequently advise lesbians, gays, or bisexuals to get sober FIRST, before attempting to raise any issues regarding sexual orientation. (The adjective "sober" might be replaced by "abstinent" in Overeaters Anonymous or "clean" in Narcotics Anonymous.) These "advisors" are usually opposed to all references to homosexuality and often make this clear to anyone who dares to mention the subject. As if sexual orientation isn't a major factor in anyone's life!

We have only to look at national statistics to know just how important sexual orientation is in the development of substance dependency. It appears that at least one person in ten suffers from addiction to a mood-altering substance or some form of dependency on compulsive behavior. Statistics from the National Center for Alcoholism about sexual minorities indicate that in the gay and lesbian community, *one in three* is addicted! These findings from the late 1980s need cautious interpretation; nevertheless, the magnitude of the problem is clear.[1]

The failure to appreciate the significance of sexual orientation in the development of compulsive/addictive behavior persists in the 1990s and continues to hinder a great deal of scientific research. Studying the incidence of disorders, in general, among sexual minorities is difficult. Research supports the contention that the stress of a homophobic, heterosexist society may play a significant role in the development of problems that prompt sexual minorities to seek help. Whether there is any direct causal relation between living in a society that officially sanctions discrimination against sexual minorities (and often condones or ignores oppressive, malicious behavior and attitudes) and the development of substance abuse problems has yet to be confirmed.

Impact on Recovery

The prevalence of alcohol and drug abuse in lesbian and gay communities can be linked to internal and external homophobia (Glaus 1989). To create the climate in which recovery can flourish, it is essential to promote physical and mental health. A key factor affecting mental health is a willingness to be honest. Each of the Twelve Step programs is built on the foundation of honesty or "H.O.W."—Honesty, Openmindedness, Willingness. Likewise, there is little hope of success in counseling unless the contract with the psychotherapist includes honesty.

Getting honest about chemical dependency is one thing; but getting honest about being gay, lesbian, or bisexual goes far deeper, for it involves who we are, as well as what we do! As difficult as revealing chemical dependency is, it is often more difficult to reveal and confront sexual orientation. Fear of losing everything—family, livelihood, home, and life—is often at issue. Rather than face the violent impact such a revelation will have on their lives, many gays, lesbians, and bisexuals choose to forego getting honest about their sexuality. As a result, many individuals return to compulsive/dependent behaviors rather than accept their own sexual orientation. The foundation of psychological health—self-honesty—is eroded by the self in denial.

We can choose dishonesty, but the toll of this dishonesty is insidious and pervasive. Lying, whether by convenient omission or by commission, is not a foundation for open and direct relationships with others. Lying creates barriers and prevents intimacy and connection between people. The existence of any barrier of this nature may be sufficient excuse to send individuals—already shaky in their commitment to change—back to old behaviors. The greater the danger that "old behaviors" hold, the greater the risk of dishonesty. To understand this intimate relation between honesty and recovery, we need to examine homophobia as a major problem standing in the way of gays, lesbians, and bisexuals with addictive/compulsive behavior.

The Problem

Homophobia is frequently discussed in literature concerning gays and lesbians. Over the past years, both its significance and complexity have been explored in terms of religious life and spiritual identity (Fortunato 1982; McNaught 1981), psychological health (Golden 1987), and relationships (Berzon 1988). Pharr's *Homophobia: A Weapon of Sexism* (1988) is an excellent discussion of the connection between homophobia and sexism. In spite of the material available in this area, the interaction between the homophobia of heterosexuals and the internalization of that homophobia by homosexuals is rarely addressed. For gays, lesbians, and bisexuals in recovery, this omission is important because of the subject's significance to the process of self-acceptance.

While it is often difficult for us to acknowledge, gays, lesbians, and bisexuals do hold homophobic beliefs. This is to be expected since sexual minorities grow up in a homophobic and heterosexist culture. To uncover the attitudes, thoughts, and beliefs we entertain about ourselves and others, we need to carefully examine these beliefs about lesbians, gays, and bisexuals.

In the West, the intolerant views of the Judeo-Christian religious tradition have formed the prevalent cultural thinking about sexual minorities. Because of fear or prejudice, Western society selectively uses biblical material to justify the oppression of those already held in contempt. This can be observed in the antigay attitudes of the religious right (Rudolph 1989). Using biblical passages to support the condemnation of homosexuality is a manifestation of homophobia.[2]

Attitudes and beliefs such as these have been fostered and passed on from generation to generation in subtle and not-so-subtle ways. Clearly, individuals who have incorporated society's attitudes and beliefs into their own way of constructing reality are not at fault. However, gays, lesbians, and bisexuals in recovery need to initiate a thorough and painstaking process to examine the impact of homophobic messages on their self-esteem, self-concept, values, attitudes, and beliefs.

It is important to identify these messages in order to examine thoughts, beliefs, and attitudes that we have incorporated into our sense of self. Without such a discovery process, the subtle but often devastating consequences of these incorporations will continue to influence us.

Growing up in a society in which homophobia is the norm, men and women who are homosexual or bisexual have internalized the message and come to believe that because they are not heterosexual something is wrong with them. Falling victims to this verdict, pronouncing themselves guilty, and needing to hide their guilt in order to live in safety, sexual minorities all too often tumble into the trap of believing that punishment and oppression are justified. It does not require a giant step to connect the suffering and victimization of being homosexual or bisexual with the suffering connected with chemical dependency.

As targets either of society's homophobia or our own internalized version of it, the burden of suffering, shame, and guilt makes it difficult, if not impossible, to access the help that is available in recovery. Low or nonexistent self-esteem, deformed self-concept, and deep-seated feelings of shame identify but a few of the devastating consequences of internalized homophobia. Just as we can observe the outward manifestation of prejudice in burnt-out neighborhoods, the rejection of the oppressed, and violence against men, women and children, so, within, the individual can be ravaged by this identical scourge.

Homophobia Begins at Home

To confront our own homophobia, we need to cease accepting it as the only way to live in this world. It is not a "given" unless we allow it to be! When we stop acquiescing to its power and pervasiveness, we find ourselves in a different environment. Our internalized homophobia steals our energy, our vitality, and influences many of the choices that leave us unfulfilled in important areas of our lives. Identification and visibility as lesbians, gays, or bisexuals helps to counteract the effects of internalized homophobia because it destroys stereotypes. Engaging in honest interactions with others without assuming that we will encounter homophobic attitudes is an important first step. A second step is refusing to remain in hiding in order to protect others from experiencing their own homophobia.

Our emotional and mental well-being depends on clearing away the internalized homophobia we endure. "Housecleaning" is essential for health. Recognizing this is essential to our recovery because getting honest with ourselves, accepting ourselves as we are, is the foundation on which to build the change process. We can never change what we do not accept. Once we deal with homophobia, it is entirely possible that other problems that have disturbed our well-being will be revealed.

Getting Assistance

It is important to get support and validation from others who have gone through the process of confronting their homophobia or who understand what the process entails. We cannot do it alone, and we need to acknowledge this. If we could have done it on our own, we may never have developed addictive/compulsive behavior.

Available to everyone are thousands of books and journals, as well as magazine articles, that provide a wealth of insight and ideas about most of the issues that trouble us. These are available in libraries and in bookstores all over the country. Publishers' catalogs are filled with titles relevant to homosexuality, as well as addictive/compulsive behavior, that can be secured by mail. These materials written by and about sexual minorities are important sources of support no matter where one lives. Getting them and reading about gays, lesbians, and bisexuals opens the door to understanding.

Next, in many cities it is possible to find gay and lesbian Twelve Step groups that provide opportunities to meet with other individuals who have been through, or are going through, the recovery process. Part II of this book, "Exercising the Twelve Steps in Your Life," provides a road map for embarking on this journey, whether you attend Twelve Step meetings or you become a member of another support group. Support groups can be found through hot lines listed in the Yellow Pages. You can call and request information about this kind of assistance. Some community agencies are resources for helping individuals find support groups in addition to providing counseling services. (See the list of resources at the back of this book for more information.)

Another alternative is to find a skilled, culturally sensitive psychotherapist who can facilitate the process of discovery and self-acceptance. With a professionally trained care provider, you can examine all of the attitudes and issues that are inhibiting growth and change. For example, a psychotherapist can help explore beliefs and misconceptions that confuse us (e.g., whether or not lesbians are masculine, whether being lesbian or gay precludes any chance of having children, or whether being gay means that long-term relationships are impossible). Investigating these ideas helps us to gain a realistic perspective about what it actually means to be lesbian, gay or bisexual. This investigation makes it possible to determine which negative beliefs about sexual minorities are serving to support a destructive attitude about oneself as lesbian, gay, or bisexual. Such beliefs can then be challenged, tested and replaced with more accurate, affirming ideas and beliefs.

Only after we have evaluated our own experience and developed more informed and balanced beliefs about sexual minorities is it possible to address and cope with negative attitudes in others. Working through our own internalized homophobia helps to create some emotional distance from the negativity that others' homophobia brings with it. We need to be able to tolerate this negativity without taking it in and applying it to our own self-concept or self-identity.

The coming-out process takes place over time, and it is important to remember that a similar process may occur with others such as family or friends. Patience and tolerance may be necessary, although we need to be self-protective and set limits about what types of interactions will be tolerated as others go through their own process related to homophobic attitudes and behaviors. Others may be so intolerant or rejecting that it is quite difficult to continue to relate to them at this time. If this occurs, it is then essential to work through the pain and loss that this rejection brings. We must do this so that this experience doesn't create permanent damage to positive self-esteem and self-identity.

Remember that it is vitally important not to jeopardize our safety, but there are ways of gradually introducing change in our lives. To experience a condition, live it in the present. For example, to create peace and harmony, live peacefully and harmoniously. Engage in activities that support self-esteem and eliminate self-hatred. Reading about the coming-out process is an excellent approach for those who are uncertain about how to go about reclaiming their integrity. Some of us choose a step-by-step process over a considerable period of time. Others do not. It is an individual decision. The most important thing to remember is that many others have made this journey, and we can be helped by them as we continue on ours.

❋ ❋ ❋

CHAPTER 6

Choosing a Therapist

Getting Started

Many people do not know how to find a psychotherapist other than to ask someone they trust for a recommendation. Sexual minorities are even more at a loss in this process. In homophobic areas of the United States, they must first circumvent the reluctance of many psychotherapists to be identified with a lesbian or gay clientele; and, second, they must overcome their own deep-seated fear of repercussions from personal disclosure. Even after getting a referral and setting up an appointment, it is unlikely that individuals seeking help will have a clear idea as to how to go about interviewing the prospective psychotherapist.[1]

Prospective clients usually have little understanding of their power and prerogatives in the interview. Nor do they understand the importance of their proactive participation in the selection process.

Because prospective clients are in pain, they are tempted to choose someone impulsively instead of undertaking a careful selection process. Choosing impulsively may help them avoid the anxiety of interviewing several psychotherapists, but it may also contribute to dissatisfaction later. After the crisis that precipitated the entry into therapy has passed, they may discover that despite the investment they've made in the therapist, they're not quite happy about the arrangement. Somehow, then, it seems too late to start the interviewing process over again.

In the process of screening prospective psychotherapists, you should request a consultation session not only to discuss your questions and concerns but also to help you assess the "goodness of fit" between you and the psychotherapist. Some therapists offer a consultation session without charge. If the client decides to engage the psychotherapist's services, the consultation session will be considered the first session of treatment and a charge will then be assessed.

Begin by inquiring about the psychotherapist's willingness to proceed in this fashion. This is a reasonable approach to pursue for sexual minorities who need to be particularly cautious about the quality of treatment they receive. If psychotherapists are not willing to schedule a face-to-face interview on these terms, inquire about their willingness to conduct a brief telephone interview with you. These may not be common practices in your area, but it will not hurt to try!

Some Basics

It is essential for prospective clients to find out psychotherapists' "rules and regulations," i.e., their expectations of the client in terms of attendance, cancellations, fees, coordination of services, and insurance affiliations. It is also important for the psychotherapist to discuss issues related to confidentiality. As a prospective client, you need to ask questions about the implications of signing insurance releases, and the information disclosed to third-party payers if insurance claims are submitted for reimbursement. Although confidentiality is important to all clients, it is particularly important for sexual minorities.

It is essential to weigh the advantages of receiving insurance reimbursement for therapy against the possible risks of disclosure of sexual orientation. When in doubt, before authorizing release of information to insurance companies, discuss the matter thoroughly and become clear about the consequences to your privacy.

It is also important to discern the psychotherapist's openness to communicating with other people in your life, such as partners, employers, and children. Involving other people may be an important part of your therapy. Prospective clients should ask what types of modalities the therapist generally uses. "Modalities" refers to whether or not the therapist works with the individual in one-on-one sessions, as part of a couple, with family members, or in group counseling. Therapists generally have areas of specific expertise as well as types of modalities that they use more frequently. It is useful to inquire about the psychotherapist's preferences as well as to what the recommended modality of treatment for your problem would be. For instance, it is helpful to know whether the psychotherapist is exclusively committed to focusing on the individual's internal processes or is concerned with processes that extend beyond the personal and into the social context.

Preparation and Training

Requesting information about the psychotherapist's preparation and training helps you to understand what type of helping professional you are interviewing. There are many different services and significant differences among psychotherapists in terms of training, specialization, and orientation.[2] Tremendous overlap exists among the treatment providers in terms of domain of interest and specialties. Some ways to distinguish providers are academic preparation, supervised practical experience, certification, length of experience, and fees for services. Following is a brief overview of what the field looks like.

Clinical and Counseling Psychologists

These two specializations do not have a hard-and-fast boundary between them. The traditional distinction was that counseling psychologists focused on the assessment, diagnosis, and treatment of individuals with developmentally related concerns, and clinical psychologists treated individuals classified as having mental illness. These distinctions have blurred considerably over the years.

Both specializations require graduates to be scientist-practitioners, i.e., professionals who are trained to conduct and understand research procedures, and to provide treatment optimally suited for the best interest of each client. Both clinical and counseling psychology hold clinical practice research in high regard, though clinical psychology doctoral programs are usually more research-oriented. Whether researcher/clinicians or clinician/researchers, the largest proportion of Ph.D.'s go into direct client service, with some having greater supervised training as clinicians than others.

After the doctorate, each must obtain licensure in order to use the term "psychologist." A *psychologist* is a licensed doctoral level clinician who has been trained to apply various forms of treatment to nervous and mental disorders (four to six years of academic and clinical training, including supervised internships and post-doctorate clinical supervision).

Psy.D's

Doctors of Psychology, Psy.D's, are a more recent addition to the scene. They have a doctoral degree in psychology (i.e., no dissertation required). These individuals are clinicians who have been trained in clinical psychology but do not have a research background. They, too, must obtain licensure to use the term "psychologist."

There tends to be a status differential between the two Ph.D. tracks, with clinical psychology programs often being more competitive and more prestigious. It is not clear where the status issue is with Psy.D.'s as yet. Professionals in these specialties often offer psychotherapy to individuals, couples, families, and groups. However, psychologists from any of these areas may teach and conduct research.

The doctorate is the terminal degree in psychology, although a few states license master's-level clinicians under the psychology heading. Most states have additional requirements related to postdoctoral supervised clinical experience. This clinical experience is approximately a year of full-time direct service to clients. (This is in addition to the 2,000 hours of predoctoral internship, which is a supervised experience required in order to obtain the doctorate.)

Psychiatrists

Psychiatrists are medical doctors with special training in psychiatry. Psychiatry concerns itself with the study and treatment of mental disorders including psychoses and neuroses.[3]

A great deal of the psychiatrist's training focuses on the appropriate use of medications to alleviate the symptoms of mental disorders. Four years of medical school, one year of internship, plus residency training in psychiatry are required. The amount of supervised experience conducting psychotherapy varies.

Social Workers

Social workers (B.S.W., M.S.W., and Doctorate in S.W.) focus not only on the internal processes of individuals but also on understanding people in the context of their surroundings. The M.S.W. degree is generally considered the terminal degree in social work. The recipient of this degree has had a broad preparation in case work and counseling, community intervention, social policy and planning, and management and administration. There are some areas of specialization such as "family preservation" and "clinical." Each of these has different types of practical training. National licensure awards the L.C.S.W. credential on completion of this preparation.

Marital and Family Counselors

Marital and family counselors are specialists who focus their work on relationship counseling with a family-systems perspective in assessment and treatment. Academic programs combine courses in assessment and treatment as well as supervised fieldwork (or internships) with clients. They are certified as marriage and family therapists (M.F.T.) by the states.

Certified Mental Health Counselors

Each state legislates different requirements for certified mental health counselors, with some states not having licensure for counselors. Training and supervised experience vary. A variety of master's-level training programs, combining academic and fieldwork experiences, are offered. More and more programs are requiring longer academic preparation to obtain the degrees in order to better prepare counselors for national licensure. Those who are prepared in this way take a national counselors exam, but some states do not recognize the national exam.

Certified Addiction or Alcoholism Counselors

Different states have different requirements for certified addiction or alcoholism counselors. A national certification exam is available, but this is not currently required for certification in all states. In most states, counselors are not currently required to have a specific formal credential, such as a bachelor's or master's degree, though in order to obtain certification an individual must meet requirements regarding relevant course work and supervised experience. Obviously, there is a great diversity among psychotherapists with this certification, ranging from individuals without any formal academic credential to those who have obtained the doctorate.

Specific Preparation

In your interview, discuss the psychotherapist's background in addictive disorders, cross-cultural and diversity counseling, and human sexuality. It is advisable to request information about the psychotherapist's preparation in terms of working with clients with problems similar to yours. Also inquire about current supervision, licensure and/or certification, and collaboration with other health care professionals. It is frequently essential to enlist other professionals in order to provide a holistic treatment approach.

After you have received answers that appear to support the work you'd like to do with this psychotherapist, inquire about the provider's understanding of homophobia, external and internal, and attitudes about sexual minorities. You might ask the psychotherapist to talk in a general fashion about a recent case with a gay, lesbian, or bisexual client. Prior experience with other sexual minorities is essential. (You don't want to be someone's on-the-job training if you don't have to be.) An easy way to determine prior experience is to ask, "What has been your own process in coming to deal with homophobia, racism, oppression, and other such issues?" After you have heard the answer, you should have more information to help you decide if you will be able to make a trusting, safe connection with this person.[4]

Psychotherapists should be prepared to discuss theoretical orientation without using jargon; they should also be able to discuss how they see the change process, and how they can facilitate change. Psychotherapists can be asked to state in a general fashion how much they see themselves as a coach, a consultant, or a "mirror." Attempt to discover how active or direct the psychotherapist is in order to determine whether this will be a good fit with your needs.

For example, you may want the psychotherapist to provide feedback and information. Before beginning a relationship, find out if the psychotherapist's theoretical orientation (or preferred style) permits such a role. Similarly, different orientations assign responsibility for change to different agents—clients, psychotherapists, the intervention, or perhaps the medication. Inquire how the provider responds to a direct request for advice, for information, for support.

Finally, inquire about the psychotherapist's policy regarding physical contact with clients, such as hugging and touching, and how social interactions are handled. This is particularly important for sexual minorities seeking treatment from a gay or lesbian psychotherapist. Gay and lesbian communities are often small and interconnected, and gay/lesbian psychotherapists are likely to come in social contact with current, former, or future clients.

Asking "the Question"

To ask or not to ask about the psychotherapist's sexual orientation? In a less heterosexist society, this question would be quite routine. In this society, however, many will find this a difficult question to ask. If you decide to inquire, be clear about why you want or need to know the answer in order to be willing to work with a psychotherapist. It is quite appropriate to share your reasons for asking the question and the importance of the answer with regard to your ability to engage in the therapy process.

This is not to suggest that asking the question will, or even should, produce an answer. Some theoretical orientations suggest that psychotherapists not answer personal questions. For example, psychoanalytic and psychodynamically oriented psychotherapists are likely to have a more distant and personally reserved posture, and be unwilling to answer any personal question. However, if the psychotherapist has answered prior personal questions, but is unwilling to answer your question about sexual orientation, it is reasonable to consider this a warning signal. Consistency is a reasonable expectation.

The psychotherapist's response and comfort level with the topic of sexual orientation can help you decide whether or not you are willing to make a commitment to work with this individual. However, sexual orientation is only one dimension of many that may influence the "goodness of fit" between psychotherapist and client. Be honest with yourself about how important the information is at this time and how much it is likely to influence you.

If sexual orientation issues are a major part of the work you want to do, you should seek out either a gay or lesbian psychotherapist or a nongay psychotherapist with sufficient training, experience, and sensitivity in this area.

Therapy: Art and Science

The consultation interview may take a full session. If it does not, and you are satisfied with the answers you have heard and time permits, you could disclose your reasons for seeking services and the recent issues that have precipitated your search. Be willing to answer the psychotherapist's questions about background, social support, interpersonal relations, and family of origin. At the conclusion of your disclosures, this session or the next, invite the psychotherapist to make a general assessment of the nature of your problem. Attempt to get a new perspective on the problem or situation you face or a plan for developing this perspective. A simple summary of what you already know is less than ideal.

Your initial goal may be quite different from the psychotherapist's recommendation. This discrepancy should be addressed in order to reach a consensus. Be sure that you are able to commit to the goal(s) selected. It is essential to be able to collaborate with your treatment provider!

If you are not sure that there is a good fit at the end of the interview, take time to think over the information. You may call back after you have interviewed other psychotherapists. If you *are* satisfied, you can test the "fit" by contracting for a specific number of sessions with some measurable objectives. For example, if your focus is on improving your problem-solving abilities, look at how treatment is affecting your ability to solve problems after a specified period of time. Be realistic about the time frame and the measures to assess progress.

Therapy is both an art and a science. The science part relates to "knowing *what* needs to be said," and the art part refers to "*when* it should be said." This may sound like a simple task; it is, however, quite difficult. Not all providers provide equally.

It is well to be aware that a certain amount of anxiety and discomfort is appropriate and to be expected in initial sessions. You are dealing with someone who is a stranger. Some theoretical orientations consider anxiety to be essential for the change process and a sign that change is occurring. One rule of thumb is that, regardless of the psychotherapist's theoretical orientation, there should always be a balance between support and confrontation. Experiencing excessive anxiety that interferes with your ability to be open and trusting with this psychotherapist indicates that you need to discuss your apprehension. If it is not possible to bring this anxiety to a manageable level, pursue another referral. If you have a persistent and prevailing sense that this is not a safe relationship in which to pursue self-discovery, trust your gut. You are the one seeking help.

When considering questions to ask a prospective psychotherapist, I (KDK) think back to an experience I had when I lost my way in a little town in Italy. I knew a few Italian words to ask for directions; however, I didn't know the language well enough to understand the fast and complicated responses to my questions. I covered my confusion with a smile and muddled along; it took awhile until, eventually, I found my way.

In interviewing a psychotherapist, you do *not* have to "muddle through." If you don't understand the therapist's answers, continue to ask questions until the answers are clear and understandable, and you feel relatively confident that this person will help you find the additional answers you need. Getting your questions answered brings you to a new level of understanding of yourself, the world you live in, and the people around you.

* * *

CHAPTER 7

Assessing Progress with a Therapist

P sychotherapy is a process in which we heal our hurts through the relationship with a trained professional who is concerned with our best interests.
The therapeutic process cannot be evaluated in the same way we would
assess a management process or decision. We may have periods in which we feel a
great deal of progress is being made, and then there are other times when it seems
no progress is being made at all. Barren periods are definitely part of the therapy
process, and, sometimes, pursuing what may seem the wrong direction reveals
far more than staying on target. All of us can learn from our "mistakes." And, in
addition, we can discover the importance of our own imperfection and fallibility
through these tangents we have taken.

As an overview, evaluation itself depends on therapeutic orientation: how it
makes us feel, or think, or change our behavior. At the start, becoming aware of
feelings, or thoughts, or behavior can take a long time. When this finally happens,
as our relationship with the therapist progresses, we can ask ourselves: Do we feel
less defensive? Do we feel more insightful? Do we feel more empowered to reach
developmental goals? Evaluation needs to take these and other similar questions
into account.

Steps of the Process

In the therapeutic setting, the care provider helps us identify the issues causing
concern and distress. After these are recognized, therapist and client together may
develop measurable objectives that will indicate progress is being made. Once this
is accomplished, setting priorities for dealing with the issues is the next step. It is
entirely possible that, in the process of setting priorities or actually beginning to
work on them, additional issues will emerge that require attention. In tackling one
problem, therapist and client may discover additional problems.

Several important qualities facilitate the skilled professional's therapeutic interactions with clients. Small (1981) identifies these qualities as empathy, genuineness,

respect, self-disclosure, warmth, immediacy, concreteness, confrontation, potency, and self-actualization.

In a 1993 study, Picucci surveyed 130 clients and workshop participants in recovery regarding the specific attributes they looked for in therapists. Their responses indicated that individuals in recovery want therapists

- to encourage growth outside the therapy setting.
- to show lack of fear in revealing the therapist's own weaknesses.
- to allow themselves to make mistakes and show their humanity.
- to be familiar and respectful of varied addictions' self-help groups.
- to engender a safe, nonjudgmental atmosphere so that shame can surface.
- to encourage the client to take healthy risks.
- to give feedback, without which therapy would be frustrating.
- to provide a role model of what a fuller recovery might look and feel like.
- to be interactive and help illuminate dynamics that are debilitating.
- to compassionately include, and have understanding of, one's "shadow-self."
- to understand that therapy is ineffective if a client is suffering a substance addiction.
- to recognize that a new approach/strategy is required if the process becomes stagnant.[1]

Cavanagh (1982) identifies these qualities as important for a therapist to have: self-knowledge, competence, good psychological health, trustworthiness, honesty, strength, warmth, active responsiveness, patience, and sensitivity. In addition, the therapist must value the client's freedom to make choices; the therapist must approach, with a holistic awareness, the individual's many dimensions and also be aware of the impact of the environment. Taking all these qualities into account provides us with some useful insights about the manner in which the psychotherapist works with us on problems.

Measurable Objectives

A useful way to think of "measurable objectives" would be to look at the symptom(s) as if the problem were solved. What would be different? For example, to reduce symptoms of depression, a treatment plan might include objectives that would address (1) sleeping too much, (2) loss of appetite, (3) irritability, and (4) difficulty in keeping up with responsibilities. Some measurable objectives that would indicate progress in the first two areas might include sleeping no more than seven to eight hours a day or eating "x" amount of calories per day or "x" number of meals per day based on what would be normal functioning. (Getting outside consultation from a nutritionist might be required to accomplish this.) For the symptom of irritability, reduced friction in interpersonal contact might be a measurable objective. Indications of progress in fulfilling responsibilities might be attending work on a regular basis and showing up on time, getting the kids off to school on time, attending classes, or following through on commitments to others.

Once the client and therapist have set the objective(s), they might draw up a target contract as to when it seems reasonable the objectives will be accomplished. Some people will be able to achieve their objective(s) very quickly, while others may take much longer; it is never possible to predict an end point—not only because of clients' motivations but also because of the many strategies that might be introduced to address the problems.

Consideration of Strategies

Determining which strategies to use depends on the therapist's orientation and our goals for therapy. Some therapists might refer a client to a psychiatrist for a pharmacological intervention. That, in turn, would mean an additional objective for the client to become compliant and take the medication. The time frame for accomplishing the objective would then need to be extended until the individual responds to the medication.

Apart from medication, it is possible that the need for other modalities may become clearer as the therapy progresses. For example, the use of group sessions, family sessions, or couples sessions might arise. Supplementary resources—such as attendance at a Twelve Step program, participation in a self-help group, or involvement with people who have other disabilities (e.g., a cancer support group, an AIDS support group)—may also be needed. Additional interventions may need to be considered, including coping-skills training, relaxation methods, or other more complex activities, such as hypnosis or dream analysis. In all of these instances, the time frame for accomplishing objectives must be realistic, as determined by the client and therapist together, and reflect the use of different interventions as factors in implementing the strategy.

Treatment Plans

Because of the complex nature of individual responses to therapy, it is simply not possible to suggest what any treatment plan might look like, what specific measurable objectives should be, or where clients should be at the end of a session or a month or a year. The treatment plan will evolve, depending on (1) what we want to accomplish for ourselves in the therapeutic process and (2) the orientation of the therapist. At the same time the treatment plan is being consciously developed, an unconscious process is taking place that can be the most therapeutic or the most harmful. This process involves the development of trust in the therapist and trust in ourselves. Skilled therapists have healthy boundaries and help clients learn to develop these boundaries for themselves. In learning to trust others and ourselves, and in learning healthy boundaries, we begin to heal. In this process, earlier symptoms begin to fade away.

Perhaps sexual orientation is a primary focus of the work we wish to do with the psychotherapist. If there is no obvious strategy based on current circumstances, a possible approach to developing a treatment plan is, first, explore internalized homophobia and identity development (see chapter 27 for more about identity development); next, address the homophobia of family and friends; and, finally, address the impact of societal homophobia and larger cultural issues.

Client/Therapist Synergy

Target contracts need to be looked at and considered for revision on a periodic basis, and progress toward achieving objectives needs to be evaluated regularly. Periodic written or verbal reports of progress may be a routine part of the therapeutic process, and receiving these can easily be made part of the contract developed with the psychotherapist.

Clients have the right, within reason, to set the direction of the work being done with the therapist, but it should be a collaborative effort. However, there are exceptions. Consider the example of "Mr. Smith." Mr. Smith has been referred to a counselor because of three arrests for driving while intoxicated. From his history, his performance meets the criteria for substance abuser. Mr. Smith, however, wants to talk about why his partner is not more helpful or why his boss unfairly insists that he come to the counselor for help. His treatment focus is that he doesn't need a treatment focus. In fact, he may be actively resistant to the idea that he has any problem at all. In this circumstance, the kind of collaboration that can be expected of Mr. Smith in designing a treatment objective is quite different from someone else who acknowledges the existence of a substance-abuse problem.

Dorothy is another example. Dorothy comes to a consultation and says, "I'm here; can you help me?" Dorothy mentions a long list of symptoms but is in complete denial about a substance abuse problem. Does the therapist confront her at the outset with, "Oh yes, you do; and this is what we're going to do about it"? Probably not. A skilled therapist will work with her so that she will come to see the nature of her problem. The point is that the therapist can help to set the direction, but the client must cooperate in working on that lead. How the therapist manages to do this will have a great deal to do with professional training.

A good mix of support and confrontation is particularly helpful. Strategies for working with clients always involve the therapists' personal approach and their theoretical orientation. Some dynamics are more difficult to articulate than others, and it is essential for us to be patient with the process and trust it if our instincts tell us that progress is being made. If we have doubts, we should discuss these with the therapist.

Outcomes

Because the therapeutic process is a delicate and complicated one involving both conscious and unconscious dynamics, conflicts may arise that are not easily resolved. One way to determine if a therapist is skilled and effective, and has our best interest at heart, is to examine the way in which we feel supported in the conflict, and how satisfied we feel about the answers. How do we feel as a *result* of the conflict? Conflict is not necessarily bad; conflict can often be good. At the end of the struggling process, in terms of how it was handled, do we feel satisfied with the way the conflict is resolved?

It is not at all uncommon for clients to want to change the objectives they originally identified. They might also want to avoid changing behavior so that the objective would not be reached. Clients may want to change the focus of their therapy because either the objective has been achieved, and they don't want to formally acknowledge this, or they are unwilling or unable to start the process toward a different objective. Many clients have second thoughts about the changes they think they want to make in their lives. Often, they really aren't ready for them.

A model for change is precontemplation, contemplation, preparation, action, and maintenance (Prochaska et al. 1992). For example, someone has told Philip he really should think about change; Philip reaches a place in which he decides he doesn't need to change; but the therapist says, "Yes, you do." A struggle begins. Some people are merely contemplating making changes; they are not really ready to start the process. A skilled and caring therapist will attempt to honor where the client is, while also attempting to shine some insight on where the client might go.

Not infrequently, a small issue is responsible for getting clients into therapy. Then, as clients feel more comfortable, and the small issue is resolved, bigger issues surface. This is a good possibility. Other people may come with a big problem. Over time, they realize how big the problem really is, and they don't want to change because change is very frightening and therefore so much more unmanageable. Maybe the problem *is* unmanageable; maybe they are not ready to take it on. A caring therapist will help them explore their fears in a nonthreatening way. Then, the client may be able to decide against dealing with these other issues and understand the consequences of this decision.

Some people may take a moratorium on dealing with issues or make an extremely short foreclosure. For example, when confronted with a vocational crisis, some individuals haven't a clue what they want for themselves. They foreclose working on the problem; rather than explore what *they* want to do and make their own decision, they go into the family business. Even though James doesn't want to be a funeral director, he resolves the conflict by premature foreclosure and goes into the family business. While some people are able to work through conflict and get a resolution; others will put the conflict on hold and have a moratorium. Their problem is not resolved. In fact, it is now compounded because their feelings of self-worth have been lowered.

Using Therapy and Getting Results

Some of us for whom therapy has been a good experience think that we have to be in therapy continuously. "In case a problem arises in the future," we have someone to help us work through it. Another model of thinking about therapy is that of the primary care physician: the individual goes to the doctor for a checkup on an annual basis, or periodically; in the meanwhile, a cold or an infection can be the occasion of another visit to the physician.

We need to think about therapy in the same way we think about other kinds of support. We don't go to an accountant once to do our taxes. We go every time we need assistance with our taxes. We should not become defensive about seeing a therapist or foster in ourselves an unhealthy dependency on therapy. A therapist with whom we have rapport is an excellent resource. We can visit our therapist over the course of time and know that we will be working with someone who can support us when the need arises.

The importance of assessing our progress with a therapist on a regular basis cannot be overlooked. Each time we do this, perhaps the single-most important guideline indicating success and progress is whether we are feeling empowered to be healthier, happier individuals.

❋　　❋　　❋

CHAPTER 8

Using This Book

We are all "experts" on our own lives. After all, who knows more about a life than the one who has lived it? The material in part II provides the opportunity to explore in depth many of the feelings and attitudes that fill our conscious and unconscious experience. It offers a structure, a map if you will, for everyone who wishes to progress in recovery. Along our journey, we will explore where we have been and the conditions we have experienced both before entering recovery and in recovery.

Much of the time we are not even aware of the fears and inhibitions that motivate us. Therefore, to initiate any kind of action to change what we do, it is essential to get as much out in the open as possible. Only then can we be clear about misconceptions and destructive conclusions. Once we acknowledge these, we have a starting place from which the task of changing old ideas takes on entirely new meaning.

There is no "right way" to journey on the path of recovery; however, certain efforts bring us farther along the road than others. Support and encouragement to initiate these efforts, along with giving ourselves permission to make mistakes, will present a therapeutic key to using part II.

Through understanding comes empowerment. Regaining control of one's life is a process of clearing out the wreckage of the past and making new connections that will encourage the process of healing. The approach here is eclectic and focused on the individual. Hearing what others share at Twelve Step meetings and in group therapy may indeed be helpful in getting in touch with one's own "stuff"; nevertheless, the most important thing is that you get to know as much about *yourself* as possible. To accomplish this, the authors have used the models and ideas of professionals in all of the health care fields, as well as information and insights available in books, articles, and doctoral dissertations about recovery from addictive/compulsive behavior.

This book focuses on the gay, lesbian, or bisexual who seeks encouragement and support to make the journey through the wilderness. Many gays, lesbians, and bisexuals—as well as heterosexuals—have already used these exercises to explore their lives and enhance their recovery. You may wish to work entirely on your own or form a small group of people in recovery interested in discussing these exercises. The journey into recovery is a daily process of self-acceptance of *our own* diversity that gradually opens out into the acceptance of others in all *their* diversity. Part II will help you to begin the journey.

✻   ✻   ✻

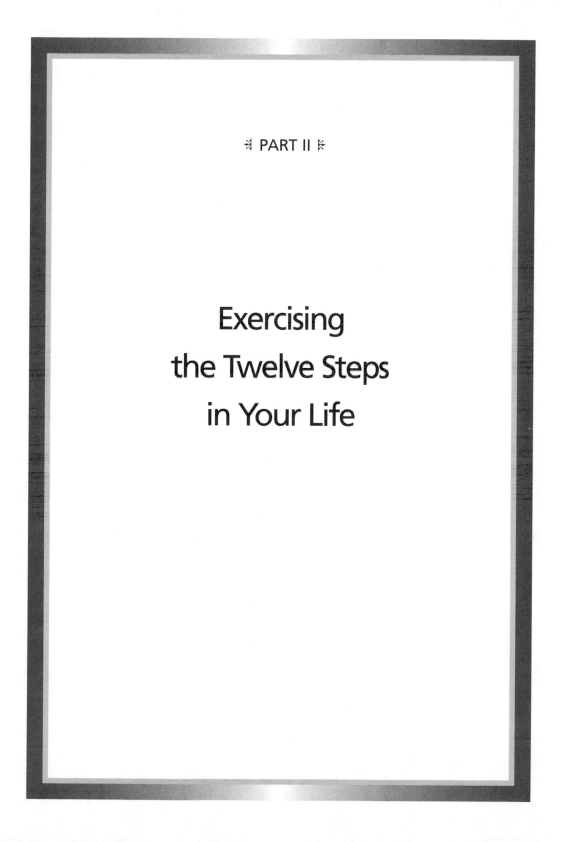

⚜ PART II ⚞

Exercising
the Twelve Steps
in Your Life

The Twelve Steps of Alcoholics Anonymous

Step 1
We admitted we were powerless over alcohol—
that our lives had become unmanageable.

Step 2
Came to believe that a Power greater than ourselves
could restore us to sanity.

Step 3
Made a decision to turn our will and our lives
over to the care of God as we understood Him.

Step 4
Made a searching and fearless moral inventory of ourselves.

Step 5
Admitted to God, to ourselves, and to another human being
the exact nature of our wrongs.

Step 6
Were entirely ready to have God remove all these defects of character.

Step 7
Humbly asked Him to remove our shortcomings.

Step 8
Made a list of all persons we had harmed,
and became willing to make amends to them all.

Step 9
Made direct amends to such people wherever possible,
except when to do so would injure them or others.

Step 10
Continued to take personal inventory
and when we were wrong promptly admitted it.

Step 11
Sought through prayer and meditation
to improve our conscious contact with God as we understood Him,
praying only for knowledge of His will for us and the power to carry that out.

Step 12
Having had a spiritual awakening as the result of these steps,
we tried to carry this message to alcoholics,
and to practice these principles in all our affairs.

From *Alcoholics Anonymous*, 3d ed. New York: Alcoholics Anonymous World Services, Inc., 1976, pp. 59–60. Used with permission. See editor's note on copyright page.

CHAPTER 9

Alternatives to the
Addictive/Compulsive Condition

Each of the Twelve Steps presents the recovering individual with an alternative approach to living. The chapters in part II explore the conditions associated with addictive/compulsive behavior. These painful conditions, along with all of the patterns developed to maintain them, keep us stuck or overwhelmed. But unless we are clear about any condition that needs to be changed, we have no reason for choosing the alternative!

By using each Step as a tool for self-revelation, we can work our way through the pain and bondage of compulsive/dependent behavior into the freedom of recovery. "Living-through" is the name given this activity; it provides the process for self-acceptance. After exploring our own personal experience in relation to the addictive/compulsive condition, we discover that the efforts we need to make in recovery are no longer vague or confusing. The chart below shows the twelve conditions most prevalent in addictive/compulsive behavior and the alternatives offered by the Twelve Steps in recovery.

TWELVE CONDITIONS & ALTERNATIVES

CONDITION	ALTERNATIVE
1. Denial	1. Acceptance
2. Isolation and fear	2. Faith/belief
3. Willful powerlessness	3. Willing, positive action
4. Self-delusion	4. Self-revelation
5. Regression/stagnation	5. Cleansing/renewal
6. Inflexibility	6. Flexibility
7. Arrogance	7. Humility
8. Irresponsibility	8. Responsibility
9. Suffering and fragmentation	9. Healing and reconfiguration
10. Backsliding	10. Self-discipline
11. Self-centeredness	11. Spiritual connection
12. Self-seeking	12. Communion with others—altruism

Because the process of recovery is a slow one, moving into the alternatives and restoring balance in all the different parts of our lives is accomplished a little at a time. Using the Twelve Steps to work through the physical, emotional, and spiritual dimensions of life reveals always new areas for recovery, no matter how far along we are in the process. In each chapter in part II, practical exercises and suggestions for action explore the route of the journey and provide an in-depth perspective for the novice and the veteran traveler.

Change doesn't occur magically or because we spend several hours with a therapist or in a group once or twice a week. Change develops through working at it, day in and day out, and finding ourselves in a different place. While comparing ourselves with others is useless and often discouraging, we can always benefit from looking at our own progress in terms of where we start out from and the movement we make forward in our journey of recovery.

The exercises in each chapter have been designed as a means of assessing progress. They create an index of change: "I used to feel this way about my hopes and aspirations; now, I feel *this* way." The workbook sections will provide you with the opportunity to extend the processing of material about the Steps, as well as focus your attention on specific ideas of change that may not have occurred to you. Someone once said, "If all you do is talk about feelings, you don't change." (The same thing can be said, "If all you do is talk, you don't change.") These exercises are about facts as well as *feelings*, and they link both together into new patterns. These patterns provide insight that can guide the development of the new thoughts, behaviors, and attitudes essential for progress.

Along with a journal notebook to write in, you may wish to purchase a three-ring binder in which to keep completed photocopied worksheets, along with additional pages you way want to interleaf. That's up to you. Over the next weeks, you will develop a great deal of information to support your recovery now and in the future. Keeping your work in a safe and secure place is a good idea in any case.

For anyone who does not use the worksheets on a regular basis, it might be important to check out what's standing in the way. Explore the reasons in order to identify important clues regarding obstacles to your own personal recovery. List a few of the reasons. After reading over your list, what do you discover about yourself? What can you do about this now? Make an entry into your journal notebook about your answers.

✳️   ✳️   ✳️

This first sequence of exercises has been developed to help you understand what change means in a very personal and specific way in your life. Change is movement from one place or state of being to another. Most of us made many changes from one city to another ("geographics"), from one relationship to another, and from one economic level to another (affluence to poverty) before we entered recovery. To understand what change would mean now from the perspective of the things we like about ourselves and the things we don't, let's show the kind of movement we'd like to make in our lives on a matrix.

Over the next weeks, you will develop a great deal of information to support your recovery now and in the future. Keeping it in a safe and secure place is a good idea in any case.

Be sure to consider the impact of sexual orientation as you explore these questions.

1. On the matrix below, place an "x" where you think you stand in each of the areas shown, and then indicate in which direction you think you'd like to move. (Assets are the things about ourselves that we like; liabilities are the things about ourselves that we don't like.) The line down the middle is the balance line.

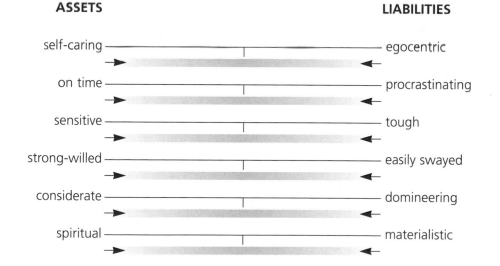

ASSETS		LIABILITIES
self-caring		egocentric
on time		procrastinating
sensitive		tough
strong-willed		easily swayed
considerate		domineering
spiritual		materialistic

You may extend this list of characteristics on additional sheets.

2. In considering the direction you wish to move with any of these assets and liabilities, what evidence do you have that any movement is necessary? Give specific examples from your present and past.

_____

_____

_____

3. Use the list below to record additional examples of the *conditions* that affected your life prior to entering recovery:

   a. *Denial:*_____

   b. *Isolation:* _____

   c. *Willfulness:* _____

   d. *Self-delusion:* _____

   e. *Feeling caught or stuck:* _____

   f. *Inflexibility:* _____

   g. *Arrogance:* _____

   h. *Irresponsibility:* _____

   i. *Feeling like a victim:* _____

   j. *Inability to keep promises to yourself or others:* _____

   k. *Self-centeredness:* _____

   l. *Self-seeking:*_____

4. Circle the three conditions that functioned most significantly in your life.

5. At the left, identify these three conditions and on the right describe how each one affected the following:

   #1: _____   a. relationships:_____

                                b. job/work: _____

                                c. health: _____

                                d. sex life: _____

                                e. happiness: _____

                                f. security: _____

                                g. (other): _____

#2: _____ a. relationships: _____

                                    b. job/work: _____

                                    c. health: _____

                                    d. sex life: _____

                                    e. happiness: _____

                                    f. security: _____

                                    g. (other): _____

#3: _____ a relationships: _____

                                    b. job/work: _____

                                    c. health: _____

                                    d. sex life: _____

                                    e. happiness: _____

                                    f. security: _____

                                    g. (other): _____

6. Of the seven areas of your life identified above (a.–g.), which was the most unmanageable?

_____

_____

_____

7. Describe the ways in which it was unmanageable.

_____

_____

_____

8. What is your definition of "unmanageability"?

_____

_____

_____

9. Visualize yourself in your most "unmanageable" situation and choose a word or a phrase that captures this image.

_____

_____

_____

10. In a few sentences, describe what "hitting bottom" meant for you in your life. Be as specific as possible.

_____

_____

_____

11. What feelings does "hitting bottom" evoke for you?

_____

_____

_____

12. When did you start working on your recovery? Is this your first time, or have you made previous attempts?

_____

_____

_____

13. What specific events led up to your most recent decision?

_____

_____

_____

14. Mention any doubts you may still have about the necessity to make a significant change in your behavior regarding substance(s), person(s), or behavior(s). Write about these doubts.

_____

_____

_____

15. How might you be avoiding facing yourself and your need to make changes *(e.g., "I'm too young," "I'm too healthy," "I'm too _____ ")*. Write about this.

_____

_____

_____

16. What reservations do you have about the need to remain committed to the changes you have set out for yourself? What conditions have you placed, if any, on your recovery? *"I'll be sober as long as I have my job, my house, my car, my relationship."*

_____

_____

_____

_____

_____

17. Identify three things about *yourself* that you find difficult to (or cannot) accept.

_____

_____

_____

_____

18. Identify three things about *others* that you find difficult to (or cannot) accept.

_____

_____

_____

_____

19. What obstacles are in the way of your recovery?

_____

_____

_____

20. What do you need to assist you in your change process? your recovery process?

_____

_____

_____

_____

_____

21. Write some of your thoughts or comments after considering these questions.

_____

_____

_____

_____

_____

22. On the scale below, circle how you feel after considering these issues.

Hopeful	1	2	3	4	5	Hopeless
Enthusiastic	1	2	3	4	5	Discouraged
Receptive	1	2	3	4	5	Shut down

23. Complete this sentence: At this moment of my life, change is

_____

_____

_____

24. Is this okay for now?   ☐ Yes   ☐ No

25. Begin a journal entry about your experience of recovery at this time. Use your notebook for this entry.

CHAPTER 10

The Paradox of Denial

CONDITION

Denial

For as long as we can get away with it, we turn our backs on anything we do not like about ourselves! We encourage family, lovers and friends, employers and strangers to believe we are the way we'd like to be instead of the way we are. When we can no longer avoid looking at the effects of our substance use or compulsive behavior, we come face to face with our own denial. For some people, this means they "hit bottom." And for as long as we pretend that we are not dependent on the substances and/or behaviors that we have allowed to run our lives, we remain in denial.

ALTERNATIVE

Acceptance

Only by accepting ourselves exactly as we are—gay, lesbian, and bisexual men and women dependent on substances or compulsive behavior—can we begin to recover.

Step 1

We admitted we were powerless over alcohol [mood-altering substances, compulsive behavior]—that our lives had become unmanageable.

Beginning recovery as a lesbian, gay man, or bisexual means that wherever we start the journey, the road winds through a threatening landscape of soaring peaks and dark abysses known only to us. From our own experiences and the stories of others, we know this is true for each of us. Sharing this journey of recovery as simply and honestly as possible is the task we are beginning, and we cherish the hope that our effort will provide others with the strength and support they need on their way into a new life.

It is especially difficult for nongay men and women recovering from compulsive/dependent behavior, and others who are not at risk, to understand what it is like for us to set out on the journey of recovery. The answer to the question "Isn't recovery the same for everyone?" is yes *and* no. At the heart of this book is the need to appreciate and respond to the differences.

The description of the journey starts where recovery begins—with the individual at the very moment of beginning: now. Unless we begin here, we cannot progress beyond yesterday. We are stuck in the past, lost in the labyrinth of what has already happened instead of open to the possibilities that recovery makes available to us.

Living in today is vastly different from living the past over again—that's like living IN my story, the way so many others do who keep repeating the chronicle of the events of their lives when acting out with compulsive/dependent behavior. Instead of being lost to it, honestly acknowledging what has already happened helps us to live *through* these events, to live beyond them into this moment. No longer remaining stuck in the past and being held hostage to it, we can enrich the present with new experiences. Life begins to belong to us in some new and authentic way instead of everything being painfully accidental.

Addiction to substances has been called "the disease of denial." This means that the very condition itself makes it difficult to admit that there is a problem. In fact, the presence of persistent denial when others who are impartial and unbiased assert that there is a problem is cause for concern. While others may be able to recognize the evidence of abuse or dependency, denial often makes it impossible for those who suffer to see the symptoms in themselves. How insidious! Addiction *is* insidious, along with being cunning, baffling, and powerful enough to damage or destroy the lives of everyone it touches. It is understandable why it would be so difficult to admit and self-apply the label of "alcoholic" or "addict" because of the stigma attached.

Compounding this condition with the denial of our sexuality (because of the stigma attached), we raise the destructive power of dependency to the maximum. In the early stages of recovery, the most common reason for gay men, lesbians, or bisexuals to return to the old habits of the past is their inability to accept being homosexual or bisexual. In the past, many of us have found it possible to endure intense pressure and strain; in recovery, by definition, there is no mood-altering substance to deaden the pain. It is a shock to many who believed they had completely accepted their sexuality to discover old doubts and fears again staring them in the face once they stop self-medicating or acting compulsively. Often, they find they need to begin the acceptance process all over again, or at a deeper level.

The Bar Scene

Many gay men and lesbians, in the daily course of their lives, spend a great deal of time in bars, clubs, or discos. The bar is frequently the center of activity and recreation for both couples and singles. Bars and discos are a place to hang out, meet friends, find new partners, and, in general, relax and enjoy life. A party in someone's home is a special occasion; a night at the bar is any night of the week. "The life," for those new to it, often focuses on the bar scene.

For many of us, at first the bars seemed glamorous and exciting in comparison with the shadow lives we lived at home in our families. The clubs were filled with new faces, people to talk to, and the kind of stimulation we had been looking for. The bars were exciting and different. As time passed, however, and as the scene grew more and more familiar, routine set in. When the glamour fades and the boredom begins, the alcohol in the glass assumes a different role. All too often it becomes the real reason for going to the bar, but by then the habit is so much a part of the routine that the truth is hard, if not impossible, to recognize. Does this sound at all familiar?

Guess I'm up for a little change of scenery tonight. Tryin' out a new bar. At least the name out front is different. Not much else inside. I'll see if I can get one of those stools at the end of the bar. Damn! That nerd ordered another drink instead of leaving. What's the matter: doesn't he have a home? If I'd gone to my usual place, I'd have a seat by now. Well, maybe I wouldn't.

The bunch drinking here looks just like the ones in my usual hang-out; haven't I seen them all before? Everyone's beginning to look alike to me. That same phony kind of cheery sullenness (or is it sullen cheeriness?) is every place I go. And the sound system, yuk. Sticky icing on a stale birthday cake. This whole scene is stale. I should know, I've lived it . . . forever! Why do I keep telling myself it's fun? Can't understand it!

But I'm here. Where else do I have to go? I'll order another drink. I didn't drive all the way downtown just to turn around and drive home! Look at that; the nerd on my left is on his way to the door. Now that feels good: perched on my favorite spot at the bar. How about another drink? Sure. Isn't that what livin' right is all about?

Variations on this monologue are endless, but the basic condition is the same: being trapped inside the bottle—or the drug, or the food, or the sex, or the dysfunctional behavior—with no other alternative except to use the fix. Chasing that first "high" is a losing game. Where are the good times? They're rare, even though we never give up searching for them. But we go on compensating for this disappointment by losing ourselves in our drug of choice. Except that after awhile, we feel we no longer have a choice. It seems to have chosen us. What began in fun becomes an absolute necessity; we cannot live without it. Seemingly, without warning, we are hooked without even knowing it. And once begun, the progress of our dependency may accelerate undetected. For some, this hook has psychological dimensions; for others, underneath the psychological dimensions are physical dimensions that create tolerance and the need to maintain a certain level of consumption to avoid withdrawal.

How Can I Tell?

Paul had just come out of the hospital after suffering severe depression brought on by excessive use of alcohol and pain medication. The previous spring, he had been hospitalized after an auto accident in which he had almost been killed. His use of alcohol before the car crash had never been a problem—except for an occasional bad hangover when he really overdid it. Paul had a very hard time believing he had become an alcoholic. He went to an AA meeting to find out how people knew whether or not they were alcoholics. An old-timer named John told him: "Try AA for ninety days: don't drink alcohol or use any other drugs for ninety days. And go to meetings. If you really don't have any problem, everything will be fine. We'll refund your misery. You can always go back to drinking."

Paul needed to find out if John was right, so he decided to try AA just to see what happened. To his absolute horror, he discovered he couldn't get through even the third day without drinking, let alone ninety! Without help, he knew he couldn't stop drinking.

Most people who use alcohol don't become "alcoholics." And we meet people everywhere who have survived serious accidents and don't become dependent on medication. Nevertheless, for Paul, the drugs the doctors prescribed and the alcohol he used to anesthetize the physical pain and the emotional despair, a dose at a time, affected his system in such a way as to create dependence on these substances without his knowing it. After the pain he had already endured, it was not surprising for him to ask, "But why me? Why has such a thing happened to me?"

Everyone who develops a dependency asks these questions. It is as shattering and incomprehensible as the demand for an explanation to the question "Why am I gay?" "Why am I lesbian?" "Why am I bisexual?" At present, the answer is an enigma. There is only one response that has made any sense at all: *Why NOT me?*

Neither running away, nor hiding, nor denial brings any relief that lasts. While we may pretend we've escaped from any obstacle that may be confronting us, when we wake in the darkness between 3:00 and 4:00 A.M., we know we are alone. It is then we are clearest that any hope for peace comes in accepting ourselves exactly as we are and moving on from there.

"Why Me?"

The question "Why me?" is at the heart of the denial system. Denial is the mask we use to protect ourselves from the reality, from the truth that we have a substance-abuse problem, or have become dependent on addictive/compulsive behavior. By asking the question, we mask the truth that it IS the way it IS. The asker begs for a different answer.

If dependency exists as a plan, it is nevertheless quite rare for someone to set out in life to become dependent on substances or behavior. It happened along the way. Dependency entails a process where the use of substances influences our physical, emotional, and mental being in greater and greater degrees. And in the place where things only happen, where we happen to something or it happens to us, we function as victims. As victims, there is no help. We are only available to be victimized.

In our denial, in our nonacceptance of the man or woman we are, others intentionally, as well as thoughtlessly, negate who we are and all that we value and act on. Living as a negative entity in a positive world is the predicament of the gay man, lesbian, or bisexual who does not accept himself or herself *and* of the individual who does not accept that he or she has a chemical or behavioral dependency. Living like this is living in a nightmare.

In this bad dream, the world is upside down; suffering is a source of pleasure. As perverse as it sounds, substance abusers find in suffering, in their dependency, something positive. The dependent individual is accustomed to pain and suffering; the victim is accustomed to pain and suffering. It becomes the norm. Denial makes it possible for this upside-down world to function. We do not have to search far for the reason. Gays and lesbians have been conditioned in our homes, our schools, our churches—everywhere in our society—to be victims and to deny that what is is not. Under these circumstances, there should be little wonder why sexual minorities are at such a higher risk for addiction.

Many people know about the risk; nevertheless, they choose to believe it can never happen to *them*. It looms as too much of a threat. The moment their upside-down world becomes shaky, they implement every defense they can think of: "I am too intelligent!" "I am too rich/poor!" "I am too young!" "I only drink beer!" "The doctor prescribed it!" "It couldn't happen to me!" "My life isn't unmanageable; I don't live in the gutter!" Defenses are legion, but all we are actually dealing with is denial. For most individuals with a dependency, it usually takes a special kind of personal calamity like a serious car accident, losing a job, the breaking up of a relationship, or a devastating medical diagnosis to come face to face with the truth that there is a problem: "I am dependent on alcohol." "I compulsively overeat." "I use sex compulsively." "I am dependent on others to feel good about myself."

No one can make another person say this and *mean* it. The individual is the only one. The acknowledgment of the label is not the point. The point is that the individual must come to the conclusion that a change is necessary because life as it is is unmanageable. While the pain may be enormous in getting to that place in which such an admission of unmanageability is possible, the relief of being able to do it is indescribable. With these words of acceptance, the way is opened to receive help. Until that moment, there is no access to the individual who has become isolated by chemical dependency or compulsive behavior.

Why is that? Dependency masks itself in many different disguises. As many as one out of three hospital beds may be filled with patients with complications arising from substance abuse. Until individuals treat the root cause of their problems, the rest of the complications go on multiplying.

Accepting the reality of the problem (whatever the degree of severity) is the beginning of the process of dealing with the unmanageability of one's life. It's as simple as that. Then why is it so difficult for gays, or lesbians, or bisexuals to accept the reality? It is through alcohol, through mood-altering substances, through compulsive behavior that so many of us believed we found the comfort and acceptance that was missing in our lives. How can we live without these "friends" who have seen us through the night? Where, after all, is there to go? Our loneliness and our isolation from society are real. Is this void, then, the alternative to drinking and using? It is no surprise when individuals with alcohol dependency give in to the drink without a second thought: "I couldn't stand living without alcohol or drugs, so don't even suggest it!"

An Agonizing Choice

Alone or in relationships, sexual minorities face an agonizing choice. Drugs and alcohol are often at the center of the connection with lovers, as well as friends. The prospect of breaking up with a partner because of substance abuse—as unhealthy or painful as the relationship might be—is as terrifying as leaving the bars for those who make them the focus of their social and "family" life. Putting up with bad is at least better than *disaster*, and many are willing to settle for that.

Nongay men and women, when they first abstain from alcohol and substances, are painfully in touch with the bitter experience of isolation resulting from the consequences of substance dependency. For gays, for lesbians, who already suffer from the isolation separating us from society, it is a double dose of despair to swallow. In a society that deprives homosexuals of their human rights and ostracizes them for their basic human desire to relate with others like themselves, there seems no place to turn. Discriminated against on the basis of sexual orientation, gay men and women face the devastating prospect of being discriminated against because of chemical/behavioral dependency *as well.* Remembering that these substances had made life a little less difficult to bear, the gay and lesbian look at denial as the only choice possible for them to make.

Chemical dependency and compulsive behavior are maintained by the defense of denial. Denial is often adaptive and keeps at bay what would overwhelm and incapacitate us otherwise. For many who are chemically dependent, this is the way to cope, to stay sane. The choice to drink or to use other drugs made it possible to put up with the cruelty and abuse, the hatred, the discrimination, the distortions of the truth that sexual minorities experience. Just like the alcohol and the other drugs, the denial of who we are, and our value as loving and responsible human beings entitled to live happy lives along with everyone else, made it possible to support the little there was left to settle for. Staying hooked on denial makes life at least a little more bearable.

But the least is far too little to settle for in a world in which every man and every woman has the responsibility of finding joy and happiness. When we become willing to look through the *other* end of the telescope at the upside-down world we settled for, we finally understand there is an alternative: acceptance—of ourselves exactly as we are, and of our task of finding joy and making our own unique contribution to life and the world around us. With such understanding, sexual minorities with chemical and behavioral dependencies can appreciate that denial is *un*natural and merely a symptom of the disorder. Instead of being the basis for uniqueness, denial forces everyone who suffers from it to live like outcasts in a foreign land.

Accepting Our Denial

Accepting denial is the beginning of recovery because when we no longer have to live in opposition to denial, its force and persistence diminishes. When denial loses its power, other alternatives appear. We may have little or no idea what a different kind of life might mean, but we can begin to understand that the way we've been living does not have to continue. It takes a long time for many of us to reach this place. We have been looking through the wrong end of the telescope for so long that we are capable only of tunnel vision until some powerful shock occurs in our lives.

For some of us, a job loss or an auto accident is the cause; for others, a different kind of shock accelerates the unmanageability of our lives and sends us spinning downward into the vortex of self-destruction. Quickly or slowly, we come to some understanding that something *must* change. Continual denial that we have become addicted results in lower and lower depths to sink to. There comes a time for some, however, when we are either sick enough or frightened enough or desperate enough to say: "No further! I'm getting off here!" Or, "I'm sick and tired of being sick and tired!"

This has been called "Step Zero: This shit has got to stop!" It is the moment, the bottom, from which recovery begins. Accepting oneself as being in such a place, no matter how little or how much one has lost, is the only way possible to receive help.

An interesting similarity exists between "coming out of the closet" as gays or lesbians, or bisexuals, and accepting ourselves as addicted. Both acts admit that there is a real life to live outside of isolation and despair, and that the choice to live it is ours. In the closet, gays, lesbians, and bisexuals pretend they are *not* this or *not* that. What a different place to be in to be able to say: I *am* this; I *am* that! This act of affirmation carries with it basic human entitlements instead of rejection and scorn. Affirmation is power, and with it now directed back to its very source—to ourselves—instead of giving it away to others, we begin the process of living a healthy life in a world that no longer has to be upside down. Coming out of the closet makes it possible for us to live as a positive force instead of as a negative one in an upside-down world.

This is exactly the courage that is essential if we are to accept ourselves as being dependent on or addicted to substances or behaviors. It is as if the whole world would suddenly collapse. Accepting oneself, however, makes it possible to receive the help we need to begin recovery into life. The act itself *is* incredibly difficult to do. Nevertheless, the fact is very simple: affirmation is the end to denial. Affirmation opens the way to accessing one's path in life again.

As a victim, such a transformation is impossible, and that is the best explanation why change cannot begin without acceptance. What makes one human being truly different from another is the way in which each of us uses our energy. Denial deprives us of energy and forces us to live as victims. Acceptance, on the other hand, is the initiation of responsible action.

No one else can do this for us. We are the only ones who can accept ourselves. Indeed, others can show us how they have done it, but unless we do it for ourselves, we must live in denial—with the world on its head, upside down. Acceptance is the first gift from the sea of recovery that we can give *ourselves*. That is why it is so difficult to grasp! Once we do, others can help us.

Sexual minorities have grown up in a world in which they have experienced shame and scorn from family, friends, and strangers. They are not in the habit of affirming themselves; they are not in the habit of trusting others to affirm them. Imagine how difficult it is, therefore, to believe that the solution to problems is not in the fix, and that there are others who CAN help us. Living upside down in the world, we have told ourselves that we CANNOT be gay and happy and sober, because that's the message society has given us. We can never discover this is a lie until we begin to live the truth. Taking the first step of self-acceptance is an incredible risk that opens on a new way of living. Many have balked at this risk, thinking that they, in their own uniqueness, could find an easier way.

Chemically dependent individuals who are gay and lesbian often fool themselves into believing it is fear of something, or someone, or the past, *instead of the fear of the unknown that change brings with it,* that makes them hang on to their dependency or that drives them back into it again. Living in dependency on substances or behavior, we *know* exactly where we will end up; in recovery, we have no idea, and that is why sobriety is such a risk. Recovery is the real challenge and not dependency. Can we do it? Are we worth such a gift? Acceptance of ourselves as being worthy can be experienced only in the act itself, and, if you have read this far, you have already begun the journey.

For those who have doubts whether or not they are dependent on substances or behavior, or are involved with people who are, there are two lists of questions in appendix A and appendix B (pages 353–356). Allow yourself the benefit of answering the questions honestly. You can do this for yourself. The rewards are waiting for you if you do, and the choice of receiving them is entirely yours. Not one gift from the sea of recovery will be withheld once you reach out for the first one: acceptance. Acceptance is the beginning of change.

米   米   米

As you begin to work through this exercise, remember to consider the impact and influence of sexual orientation on your attitudes, beliefs and behaviors. After you have answered the questions in appendices A and B (pages 353–356), consider how you feel about your life and your future. How do your answers to these questions contribute to your motivation to change?

※   ※   ※

For those who are, or may consider, attending a Twelve Step program, sponsorship is recommended as a source of support, encouragement, information, suggestions. Others who do not wish to attend Twelve Step programs will need to find support and coaching from other knowledgeable and capable sources. Such sources may include a single individual (psychotherapist, friend, spouse) or a group.

※   ※   ※

Perhaps you know individuals already in one of the Twelve Step programs with whom you could talk about dependency on substances or compulsive behavior, or codependency. Arrange to meet them and discuss some of your concerns. Give yourself the opportunity to learn what they did to find help. Conduct the conversation as an exercise in listening.

If you do not know anyone in a Twelve Step program, consider finding a psychotherapist who can assist you in undertaking a change process. See part I, chapter 6, "Choosing a Therapist" (page 45).

※   ※   ※

Once you have begun to gather new information, write down your thoughts about what you heard and its significance for you at this time.

※   ※   ※

Alcohol, other drugs, and/or compulsive behavior(s) have been a powerful influence in our lives. Far more powerful, perhaps, than we have been willing to admit to ourselves. The condition we know so well is one of denial—that there is nothing wrong with us, and that everything in time is going to be okay. Getting in touch with the realities we have been denying or avoiding is often painful and always startling. We need to look at what comes up for us as we respond to questions that explore the condition of denial and point to the alternative of acceptance.

1. In which areas of your life did you feel most "powerless" and unable to make changes?

   _____

   _____

   _____

   In which areas of your life do you feel most capable of making changes?

   _____

   _____

   _____

2. "Powerlessness" means _____

   _____

3. What are your reactions when you consider the idea of being "powerless" over chemical dependence or compulsive behavior? Be as specific as possible.

   _____

   _____

   _____

4. At this time in your life, identify the most significant/powerful

   People:

   _____

   _____

   Places:

   _____

   _____

   Things:

   _____

   _____

5. If you have made other attempts in the past to begin recovery but were unsuccessful, what role have these people, places, and things played in your life?

_____

_____

_____

6. How did you feel about the role played by these people, places, and things in the past?

_____

_____

_____

7. Have you reached any conclusions about what you must do now to handle problems that result from any of these issues?

_____

_____

_____

8. Your support system before entering recovery was made up of the following people:

_____

_____

_____

9. Your support system in recovery is made up of these people:

_____

_____

_____

10. What are some of the characteristics you appreciate in them?

_____

_____

_____

11. What characteristics or attitudes of other people do you need to guard against? What are the implications of these insights?

_____

_____

_____

12. Take this opportunity to consider the past few years and draw a time line on which you can place significant events that reveal your progression of abuse/dependency/ addictive/compulsive behavior. Start with the twelve months immediately prior to entering recovery or from the earliest memories you have of problematic behavior. (Indicate the events or behaviors on the line below the year.)

Year _____

_____

_____

Year _____

_____

_____

Year _____

_____

_____

Year _____

_____

_____

Year _____

_____

_____

Year _____

_____

_____

(Use additional time lines to go back as far as you can remember.)

13. Create a "life line" noting with an "x" significant events such as losses, traumas, triumphs, and illnesses. (See the example below.)

X
high school
graduation

X
college
graduation

X
marriage

X
promotion at
work

X
DWI

X
car
accident

X
father's
cancer diagnosed

14. On your life line, write the names of people, places, and things you associate with each event.

15. What new connections are you able to make between these life events and your history of substance use/abuse? Explain.

_____

_____

_____

16. Imagine Denial and Acceptance as two opposite ends of a rope. Where do you place yourself on this continuum? Consider what tension there is for you as you make this choice.

Denial   **Acceptance**

17. What does "acceptance" mean for you?

_____

_____

_____

18. Are there any issues in the way of your being able to accept the need for change in your life? Explain.

_____

_____

_____

19. If you see yourself as dependent on substances or compulsive behavior, visualize yourself as Bambi and your dependence as a monster from a horror film, such as Godzilla. Imagine that every time you attempt to prove yourself _powerful_ over your monster, this is like "Bambi meets Godzilla." How do you feel about this attempt to control the impossible? How does this image relate to your prior experiences? _(Use as many sheets of paper as you need to explore these questions.)_

CHAPTER 11

The Wilderness of Isolation

CONDITION
Isolation and fear

ALTERNATIVE
Faith/belief

We felt lonely and afraid. If we were hoping that the bars and the clubs would change all this, we found out they didn't. We began to feel even lonelier and more frightened as time went on. Whatever we used for a fix became our bosom buddy. We came to rely on it—until we began to notice that we were becoming even *more* frightened and *more* alone than before. We found ourselves in a corner with nowhere to turn. Physically, emotionally and spiritually, we became desperate in our feeling of hopelessness.

The antidote to compulsive/dependent behavior is faith in a Power greater than ourselves. Developing this faith opens the way to help and hope.

Step 2

Came to believe that a Power greater than ourselves could restore us to sanity.

Compulsive/dependent behavior is like an elevator ride to the bottom of the universe. At any stop along the way, we can get off if we make a conscious decision to get help. The most common response is to insist that nothing bad has happened yet, so there is no reason to end the joyride.

Nancy, a twenty-two-year-old lesbian, is indignant at the mere suggestion she might have a drinking problem. She speaks for many who refuse even to consider getting off the elevator:

> *Listen, I'm not like those drunks! I've got a job; I've got an apartment;*
> *I've got a lover! Does that sound like someone who's hangin' on to the*
> *curb looking for the next drink?*

Even though Nancy couldn't get through a day without a six-pack and several vodka tonics, she hasn't *yet* experienced the full effects of chemical dependency on her life. The three letters *Y E T* are initials that stand for *You're E* ligible *Too*. If it hasn't happened yet, for many people it may be just a question of time before the ride hits the bottom.

Stepping Off the Down Elevator

Denial, as we have already seen, is a powerful force, and the evidence of YET— if it isn't too weighty—requires little effort to dismiss. Many must prove this to themselves, but there are a few who are willing to let others carry on this research. We are the lucky ones who get off the elevator before YET happens.

Lucky is hardly the way most of us in our first few days of abstinence would describe ourselves. The physical symptoms of chemical withdrawal are painful and many of us require professional attention because of the danger the body is exposed to. The body fights back to secure the "fix" it has been deprived of, and the mind and the emotions are willingly enlisted in this combat. It feels like living in No Man's Land on a battlefield; it is a wilderness in which everything else seems unreal except *my* pain, *my* confusion, *my* terror. Most of us who experience the pain and anguish of withdrawal ask: "Is this why I stopped drinking? Is this what putting down drugs gets me? You've got to be kidding!"

During those initial days after deciding to find out what it feels like to be abstinent, we are often baffled by what people do with their lives day and night who do not use any substances or compulsive behavior! Abuse of these may have become such an entrenched part of our routine that being without them seems UNnatural. We are lost, totally lost without them. All sense of security vanishes and we feel hopeless we will ever get it back again. One of the most frightening things we tell ourselves when we are in a bad place is that it will ALWAYS be like this—"I will never feel better again." We tell ourselves that unless we drink or use or act out, we will die. In the wilderness, this is the voice we know best, and it finds us any hour of the day or night.

But that voice in our head that tells us this is a liar. It's our compulsive behavior that says to us: You can't make it without ME! (whatever the substance or behavior is). We can answer back: "When I start thinking like that, I know it's my stuff talking to me. And you know something? If I listen to that insanity, then I *am* insane! When I live in recovery, I'm not."

Without help, it is almost impossible to hear the sound of any other voice. As remarkable as it may seem, we ARE able to listen to other individuals in recovery who tell us how *they* made it through this place and are still alive to talk about it.

> *I know all about the stuff I'm using. I'm an expert! Where to get it, my sources, the prices and when. It's my whole life. Everything I did centered on my addiction. I can't trust anyone who can't understand this. That's why if I'm going to get through this wilderness, I've got to hear it from others just like me who have already done it. I've got to hear it from people who talk my language, not doctors in white coats who talk in words only they can understand.*

Some individuals have put down the drink and "white-knuckled" it on their own. As far as they are concerned, they don't need anyone else to support their efforts at abstinence. However, except for not abusing other substances or indulging in a specific compulsive behavior, their lives often progress very little beyond this point. For them, it will not be long before compulsive behavior begins in other areas, like work, sex, or relationships and with other substances, like cigarettes, pills, or food. The pain starts all over; this time in a new place.

Choices

In dependency, there are no choices: nothing will satisfy us except the substance on which we depend. In sobriety, in abstinence, in recovery, there are an infinite variety of choices. One of those choices is to participate in a Twelve Step recovery program.[1] In these meetings, we can hear from others who have been in the same place before us, or who are there right now, exactly where we are. What a shock it is to discover that there are others just like ourselves!

I am alone: I am NOT alone.

This is an amazing paradox; just when we believe we are totally alone, without a relationship or any of the friends from the life we have been leading, just when we find ourselves in the midst of the wilderness, we can see gays and lesbians just like us at AA meetings, Narcotics Anonymous meetings, Overeaters Anonymous meetings. Is this possible? Is there really life *outside* the bars? Are there others who have left relationships centered on booze, substances, or compulsive behavior and still survived? Can we live without the world upside down? Can we trade such a world for a life in this new wilderness?

These questions can be answered if we are willing to collect the data needed to support the evidence. We can begin by answering seven questions about our lives in addiction:

1. How happy, comfortable, or secure were we without our "fix"?

2. What about the people around us: how happy, comfortable, or secure were they?

3. What was actually happening to us most of the time we thought we were "having fun"?

4. What was it like to come down off the "high"?

5. What do we have to show for it?

6. What kind of success did we have in finding someone to share our lives? (Was our primary relationship with our "stuff" and not someone else?)

7. What made us believe we couldn't live outside our habit?

As we begin looking at these questions, it is possible to see that we carefully surrounded ourselves with others like ourselves just to make certain we would never stop to ask such questions. What all of us had in common was that we deluded ourselves and abused ourselves in the same ways! The proof of this is that we never allowed anyone who thought differently to get close to us.

The temptation to continue with the delusion and the abuse is intensely powerful in the early days of abstinence; it is a temptation to choose the "safety" of the upside-down world over the hazards of life in the wilderness. Considering that we had managed to live our lives and establish some semblance of comfort with our drug of choice, this temptation appears to make a great deal of sense. Until we review the evidence. Living in the way that we did wasn't as fabulous as we thought it was. And we weren't the happy souls we thought we were, either. Is it just possible, now, that this wilderness in which we find ourselves isn't the place we think it is?

Experiencing ourselves as children, lost children, terribly uncertain and in need of help, we may begin to see how rigorously we supported our lives and defended ourselves against being in such a vulnerable state. It is also possible to see how this attitude about being able to manage things in this upside-down condition actually prevented any change from ever occurring.

The Wilderness

What if the wilderness we're in is a place for growth, a place for change? Instead of its being a setting in which the only alternative is to abuse our systems to fill the void that has eaten away at us, perhaps in the wilderness we have the space and the time to get into action, real action. Perhaps it is a zone in which we can discover who we are and what we can do without alcohol, other drugs, or compulsive behavior to confuse us. In this place, we may just begin to be able to see our lives in a different way.

A line in the Talmud, a remarkable book of wisdom that has survived many centuries, says, "I do not see the world the way it is, I see the world the way I am." As individuals with compulsive/dependent problems, we see and live in a compulsive/dependent world. In early recovery, we are often terribly disoriented and experience a loss of almost everything familiar because we have stopped using the substances that made it all "intelligible." It will take time to create a new sense of order and familiarity, and in this wilderness we can meet and discover others, just like ourselves, who are just as disoriented.

Our lives are the reflection of what we value. When we value things, we fill our lives with things; when we value people, we fill our lives with people. And when we begin to value abstinence, our lives begin to reflect a world very different from the one we knew before. Is it any wonder that we are dismayed and frightened by it?

At group therapy sessions, or Twelve Step meetings in which others share their experiences, we begin to receive glimmers of understanding about the isolated and isolating lives we lived. Instead of being a mark of our uniqueness, as we thought, we discover that isolation is but a symptom of our condition. Through the voices of others, we begin to hear things we have never heard another person speak, things we never believed possible—except inside our own head. Listening to others like us who have lived as sexual minorities share their most intimate secrets, we hear the story of our own lives. That is powerful; and we make a powerful identification with it.

Unless we can identify with the experience others share, some of us are unable to feel the understanding and strength that other individuals in recovery can bring us. In nongay meetings, many of us may struggle to realize any kind of identification with the others in the room. We may find ourselves feeling like strangers in these meetings, and our own deep sense of isolation may even be accentuated. For many of us, in order to feel the power, the speaker needs to know *our* suffering. Twelve Step meetings for sexual minorities have grown in number all over the world, and they have provided the opportunity to meet and hear others whose story—"her-story" and "his-story"—can be told in an environment of understanding and acceptance. Wherever and whenever identification occurs, race and ethnicity and sexual orientation are transcended, and we are able to hear the whole message of recovery.

Some recovering individuals may take months or years to find their way to this kind of meeting. One aspect of isolation is homophobia, and we must deal with this crucial issue in recovery. Twelve Step meetings for sexual minorities are of tremendous help in coming to grips with the complexity of how homophobia works in the lives of gays, lesbians, and bisexuals who have become addicted.

In our society, homophobia is the rule and not the exception. Children growing up with nongay parents experience it whether they live in the midst of a warm and loving family or a loveless one. Boys and girls are raised with fears about "different" people, and feelings that in any way reflect sympathy or identification with "those kind of people" are shunned.

At the same time children learn to mistrust certain feelings in themselves, they begin to mistrust the parents who invalidate these feelings. It is not uncommon for children with same-sex feelings of attraction, growing up in a nongay household, to believe they don't belong there. They may even believe themselves to be adopted instead of being the natural offspring of these adults who make lies out of their innocent, honest feelings. Having these basic feelings invalidated is one of the best reasons for mistrusting the source of invalidation.

It is also one of the best reasons for the development of a highly judgmental, hypercritical attitude toward others: "If that's what they think about me, then this is what I think about *them*." Gays, lesbians, and bisexuals, having grown up in a homophobic society, are often among the most critical people in the world. This is apparent in their conversations about many subjects, especially about *other* gay men and lesbians. As the best defense of our lifestyle, many of us have chosen to be critical of everyone and everything. This defense is a first-attack offense.

It Begins with Sharing

At Twelve Step meetings and group therapy sessions, instead of the criticism and one-upping that we are used to, we hear others share about their lives. This has an unusual effect on us: we begin to identify with our own survival power. The stories of others give us courage. With this courage, we begin to redirect our energy toward getting and maintaining abstinence. Have we not spent years in using our energy to hide the truth about our sexuality? We are experts in secrecy and denial. But with other gays and lesbians in recovery, hearing others talk about it so openly, the way clears for us to begin to refocus this previously misdirected energy instead of slipping back into old patterns.

Surrounded by others sharing their experience honestly in language so familiar and yet so different from the bar scene, we may sit silently for a while. It should not be too long, however, before we become a participant in sharing bits and pieces of our own story: "If this is what it's like to feel lost and scared, I might as well put in my two cents!"

And the moment we open our mouths in this wilderness, we are confronted with the realization: we are not alone. As we add our voices to the others, we hear in the sound we make together the power greater than ourselves that has always been there, ready and waiting for us to seek help. The dead end we reached was the effect of the substances we used, and of growing up in dysfunctional families; it was not because of our lack of entitlement in the human race that is *both* gay and straight. In hitting bottom, we reach a place in which we discover that *we* are the ones who think of ourselves as isolated and completely alone. We are the reflection of our self-delusion: since things didn't work out the way we thought they should, we cut ourselves off from others, from the kind of connection and help that is available to everyone in life.

In the support that flows from the group, there is a strength that we never had on our own. Acknowledging the group acknowledges also the power that is in all of us if we work together at the task of recovery. Sharing problems together reduces the magnitude of the problem for some reason, some miraculous reason. We come to this understanding, however, only after we have reached a place in ourselves where we are available to this help. This, it is important to see, is not a condition of helplessness, because those who believe that they are helpless are *not* available for help. The person who is available to be helped is never helpless.

When we are available to be helped, we can begin to believe there is help for us. We remain completely isolated for as long as we believe that we are helpless.

The delusion of the bar scene is that, in it, we felt we were free to be ourselves without hiding, because there were other isolated people *just like us*. But we made no efforts, or few efforts, to make any real connections beyond escaping. With or without anyone else, we escaped into our loneliness. We "fixed" ourselves so that we would not feel the pain, and we came to trust this solution because it helped relieve the pain . . . until it became the source of the agony itself.

When the world turns around and is no longer upside down, the way out of not feeling the pain is through allowing ourselves to feel it! Instead of avoiding the feelings, as we have done in the past, we discover an alternative we never knew before. The best explanation for this comes from a woman who shared the following at a lesbian and gay Twelve Step meeting:

> *I have a really wonderful therapist who told me this not too long ago when I was completely unable to recreate my feelings about something that had happened to me. She said that pain, emotional pain, the really bad pain that comes and you're afraid you're not going to be able to hang on, lasts between four to nine minutes; and then it's gone.*

It might come up again, but it's just four minutes you've got to get through, or a little bit more, and then something else happens. So, my whole story about my alcoholism is what I have done to avoid those four to nine minutes.

Instead of escape into using substances or compulsive behavior to end the pain, it is through having the courage to experience it that we can pass beyond the pain. These men and women may not tell us this in their stories; nevertheless, it is possible for us to see and to hear that is what happens *to them*. And if it happens to them, we can wonder whether the same thing will happen to us. We may find ourselves saying, "This is not the place I thought it was going to be! These other people who have stopped using alcohol/drugs/compulsive behavior sound so different. Somehow they've tapped into some courage they never had before. It's in their voices, even though there's no explanation for it." Others of us may say nothing because we are too frightened to speak—even to ourselves.

"H.P."

It is a moving experience to sit in groups with gays and lesbians and bisexuals and listen to others share honestly their pain and suffering. In what others share, many of us may begin to feel a power that exceeds any single individual's strength or courage. We may identify this power with the group itself. For others, the power they feel is given a name: "H.P."—Higher Power. And for still others, who choose to call it God, the experience of a power greater than themselves helping them into recovery is a reconnection with a positive force in their own past from which they have isolated themselves.

Observing the changes that begin to happen in others like ourselves makes it possible to begin to believe it can happen to us. That we are NOT excluded from a connection with a Higher Power, with God, is a major breakthrough for most sexual minorities to experience.

Homosexuality and homosexuals have been disowned and blacklisted in the doctrines of the major religions of the world. Because of this, many gay men, lesbians, and bisexuals have lived believing that they were cut off from God for most of their lives. Cast out, scorned, and rejected by the very ministers who could have helped us remain close to the support of a loving, caring source of strength and inspiration, many of us bear the scars of religion's abuse on our psyches, if not our bodies. Because of this, many of us lost faith in a Higher Power.

In recovery, we discover that we no longer have to suffer this deprivation and abuse. Through OUR availability, we discover the beginning of a connection with a power greater than ourselves. For many of us, this may take quite awhile in recovery. But no matter how long it takes, through the painstaking process of recovery, we begin to believe in this power because we see it acting on the lives of others, as well as on our own lives. Power in action is very convincing.

> *Ya know, there's a place inside me, I don't know where it is, that I can feel comfortable—good about myself. That's Higher Power enough for me!*

Unlike heterosexuals, sexual minorities have to pass through *both* edges of denial—compulsive/dependent behavior and homosexuality. That is why it takes many of us longer to take the Second Step: "Came to believe that a power greater than ourselves could restore us to sanity." The process begins with coming to believe in the help that is available to us to recover and expands as we come to believe in ourselves as worthy of recovering. Our development of self-esteem as homosexuals and bisexuals is therefore directly related to recovery from dependence on substances and behavior. "Until there is somebody home, Higher Power can't get in!"

Valuing ourselves enough to honestly answer the questions about the role that substances or compulsive behaviors play in our lives, we embarked on Step One. Coming to believe we don't have to face the consequences alone—that there is help for us—gets us started on the Second Step. By allowing ourselves to take it, we can begin to reverse the direction of that elevator ride to the bottom of the universe. And as we begin to move upwards, we create a new connection with other members of the human race. Just as we were killing ourselves with alcohol and drugs in our descent, so we are able, through believing in a Power greater than ourselves, to find our way back into life in recovery.

Psychologist Carl Jung wrote about the importance of spirituality to recovery in a letter to Bill Wilson, the cofounder of Alcoholics Anonymous: *"You see, 'alcohol' in Latin is* spiritus, *and you use the same word for the highest religious experience as well as for the most depraving poison. The helpful formula therefore is:* spiritus contra spiritum."[2]

Jung's insight provides us with a life-restoring prescription: treat alcohol dependency with spirituality. Through sharing our experiences with others who are just like ourselves, we may be able to develop the spiritual connection that is central to our recovery from the dependency. What a paradox exists in recovery!

Paradoxes

We encounter many paradoxes on our journey into recovery. It is only when we come close to losing our lives that we become willing to consider the prospect of living differently. It is true for countless numbers of people. Identifying more of these paradoxes provides a source of additional insight:

- when we think we are most alone, we find ourselves NOT alone;

- becoming as vulnerable as children makes it possible for us to receive the courage and strength it takes as adults to enter recovery;

- not by escaping but by living through the pain, we find the way to end it;

- in the stories of others' madness we are able to discover sanity for ourselves;

- help comes when we realize that we are no longer helpless;

- this wilderness in which we find ourselves from time to time on our journey is not the end of the world but the beginning of a new one!

Twelve Step programs are crammed with paradoxes, such as "Surrender to win!" or "You've got to give it away in order to keep it!" It is no accident that these figure so prominently in the process of recovery. Change is a terrifying process for everyone, and, in order to embark on it, the individual must reach a state of willingness. The paradox of death in life is well-known to those suffering with chemical dependency; and the despair of gay people who contemplate suicide as a way out of their anguish is an experience with which many homosexuals can identify. Paradox provides a synthesis of irreconcilable extremes and creates a paradigm, a model in words, for realizing what appears to be impossible.

For many gays, lesbians, and bisexuals, recovery often seems like an impossibility. Perhaps a major reason for this sense of hopelessness and despair is the apparent invincibility of addictive/compulsive behavior. Recovery, itself, is a paradox because it is more easily seen in others than in ourselves. In addition, the moment many individuals use alcohol or drugs again, they experience that their substance dependency has advanced much further than where they left off. The paradoxes help us to remember that we are only one "fix" away from the man, from the woman, who was dependent on substances or behavior.

It takes great courage to face this. Where does this courage come from? It comes from recovery itself, where, over and over again, we hear the words in the message both the newcomer and the old-timer bring us: *We can do it!* As we begin to believe this, we understand that it is our self-defeating attitudes that tell us we can't.

❋　　❋　　❋

In your notebook, record your responses to the questions that appeared earlier in this chapter. Consider making several entries over the period of a week.

1. How happy, comfortable, or secure were you without your "fix"?

    _____

    _____

    _____

2. What about the people around you: how happy, comfortable or secure were they?

    _____

    _____

    _____

3. What was actually happening to you most of the time you thought you were "having fun"?

    _____

    _____

    _____

4. What was it like to come down off the "high"?

    _____

    _____

    _____

5. What do you have to show for it?

    _____

    _____

    _____

6. What kind of success did you have in finding someone to share your life? (Was your primary relationship with your "stuff" and not someone else?)

    _____

    _____

    _____

7. What made you believe you couldn't live outside your habit?

_____

_____

_____

❊   ❊   ❊

If you are able to attend a Twelve Step meeting, ask at least one person for a telephone number. Call the number that day or the next. Not only when you feel good but also when you don't, start getting in the habit of connecting with others—letting them know how you are feeling. Building a network of sober, recovering friends begins with the call you make today, so don't wait for tomorrow to do it. Be sure to remember that whomever you dial, they need your call as much as you need to call them. (You can always begin by asking, "Is this a good time to call?" If it isn't convenient for that person, call someone else. And if it is convenient, whoever answers will most likely be pleased that you were thoughtful enough to ask.)

❊   ❊   ❊

In the Workbook exercises that you have completed, you have considered the way you lived your life prior to entering recovery. This material will assist you in defining a perspective that is important for working on Step One. The condition of *denial* has been brought into focus for you in a very special, personal way. Now that you've had a chance to think about this condition from your own individual viewpoint, let's take this opportunity to look at it creatively.

8. In the space below, draw a picture, sketch a face, use stick-figures, or just doodle: what does DENIAL look like in your life?

9. Describe your picture in a few sentences.

_____

_____

_____

10. Much of what you have been in denial about is usually the basis for _isolation_. List a few reasons that may occur to you now for isolating yourself from others.

_____

_____

_____

11. What are some of the things you continue to _isolate_ yourself over now?

_____

_____

_____

12. "In our isolation, we were afraid; in our fear, we chose to isolate ourselves." Consider this statement in terms of the way in which you lived before entering recovery. Do you identify with this? How did you experience isolation and fear?

_____

_____

_____

13. From your childhood, recall an experience in which you were frightened of something real or imagined.

_____

_____

_____

14. How does this memory carry over into your present experience of being fearful or frightened?

_____

_____

_____

15. Before entering recovery, many of us have had "close calls." We pride ourselves that this or that never happened to us—yet. Here is a chance to record a few of your "YETS"—those things which, from your perspective, might have happened had you continued on the down elevator.

_____

_____

_____

16. Imagine a time sequence of these events that haven't yet happened. What is your estimate of the amount of time it would take before they might occur? *(Example: DWI—1–3 months; jail—3–6 months, lose the job—6–8 months.)*

"YETS"	Time Sequence
_____	_____
_____	_____
_____	_____
_____	_____
_____	_____
_____	_____
_____	_____

17. Going from the hypothetical to the actual, what were some of the grisly things that happened to you before beginning to work on recovery? And what are the feelings you associate with these events?

Events	Associated Feeings
_____	_____
_____	_____
_____	_____
_____	_____
_____	_____
_____	_____
_____	_____

18. How often do memories of these experiences come up for you now? How do they act on some of your present concerns or fears?

_____

_____

_____

19. At the present time, what "people/places/things" make you feel the most vulnerable:

People:

_____

_____

Places:

_____

_____

Things:

_____

_____

20. Which areas are still the most sensitive and easily start your "motor" going either in fear or anger or hurt?

- [ ] family
- [ ] lover
- [ ] job/work
- [ ] legal problem
- [ ] money
- [ ] health
- [ ] other_____

_____

21. What is the worst-case scenario if three of your worst fears ever occurred:

#1 _____

_____

#2_____

_____

#3_____

_____

22. In what ways do you use these worst case scenarios in your life today?
(Add others in your repertory.)

☐ to feel like a victim   ☐ to isolate

☐ to run away   ☐ to escape in imagination

☐ to revert to early behavior   ☐ to get angry

☐ to explode with emotion   ☐ to experience another trauma

☐ to tease or threaten yourself ☐ _____
   with a drink, a drug, acting-out
                                 ☐ _____

23. What is the likelihood of any of the worst-case scenarios actually happening?
(Please circle.)

Very Likely   **Very Unlikely**

#1	1	2	3	4	5
#2	1	2	3	4	5
#3	1	2	3	4	5

24. If you needed help to handle any of them, to whom would you turn?
(Check as many as apply.)

☐ sponsor   ☐ therapist

☐ friend   ☐ spouse/partner

☐ parent   ☐ other *(identify)* _____

_____

25. Describe your relationships with the people you loved before beginning recovery.
What did "love" mean to you?

_____

_____

_____

_____

_____

26. What impact, if any, did emotional, sexual or physical abuse play in any part of your life? How did you experience it?

    Childhood:

    _____

    _____

    Adolescence:

    _____

    _____

    As an adult:

    _____

    _____

27. What impact might these experiences have on your current functioning? *(i.e., work, interpersonal relationships, etc.)*

    _____

    _____

    _____

28. Thinking back to your youth or childhood, make a list of the things you valued.

    _____

    _____

    _____

29. What are the things you valued before entering recovery?

    _____

    _____

    _____

30. What are the things you value now?

    _____

    _____

    _____

31. What do you NOT value at the present time?

_____

_____

_____

32. Draft a definition of "sanity" that links what you value at this time with your life in recovery.

_____

_____

_____

33. Do you believe you are capable of being "restored to sanity," as you read in Step Two? If not, why not?

_____

_____

_____

_____

34. How open-minded are you about the possibility of receiving help in order to make progress with Step Two?

_____

_____

_____

35. List things you feel comfortable about sharing with others.

_____

_____

_____

36. What are some of the things you feel you *cannot* talk about?

_____

_____

_____

37. What stands in the way of sharing these issues?

_____

_____

_____

38. With whom might you consider sharing these issues, if necessary?

_____

_____

_____

39. Make a list of the things you have turned to others for help with.

_____

_____

_____

40. What happened when you did this? How do you feel about this? What did you learn?

_____

_____

_____

_____

_____

41. What's the difference between "I'm helpless," and "I need help"?

_____

_____

_____

42. What words best describe your feelings about Step Two?

_____

_____

_____

43. Step Two, for many people, evokes a conflict because of their experiences with religion. (This is particularly problematic for many sexual minorities.) It is possible to see Step Two in terms of spirituality and not in terms of religion. How do you rate your spiritual availability?

Available   **Not Available**

1	2	3	4	5

44. If you have a Higher Power, how big is it? What happens if your H.P. is even bigger than that? Keep going further and imagine your H.P as even bigger than that. Is your Higher Power big enough? Give yourself the opportunity to fill some pages in your notebook with your idea of H.P.

_____

_____

_____

45. If you have difficulty in seeing how Step Two might be relevant for you, what is an alternate source of spiritual support in your life? *(e.g., circle of friends, family, nature, art, music, yoga, martial arts, sports, etc.)*

_____

_____

_____

46. Based upon your answers to these questions, how will you translate these insights into action?

_____

_____

_____

CHAPTER 12

Taking Positive Action

CONDITION
Willful powerlessness

Even though individuals who are dependent on substances/behavior may not be conscious of this in their lives, they are not in control of their choices. Denial of this fact merely supports dependency. People succumb to the need for substances/behavior that can relieve the compulsion and provide relief. Energy is directed toward whatever rewards relief. On their own, individuals are caught in the web of dependent behavior.

ALTERNATIVE
Willing, positive action

Getting help is the beginning of positive action. By making a conscious effort to seek help, we embrace the process of healing.

Step 3

Made a decision to turn our will and our lives over to the care of God as we understood [God].

What a strange and frightening threshold we cross when we exit the upside-down world we lived in and enter the wilderness of recovery! Accepting the fact that we are not alone in this unfamiliar place is often both a surprise and a great relief. But what we are supposed to do about this now becomes the source of massive confusion.

Newcomers often share stories which confirm that, contrary to their deepest conviction that they are unique, they suffer from the double bind of denying both their substance/behavior dependency and their sexual orientation: "Who me, substance problems? Who says I'm (gay)(lesbian)(bisexual)?" What a hurdle to leap! In recovery, we are told that we are powerless, that compulsive behavior has run our lives—and the evidence of this is too vivid to contradict. But are we supposed to wallow in this condition of powerlessness for the rest of our lives? That's no way to live!

The Confusion of Powerlessness

Many newcomers, as well as old-timers, in recovery remain stuck in an intense conviction of their powerlessness. When we hear them speak, it seems they have merely exchanged one nay for another within their long history of denial. Their old tapes continue to operate in the new wilderness: "There's absolutely nothing I can do to change my life! I'm powerless."

As protection against relapses, they hang on for dear life to the belief in their own powerlessness. An interesting variation on this is the newcomer in early recovery who adamantly refuses to look for employment. These individuals insist that money in their pockets opens them to the risk of buying alcohol or drugs. Without money, they feel they have no alternative except to stay abstinent. Convincing themselves that their poverty *is* powerlessness, these people believe that staying broke will make it impossible for them to pick up their old habits again and fall back into addiction. Some people will think of anything! This kind of thinking is illogical and counterproductive to long-term change and recovery.

Such people will stay stuck by asserting their own power to *refuse* to change. This refusal is solid evidence that they *do* have the power to change—if they choose to work at it. How difficult it is for them to turn the telescope around. But it is possible to see ourselves and the world through the other end of the telescope! Acknowledging limits allows a person greater power over what is contained within those limits. The Twelve Steps of each of the anonymous programs provide tools, fellowship, and support to change that which is possible to change. Once the fog of chemicals or compulsive behaviors has lifted, it is time to think about making appropriate and positive change with the aid of the Twelve Steps or other sources of support.

If it were true that individuals had lost *all* power to influence or direct their lives, then they would have been unable to attempt Step One and Step Two—"admitting we were powerless over alcohol—that our lives had become unmanageable" and "coming to believe that a Power greater than ourselves could restore us to sanity." We need the assistance of our will in order to accomplish each of these. By directing our efforts to taking these Steps, we prove to ourselves that we have NOT lost the ability to change our lives.

Acknowledging we *can* recover is crucial to our recovery. When we do this, we again assume the responsibility we had surrendered. We understand that we no longer have to live at the mercy of our compulsive/dependent behavior. Accepting that we are responsible for creating a new and abstinent life for ourselves is often terrifying. "If I *do* have a choice whether or not I will drink or use, once I begin the process of recovery, then I also have the responsibility of making that choice!" *Choice goes hand in hand with responsibility.*

Victims

If we believe ourselves to be completely powerless, this promotes the idea that we are victims, and, consequently, recovery is even more a wilderness. This is so because, before, when feeling victimized, we had our source of "reliable comfort." Without this comfort, the pain of feeling like a victim is so much greater. Let us acknowledge the fact that we can victimize ourselves by our attitudes in both settings.

A better understanding of this destructive type of attitude helps us avoid a pitfall for the individual in recovery. We are all experts on ourselves, and one thing our expertise appreciates is our ability to suffer. Compulsive/dependent individuals are experts on suffering. For some, feeling bad is so normal that feeling good feels bad. The shame and disgrace we endured provided us with a deep reservoir of worthlessness. For any and all the reasons under the sun, we were martyrs to everything and everyone that had harmed us. As martyrs, we deserved our punishment—we were worthy of our suffering. This is a hard habit/attitude to change.

As victims, we were able to manage and have some sense of control over our world. This is "victim power." Whatever harm came to us, and the list of harms is endless, we could always look at it as proof of how deserving we were. The stripes of our punishment fell on us from all sides, and we could suffer with an earnest conviction of our worthiness in receiving them.

A therapist has suggested that "every alcoholic is addicted to suffering." Consider this possibility in your own life. You won't be alone if you find yourself retreating within the security of self-righteous denial. The suggestion that we might for one instant have gotten pleasure out of suffering may seem too ludicrous to accept. Underneath, however, this revelation now asks us to examine our lives as victims in control of each misfortune and unhappiness that knocks on the door.

Whether the problem is health, work, or family, we are always ready with the response, "See, what else would you expect to happen to someone like me?" Or, if something good happened, it could only be a mistake or an accident, and we dismiss it easily or turn it around to be used in a negative way. This condition of willful powerlessness is immensely difficult to give up, for it proves us right in a world in which we're always wrong. None of us have even a clue what will happen when we deprive ourselves of this power to explain our lives as victims who deserve their suffering. Giving up our victimhood, what will become of us? It's the unknown.

The recognition that we can change this condition, that it is our choice to get help and our responsibility to use it, brings us to the edge of taking the Third Step of the journey into recovery. If we are experts on suffering, we are probably novices about using our energy in a positive way. We have little experience with it, and it is a terrible burden, an obstacle that blocks our path. In the past, what have we done with obstacles like this one? Simply, we used alcohol or other drugs or acted out in some fashion or other. But now, without the crutches that got us through difficulties, we may feel lost or even helpless. This sense of helplessness causes intense confusion in recovery: we identify helplessness with powerlessness and see no way to find safety except to turn back.

For gays, lesbians, and bisexuals, the temptation is even greater to turn back from what appears to be utter chaos in which there are no supports, no reliable source of comfort. Without a safety net of any kind—neither substances nor compulsive behavior—the high wire act we have perfected during our lifetime now seems an impossibility. Many resist taking the next step, and this effort constitutes the turning point.

Our Old Ideas

Of all the difficult things we must give up, our old ideas are the hardest. For years, these old ideas have flourished in the garden of our minds and spirits. They have become planted so firmly that they have taken over. To some of us, it may even appear that these weeds are all that grow there now. The process of recovery is one of gradually rooting out ideas that are no longer of any help or use. This process makes room for new ideas that bring new life and growth again into the garden. We can begin by acknowledging that the weather, "the climate" of our minds, may not always be favorable for such efforts. We cannot delay doing this if we are to make our way forward beyond this place.

Working honestly and consistently at taking Step One and Step Two has already had an impact on us. We have identified the problem that exists in our physical and mental life: the unmanageability and insanity of compulsive behavior. Because Step Three identifies the problem that exists in our spiritual life, it is no wonder that we hesitate!

For a complex variety of reasons related to the way in which we grew up and were loved or not loved, some of us may have thought of ourselves as emotionally handicapped. In this predicament, our inadequacies and helplessness got certain kinds of responses from others that removed the necessity of being responsible for ourselves. Many people in recovery know that these emotional handicaps are serious, but when it comes to *spiritual* helplessness, most of us feel completely lost in the wilderness. This is much more than we bargained for!

Many gays, lesbians, and bisexuals have grown up in Western religions in which bigotry and hypocrisy have flourished. Because of this, they were prevented from developing and evolving a healthy spiritual center in their lives. Scorned, shunned, and punished for their homosexuality, some have turned their backs against any possibility of spiritual comfort and support. The spiritual abuse we have suffered from many denominations has left us too harmed ever to trust religious leaders who preach bigotry and hate instead of love!

What words does a lesbian use who has never felt she could pray to a God from either the Old *or* the New Testament? What prayer does a gay man say who has been abandoned by his family and his church? For example, Dignity services (Dignity is an organization of gay and lesbian Catholics) in a major Northeastern city have often been held in the basement of a church of a different denomination. What does that say to Catholics who attend this service about their connection to the deity of their religion? (So much can be said about these issues that is beyond the scope of this text. The list of references at the back of this book provides sources of information on these topics.)

To compensate for this spiritual deprivation and hardship, homosexuals and bisexuals sometimes affirm themselves in very different ways. "If God doesn't want to have anything to do with us, then we don't want to have anything to do with God! We don't need God, spirituality, or any mumbo jumbo like that in our lives, and we refuse to invoke the name of God in prayer in any and all things. We're fine, on our own, just the way we are, thank you. And we don't need anyone who thinks we're not!" Some "go it alone" in total silence. Others have formed groups in which to worship (like the Metropolitan Community Church) or returned to non-Christian based theologies. There is a growing movement on the part of some denominations (Episcopal: "Project Oasis"; Lutheran; Quaker; Jewish) to begin to minister to sexual minorities. Much more effort and increased visibility on the part of mainstream religions are essential.

In recovery, as we continue the journey, we need to let go of the attitudes and beliefs that we learned about ourselves as sexual minorities (and about others who are not sexual minorities). Instead of isolating ourselves, we have to find ways that affirm ourselves and allow us to fully participate in spiritual growth and community. As difficult as it may be, sexual minorities can benefit greatly by preparing to make themselves available to spiritual awareness and growth in a new way. This requires thoughtful risk taking, careful choice, and a willingness to pursue new possibilities.

Popular culture communicates deep philosophical truths in many ingenious ways. One of the least tedious is the bumper sticker. Two of these gems seem apt here: *Please Don't Walk on the Water;* and the other, the simple acknowledgment: *Not God!* Each one suggests how we may understand what needs to be done in order to take the Third Step. The spiritual dimension of our lives, often already under siege because of messages from oppressive religious doctrines, was further taken over by dependence on substances. Thus spiritual despair has often resulted. By refusing to continue to ascribe to such external attitudes, new possibilities open up. This process requires letting go of old messages about our spiritual meaning, self-worth, and personal value, as gays, lesbians, and bisexuals, and taking responsibility for creating new visions of and for ourselves.

Such a change process does not happen overnight; malnutrition is not a condition corrected with one or two meals. Spiritual deprivation is not resolved overnight either. It may take days or months or years (of therapy groups, Twelve Step meetings, or other interventions) for us to begin to allow nourishment from the spiritual food that others share to enter our lives. People experience a "spiritual awakening" at different times. This takes as long as it takes. Remember the long distance we travel just to find our way into the meeting or therapy rooms in which we can get help. Gaining sustenance from what is said there requires time and patience.

Alcoholism *is* cunning and baffling; compulsive behavior is destructive and often lethal. We need to constantly remember that the power restored to us in early recovery can once again be diverted back into old habits. This is a crucial reason for surrendering it to a power greater than ourselves who can provide us with good, orderly direction. It should come as no surprise that the old familiar willfulness is always ready and waiting to yield to old habits. Turning this will over to a Higher Power offers insurance against slipping back into addictive/compulsive behavior again.

Perfectionism

Another old idea of gigantic proportion in the lives of many sexual minorities is the unattainable goal of perfection. This idea is an example of extremist, all or nothing thinking. Using perfectionism to stand as the opposite limit from the zero of victimhood, we filled the void in between. This notion is deeply ingrained in everyone who has lived in addiction, gay or nongay. For many sexual minorities, however, being the best has often meant choosing different kinds of goals from nongay men and women. For example, some gay men have considered certain avenues of expression or competition closed to them. They have devoted a great deal of time and energy in pursuit of appetite gratification. The stories they share about their sexual exploits are clearly demonstrations of "besting" any other competitor around.

Many other sexual minorities, to prove themselves outstanding professionals, become "workaholics" and devote incredible amounts of energy and time to the task of being the best in their jobs and hobbies. This experience shared by Arthur is common:

> *From his college days into his career as an architect, Arthur prepared for examinations, conferences, and presentations, for everything, in a way that went far beyond what was necessary or helpful. He was always ready for a siege even though he might be going on just a reconnaissance mission. He used alcohol more and more to make life bearable, until, after a long sequence of blackouts he was almost killed by a seizure.*

In recovery, we discover there is a middle range between the best or the worst. In the middle range, we discover opportunities to develop different kinds of lives. We no longer need to swing from being victim to victor, from being damaged goods to heroic gods and goddesses. We begin to develop our personhood and stop trying to walk on the water, and we learn what it is like to give up playing God.

The pedestal of perfectionism stands in the way of discovering the middle range. This pedestal needs dismantling. Sometimes it can be done only one brick at a time. Attending Twelve Step meetings may assist the process because we can learn how other people are working on this task. From insights we get from others about what they are doing, we can begin to understand how we can get our own obstacles out of our way. Their sharing helps remove the bricks from their path, and when we get up enough courage to tell our own stories, we discover a tiny bit more room in which we can also move forward.

Developing a Spiritual Center in Recovery

Sharing our experience clears away space for recovery. Gradually, we develop a spiritual sensitivity that is different from the religion-centered training we had from any church or any clergy in our entire lives. It is a phenomenon many have known, even those who are most negative about religion, prayer, or a Higher Power. The gradual development of a spiritual dimension in our lives begins with sharing our experience, strength, and hope with others who do the same with us. When we clear away the cluttered shambles of our past, the space we create begins to be permeated with a new spiritual vitality. The development of a spiritual center within us is the result of this new energy operating in our lives.

Healing is an unusual phenomenon to describe. There is something inexplicable, miraculous, about it. Some individuals who have suffered great physical, emotional, and mental ravages, contrary to all expectation, have made unbelievable progress in recovering from the effects of addictive/compulsive behavior. Others, with apparently much less damage to their systems, have succumbed to organ malfunction and the complications of heart, liver, or other diseases. Physicians confess their inability to account for these amazing results, and, while scientific evidence can provide data, it does not answer the deepest question of why one person recovers and another succumbs.

It is not the need of the individual but the commitment, the *wish*, of the individual that counts. An often-quoted slogan captures this idea: "AA is not for those who need it but for those who want it." This applies, as well, to families, lovers, and friends. How difficult it is for them to accept that it is not *their* wish that counts! It must be the one who suffers from the disorder who wants to begin recovery. We must want it for ourselves or else the attempt will be short-lived and doomed to failure from the start. We may enter recovery for many reasons; however, until we want it for *ourselves,* our recovery house will stand on a shaky foundation.

But, once again, the familiar paradox appears. Even though it is the will, the wish that must operate, we must get out of our own way in order to allow the recovery process to set in. When individuals refuse to have faith in a power beyond themselves and insist on running the show in the same fashion as they did in addiction, they discover they are back again in the driver's seat. They are driving without any understanding of the terrain in which they find themselves or the vehicle they drive. Isolated from the healing forces that flow to them through others, they are once again on a collision course with addictive/compulsive behavior.

Many of us have lived close to danger knowingly and unknowingly. Risking position, health, and very existence to continue using alcohol and other drugs and/or compulsive behavior, we become accustomed to taking extravagant risks—living dangerously. In the dysfunctional homes many of us grew up in as children, ominous situations were not at all uncommon. As adults, many continue to confuse danger with sex, love, or intimacy. It is ironic that in early recovery there is such enormous fear of risk taking. It has been suggested that when we are under the illusion that we're in control, we love living on the edge—with all its anxiety. Without that illusion, we balk at the brink. The basic rules for the child growing up in a dysfunctional family are: Don't Trust; Don't Feel; and Don't Talk.[1] Taking Step Three is therefore the most difficult of all in early recovery. Those three rules are the reason why so many back off. Without any faith or belief in anyone except ourselves, if that, it seems impossible to turn over our will to any one or any thing, particularly a Higher Power who is still aloof and alien. It feels exactly like stepping off from solid ground into nothingness and expecting to be supported by something that might not be there.

However, many recovering sexual minorities have found a way to take this Step even though they considered themselves unbelievers or outcasts of any and all religions. They took Step Three by acting AS-IF they believed they would be helped. They allowed themselves the same benefit as those who did believe in the healing ability of a power greater than themselves to assist them in their recovery. They made a leap into AS-IF, and they refused to allow their unbelief to get in their way!

Help Is Available to Us

The Steps, the meetings, and the literature available in the rooms before and after people share their stories provide us with sources of help we can use for the journey. An additional source of support is the idea of sponsorship. Twelve Step programs have developed this concept to provide the recovering person with concrete suggestions about how to maintain a program of abstinence on a day-to-day basis. Sponsorship should not be considered as a substitute for psychotherapy, educational or vocational counseling, legal advice, spiritual guidance, or financial planning. All sponsors need to know about is how to maintain abstinence. They are asked to provide information about how *they* coped with the challenges of their recovery process. This is the sum of their expertise as sponsors. It is essential to have realistic expectations about their capabilities. Sponsorship may not be a tool that you choose to make part of your change process. Even if it is, consultation with appropriate service providers for problems other than maintaining abstinence— such as legal, marital, or financial problems—is definitely recommended.

Participating in groups, working the Steps, and reading recovery literature make us available to the suggestion that we find someone who can help us apply these tools in our daily lives. By the time we reach Step Three, it makes sense to follow through on that recommendation. This is a big decision for many of us; nevertheless, choosing someone we trust to talk to on a regular basis is part of a program of recovery. Let's consider why.

In Twelve Step programs, a sponsor is someone who has gone through the hell of early recovery and the hardship of entering and making progress in this new venture. Enlisting the support of a person just like ourselves, we begin to leave our isolation behind and acknowledge hope, as well as help, from this individual whose recovery we admire and wish for ourselves. The person we choose to help us find our way on our journey is someone with whom it is possible to form an intimate human connection with life beyond our previous experience of it. We need to learn how to do this. It is likely we would not be where we are now if we had learned this before.

Heterosexuals in recovery are encouraged to choose sponsors of the same sex. For sexual minorities, it is often a good idea to ask someone of the other sex or someone with whom there is likely to be little chance of developing romantic or sexual feelings. Sponsors are chosen not for romance but to help us with our recovery! It is helpful to choose a sponsor who can help focus on the basics of maintaining abstinence in early recovery instead of fanning the flames of romance or sex.

One good way to discover how well you work together is to ask someone to be a temporary sponsor. Set a time limit of one to three months in which to find out if you get the support and direction you need in the way that you need it. Either you or the sponsor can identify reasons for going on together or choosing a new temporary sponsor at the end of this period. Sponsorship is always a two-way street. It must work for the sponsor as well as the sponsee.

Remember that these individuals we have asked to help us are not chosen for life; we can change them when we decide to. We may also have several at the same time, depending on our needs. Choosing and working with a sponsor is useful in launching positive action to support recovery. Review this brief checklist in considering people you might ask to be a sponsor:

Do these individuals have...

- sufficient length of time in recovery, along with a solid understanding and commitment to Twelve Step programs?
- a positive attitude toward recovery in themselves and other people?
- an honest way of sharing the details of their own addiction and the work they are doing on themselves in recovery?
- open-mindedness in handling problems and considering alternatives?
- the time and availability to work with you?
- sound suggestions to offer, and can you count on these being shared with you?
- personal characteristics that encourage your trust? (In addition to age, sex, etc., these include respect for anonymity and confidentiality.)
- the tough-mindedness to call you on old ways of thinking and acting?
- the kind of self-esteem that encourages your own self-esteem?
- the kind of recovery you want for yourself?

If you have not found a sponsor by the time you begin to work on Step Three, it is a good idea to (1) set yourself the priority of getting a sponsor (or a temporary sponsor); (2) approach people you are considering, and discuss sponsorship with them; (3) accept your efforts as positive, instead of rejecting yourself when others decline your request. It's not by burying our heads in powerlessness but by taking positive action that we progress on the journey.

Whether we find it easy or difficult to accept the idea of the Third Step, we can use the sponsor to extend the entire opportunity of recovery for ourselves. Having a sponsor who is knowledgeable about working the Steps and who is willing to work with us is like having the help we need on-line. We make it much easier on ourselves when we use all the available tools to assist us in our recovery process.

Another tool is a prayer that has sustained many of us on our journey in time of crisis as well as in repose. It is often recited at the beginning or the end of Twelve Step meetings, and the first two verses are familiar to many hundreds of thousands of people in and out of recovery. The entire prayer, written by theologian Reinhold Niebuhr, may be of special help to those who already experience a connection with a spiritual force and who wish to call on this power to assist recovery:

The Serenity Prayer

God grant me the serenity
To accept the things I cannot change;
Courage to change the things I can;
And wisdom to know the difference.

Living one day at a time;
Enjoying one moment at a time;
Accepting hardship
As the pathway to peace;

Taking, as God did, this
world as it is, not as I would
have it;

Trusting that God will make all
things right if I surrender
to God's will;

That I may be reasonably happy
in this life, and supremely
happy with God forever in
the next. Amen

When we step beyond the threshold on Step Three, we initiate the kind of action necessary at this moment in our journey into recovery.

❋   ❋   ❋

Identify certain activities in which you can observe your perfectionism or extremist (all or nothing) thinking in operation. After observing these in action, ask yourself how important perfectionism or extremist thinking is to you in completing the tasks at hand. Then, whether you might be able to get along without them. Are you willing to attempt this? If you are, for ten minutes or half an hour at a time, allow yourself the luxury of accepting things and people *exactly as they* are without changing anything about them. Then try it for an hour or two, and then an afternoon or an evening here and there. We get valuable feedback when we check with ourselves how much lighter it feels to live without perfectionism or extremist thinking. It is also possible that the loss of such a weight may be too unsettling and require considerable attention and monitoring.

❊   ❊   ❊

Record in your journal several days' worth of entries concerning this different experience with perfectionism; with extremist (all-or-nothing) thinking.

❊   ❊   ❊

1. Take a blank page in your journal and draw a small circle with your initials in it. Then, in other circles that you draw around the first circle, write the initials of the significant people in your life—spouses/significant others, members of your family, friends, your employer, coworkers, etc. Place these circles, either close or distant to your circle, to indicate their approximate relationship with you.

2. Now, do this same exercise again on another journal page, except this time draw the circles to indicate the kind of relationship—close to distant—that you would LIKE to have with these individuals.

3. In your own words, explain what the change or difference means to you. What do you hope will result from this change?

_____

_____

_____

_____

4. What action(s) will you initiate to encourage this change?

    _____

    _____

    _____

5. In addition to what you can do, what additional support/assistance do you need?
    Who can provide this?

    _____

    _____

    _____

6. In chapter 10, when you defined "powerlessness," what images came into your
    mind?

    _____

    _____

    _____

7. How would you describe yourself being powerless in a situation? After you have
    done this, describe yourself in a situation in which you feel like a victim.

    _____

    _____

    _____

8. Victims have certain common characteristics. Identify as many of these characteristics
    as you can think of and then draw a picture of a "victim" and give it a name. (Use
    colored pencils to enhance your picture.)

9. "Victims attract bullies." What element of truth is in this statement? What power or attraction, if any, does this dynamic have for you? as the victim? as the bully? Explore.

_____

_____

_____

10. When recalling a crisis in your life, in what ways did you act as a victim or as a bully?

_____

_____

_____

11. What are your thoughts and feelings _now_ about your behavior in that crisis? What have you learned about yourself?

_____

_____

_____

12 In what ways might these feelings be connected with a sense of powerlessness? What other circumstances in the past produce similar feelings? Identify them here.

_____

_____

_____

13. At the present time, what decisions do you feel comfortable making? What decisions make you feel uncomfortable?

Comfortable decisions:

_____

_____

Uncomfortable decisions:

_____

_____

14. Check off below the efforts/activities in which you use your energy to make progress in your recovery program.

- [ ] a. not practicing addictive/compulsive behavior
- [ ] b. attending Twelve Step or self-help meetings
- [ ] c. working each day on the Steps
- [ ] d. reading recovery literature
- [ ] e. doing a regular service commitment
- [ ] f. staying in contact with sponsor/friend
- [ ] g. sharing recovery with others
- [ ] h. using the telephone daily to be in touch with other recovering people (including those new in recovery)
- [ ] i. maintaining a daily journal
- [ ] j. spot checking yourself; end-of-day inventorying
- [ ] k. meditating/praying/exploring your spiritual nature
- [ ] l. eating a balanced diet
- [ ] m. getting adequate rest
- [ ] n. checking out with a physician any troubling health issues
- [ ] o. physical exercise
- [ ] p. individual therapy
- [ ] q. group therapy
- [ ] r. couples therapy

15. Circle those six you like to do best. Explain.

_____

_____

_____

_____

16. Of those remaining, choose *four* you enjoy least (but think may be helpful to you) and write (1) what you dislike about doing them; and (2) what kind of support you need in order to do them.

_____

_____

_____

※　　※　　※

For those who are, or may consider, attending a Twelve Step program, sponsorship will be recommended as a source of support, encouragement, information, and suggestions. Others who do not wish to attend Twelve Step programs will need to find support and coaching from other knowledgeable and capable sources. Some of the following questions may be of assistance in developing an alternative support system. This may consist of a single individual (therapist, friend, spouse) or a group.

※　　※　　※

17. At this time, I (do/don't) have a sponsor. *(Underline one.)*
    If you have had a sponsor in the past, what changed this relationship? What were your expectations of the sponsor? On reflection, how realistic were these expectations?

    _____

    _____

    _____

18. If you *do not* have a sponsor, write your reason(s) for not having one. (If you have a sponsor, how have you benefited from the relationship?)

    _____

    _____

    _____

19. What are the steps you took to find a sponsor? (What are the steps you need to take to find a sponsor if you don't have one?)

    _____

    _____

    _____

20. What capabilities did you look for (are you looking for) in a sponsor?

    _____

    _____

    _____

21. What characteristics do you admire about your sponsor? (If you don't have one, you can answer this when you do.)

_____

_____

_____

22. What do you like best—and least—about having a sponsor? (Or, if you don't have one, what do you like best and least about the idea of sponsorship?)

_____

_____

_____

_____

_____

23. What issues do you discuss with your sponsor? Are there certain areas of your life that you do not share? What are your reasons for not sharing? (If you do not have a sponsor, what issues do you share with others in your recovery group?)

_____

_____

_____

_____

24. Prior to entering recovery, what did the word "intimacy" mean to you? How does sponsorship now relate to intimacy?

_____

_____

_____

_____

_____

25. List some of your "old ideas" about intimacy.

_____

_____

_____

26. List some of your "old ideas" about authority figures.

_____

_____

_____

27. What are some of your "old ideas" about God/Higher Power?

_____

_____

_____

28. Identify the origins of these old ideas about God/Higher Power, if you can.

_____

_____

_____

29. When you first heard the Third Step phrase "God as we understand God/H.P.," what did it mean to you?

_____

_____

_____

_____

30. From what you have experienced so far in your physical and emotional recovery, what do these words mean to you at the present time?

_____

_____

_____

31. You have also heard the expression "to turn something over." When you hear others say this, or when you say this, what does this mean to you?

_____

_____

_____

32. Are there any "old ideas" in the way of turning your will and your life over to the care of H.P.?

_____

_____

_____

33. What kind of support do you need in order to take Step Three?

_____

_____

_____

34. What actions can you take to get this support?

_____

_____

_____

35. Some people think of Step Three as they would think of juggling. Imagine yourself juggling your problems (i.e., throwing them in the air and then putting your attention on the next issue—having confidence that at the right time you'll come back to the issue that you let go of). Let your imagination play with this. How does this connect with your understanding of the Step? In what way can this image be helpful to you? *(Explore this below.)*

_____

_____

_____

_____

_____

_____

_____

_____

_____

CHAPTER 13

The Basics of Recovery

Steps One, Two, and Three provide the foundation for everyone interested in implementing a self-help approach in the recovery process. Detoxification or the introduction and use of other drugs to wean the individual away from chemical dependency is merely the preparation some of us need to begin the recovery process. However, unless we begin to change our habits, what we do and how we do it, we merely stand on the threshold of recovery. To cross it, to begin solidly on the journey of recovery, the actions identified in the first three Steps are absolutely required, and there can be no compromising with them.

However, there are many possible sources of distraction. For instance, after such a long experience of isolation, some gay, lesbian, and bisexual newcomers are overwhelmed and confused when others in recovery take a personal interest in them. This may generate instant lust. (This temptation is not confined to sexual minorities.) It is easy for many people to confuse intimacy with sexuality, which then complicates or derails the recovery process.

Individuals, especially those who may have seen their problems as the result of the lack of a significant romantic attachment, may enter into a relationship too early in recovery. They may be tempted to stop working on themselves and instead focus on the relationship to the exclusion of all else. This type of distraction—fusion with another—will inevitably cause pain. When we remove the focus on recovery from ourselves and transfer it to another person, we risk becoming addicted to that person. This is quite a perilous predicament if the object of our attachment is another individual in recovery (Halpern 1982). The relationship may lead to codependency following substance dependency or compulsive behavioral problems.

A useful analogy for the recovery process is learning a new dance routine. First we need to know the basic patterns before we can begin to complicate the choreography. Once we know the footwork, then we can begin to improvise. Before we can have a successful relationship with someone else, we need to have a successful relationship with ourselves. This takes time and effort for individuals who are used to being dependent on chemicals or behavior. This is not to say that a relationship is impossible. However, it is a complication that may increase the risk of relapse.

All too often, people in early recovery choose partners with whom they can replicate their previous patterns, or they interact with new partners in such a way as to recreate past dynamics. This is quite likely to promote unhappiness or dysfunctional behaviors of one sort or another.

Before attempting a partnership, we need to focus all recovery efforts on ourselves, if possible, while we make the first three Steps our own. Once the Steps become familiar and we are able to work them with some confidence, it is possible to learn a new dance with a partner.

Considerations about the potential distraction that intimate relationships may pose also apply to other sources of distraction, such as career, education, and economic lifestyle. It is not necessary to put all of one's life on hold, but it is important to have clear priorities and to make an unequivocal commitment to recovery.

Some people decide to stop working the Steps after they master the first three. Others may add a few Steps as they find convenient, particularly Step Twelve. The danger of this approach is that it doesn't promote a complete transformation of the individual. With an incomplete transformation, the individual may be deluded that the change made was sufficient when, in fact, there is a great deal of potential for additional growth and change to be explored. Without such exploration, individuals may encounter difficulties later in recovery and not understand the source of their discomfort.

The foundation for recovery is built on the first three Steps. When problems arise in doing any of the remaining nine Steps of the program, the reasons can often be found in basic work left undone on Steps One, Two, and Three. Thus, it is a good idea to review these Steps at this time to check if there are any loose ends and to see what might remain for our consideration.

Now that we are on our way at working at recovery, we can see how much our lives before this period were lived in denial, fear and isolation, and willful powerlessness. The roots of these *conditions* extend deep into our childhood and, for many of us, into the dysfunctional families in which we grew up. Some of the questions we responded to have exposed connections with the past that we had buried, neglected, or denied. We are on the right track when we understand that this is only the beginning, for, as all programs of recovery reassure us, "more shall be revealed."

We progress in our recovery through our willingness to bring our "secrets" into the open, to acknowledge them to ourselves, and to discover that it is possible to reveal them to others. The intention is not to dwell on the pain of the past, but to clear out that wreckage in order to get on with our future. That is why the first three Steps focus on the *alternatives* to this condition: acceptance, faith or belief, and positive action.

❈   ❈   ❈

❋   ❋   ❋

Let's consolidate our understanding of Steps One, Two, and Three. From your own perspective, what do they mean in your life at this time? Record your thoughts in your journal.

❋   ❋   ❋

1. Think of the way Steps One, Two, and Three function in your life. Relate actions you have taken in your life to the first three Steps.

    Step One:

    _____

    _____

    Step Two:

    _____

    _____

    Step Three:

    _____

    _____

2. "God grant me the serenity to accept the things I cannot change; courage to change the things I can; and wisdom to know the difference." Instead of merely reciting the Serenity Prayer, use it to inventory your present understanding of:

    a. those things you *cannot* change =

    _____

    _____

    b. those things you *can* change =

    _____

    _____

    c. those things you need help with, or advice about, in order to know if they belong in a. or b. =

    _____

    _____

3. To focus and personalize your understanding of recovery, develop a working definition of some key words in the Serenity Prayer:

a. "acceptance":

_____

_____

b. "courage":

_____

_____

c. "serenity":

_____

_____

4. How do each one of these definitions relate to any of your old ideas?

_____

_____

_____

5. Do any other old ideas invite particular scrutiny at this time? *(e.g., how rich and wonderful your life was before beginning recovery; your uniqueness; your religion; your spirituality)*

_____

_____

_____

6. Identify any workbook questions that came up in the first three chapters on Steps One, Two, or Three, that gave you particular difficulty. List them below and put a letter beside each, indication that you need to go back to it: **(a)** as soon as possible; **(b)** in the next few months; **(c)** after maintaining a year of abstinence.

	Timetable
Step One Questions	*for Review*
_____	_____
_____	_____
_____	_____

	Timetable for Review
Step Two Questions	
_____	_____
_____	_____
_____	_____

	Timetable for Review
Step Three Questions	
_____	_____
_____	_____
_____	_____

7. What progress have you made getting support for your recovery process? *(e.g., sponsor, therapist, friend)* If you have accomplished this task, complete the *Temporary Sponsor/Permanent Sponsor Action Plan* on page 138. Then complete the *Support Group Action Plan* on page 139.

    _____

    _____

    _____

    If you haven't found a sponsor, therapist, or recovery coach, what additional efforts do you need to make to find one?

    _____

    _____

    _____

❋   ❋   ❋

In early recovery, it is often very difficult to sort out feelings from facts. We have attempted to use the first three Steps to look at the facts of our lives and allow ourselves, perhaps for the first time, explicit permission to have the feelings that come up for us. Let's take this opportunity to examine our recovery with this same perspective.

❋   ❋   ❋

8. These are a few pertinent facts about recovery at this very moment.

    a. I began _____ days ago.

    b. I have attended _____ meetings.

c. I have been reading these books to support myself: _____

_____

d. I have a sponsor whom I am in touch with _____ times a week.

e. I regularly call these program people on the phone: _____

_____

f. I have had _____ sessions with a counselor.

Write additional pertinent facts about where you live, your job, etc.

_____

_____

_____

_____

_____

_____

9. a. How do you *feel* about your recovery at the present time?

_____

_____

b. What do you like about it?

_____

_____

c. What do you think could be improved?

_____

_____

d. What would you change completely?

_____

_____

10. What are some of your observations about your own, and other people's, perfectionism?

_____

_____

_____

11. What progress are you making in your efforts to deal with perfectionism and extremist, all-or-nothing thinking?

_____

_____

_____

12. Imagine yourself accepting people and things exactly as they are. What would it be like? Practice accepting people and things *exactly as they are* for ten to thirty minutes at a time; then record your experience after doing this exercise several times.

_____

_____

_____

13. Look at some of the following paradoxes you may have heard at Twelve Step meetings. Add others you know about. Indicate if the paradoxes are easy or hard for you to understand.

- "Surrender to win" ☐ Easy ☐ Difficult

- "You've got to give it away to keep it" ☐ Easy ☐ Difficult

- "We find strength when we admit we are powerless" ☐ Easy ☐ Difficult

- _____ ☐ Easy ☐ Difficult

- _____ ☐ Easy ☐ Difficult

- _____ ☐ Easy ☐ Difficult

14. Which one(s) seems the most helpful to you?

_____

_____

_____

15. Is there anything you've heard in working on the first three Steps, either from someone else in the group or at a meeting, that causes you concern or confusion, or is just an "obstacle" in your recovery path?

_____

_____

_____

16. Draw a picture of your path in recovery; then color it.

17. Where do you stand along the path? Go back and put yourself in the picture.

18. Write today's date:_____

In six months, what would you like your relationship to be with:

a. Your biological family:

_____

_____

b. Your spouse/significant other:

_____

_____

c. Your friends:

_____

_____

d. Your job/work/boss:

_____

_____

e. Your finances:

_____

_____

f. Your living situation/house or apt.:

_____

_____

g. Your health:

_____

_____

h. Other:

_____

_____

19. Look again at question 2 (page 127). Add to your Serenity Prayer inventory the appropriate letters of the entries you have just made above.

_____

_____

_____

❋   ❋   ❋

You now need to set up a plan of action that will make it possible to specifically work on those things you believe you are able to change. You will work on this task by completing the Action Plans on pages 135–139. (It is possible that you will discover you were mistaken; nevertheless, you believe you can presently do something to change the circumstance, and that is important for now.)

The Action Plans that follow will identify (1) specific tasks you will undertake; (2) the people who can support you in your efforts; and (3) the length of time you think it will take to complete the tasks. Recovery requires action, and by getting into action we merely affect the opportunity for change: we do not control it! We advance our recovery as long as we do not attempt to project any outcome of our efforts. Planning provides a source of guidance for our efforts; it is not the basis for evaluating ourselves OR our recovery program. The value is in the action. The results are often outside of our control and therefore need not be the basis on which we judge the value of the effort!

❅　　❅　　❅

Here is a sample Action Plan using the matrix that you will find on the succeeding pages. *Improving family relationships* is the area for change that has been developed. The sample shows the tasks that need to be undertaken, the people who are necessary/helpful to perform the tasks, and the length of time they will take. (It is helpful to identify *start-up* and *completion* dates for tasks.)

SAMPLE ACTION PLAN

AREA FOR CHANGE:
Family Relationships

Tasks to Be Completed	Individuals Needed	Time Line
1. Write letter to mom & dad	self	today; 2 days
2. Phone sister	self	tmrw. 1 day
3. Phone brothers	self	nxt. weekend
4. Phone aunt	self	2 wks. (-3/15)
5. Plan visit to: ———	travel agent	3/15-3/20

---

20. Once you have completed the Action Plans, work on developing the list of tasks you need to complete for each of the areas you identified as things you *can* change.

21. Review your Action Plans from time to time and make note of your progress. *(See page 139.)*

MY ACTION PLAN

AREA FOR CHANGE:
Family Relationships

Tasks to Be Completed	Individuals Needed	Time Line
1. _____	_____	_____
2. _____	_____	_____
3. _____	_____	_____
4. _____	_____	_____
5. _____	_____	_____

MY ACTION PLAN

AREA FOR CHANGE:
Other Relationships

Tasks to Be Completed	Individuals Needed	Time Line
1. _____	_____	_____
2. _____	_____	_____
3. _____	_____	_____
4. _____	_____	_____
5. _____	_____	_____

MY ACTION PLAN

AREA FOR CHANGE:
Employment

Tasks to Be Completed	Individuals Needed	Time Line
1. _____	_____	_____
2. _____	_____	_____
3. _____	_____	_____
4. _____	_____	_____
5. _____	_____	_____

MY ACTION PLAN

AREA FOR CHANGE:
Housing

Tasks to Be Completed	Individuals Needed	Time Line
1. _____	_____	_____
2. _____	_____	_____
3. _____	_____	_____
4. _____	_____	_____
5. _____	_____	_____

MY ACTION PLAN

AREA FOR CHANGE:
Education

Tasks to Be Completed	Individuals Needed	Time Line
1. _____	_____	_____
2. _____	_____	_____
3. _____	_____	_____
4. _____	_____	_____
5. _____	_____	_____

My Action Plan

Temporary Sponsor

Name: _____

Address:_____

Phone Number: (Work) _____

Phone Number: (Home) _____

Best times to call: _____

Dates contacted & issues discussed:

_____

_____

_____

Permanent Sponsor

Name: _____

Address:_____

Phone Number: (Work) _____

Phone Number: (Home) _____

Best times to call: _____

Dates contacted & issues discussed:

_____

_____

_____

MY ACTION PLAN

Support Group

	Name	Telephone Numbers	Best Time to Call
1.	_____	(Work) _____	_____
		(Home) _____	
2.	_____	(Work) _____	_____
		(Home) _____	
3.	_____	(Work) _____	_____
		(Home) _____	

MY ACTION PLAN

Action Plan Review

Date	Comments	Follow-up
_____	_____	_____
_____	_____	_____
_____	_____	_____
_____	_____	_____
_____	_____	_____

22. For the next week, stand in front of your mirror five minutes each day and say: "I can begin to be loyal to myself *today!*" Record what comes up for you after each session.

Monday:

_____

_____

Tuesday:

_____

_____

Wednesday:

_____

_____

Thursday:

_____

_____

Friday:

_____

_____

Saturday:

_____

_____

Sunday:

_____

_____

23. Consider repeating the mirror exercise for the following week(s). Record the responses in your journal.

24. After several weeks of responses, identify the major themes you discover in them.

25. Arrange the themes in order of priority for discussion. Discuss with your sponsor those issues that relate to your ability to remain abstinent. Discuss with a therapist issues that do not come within the domain of abstinence.

If you do not have a sponsor or another person committed to assisting you in your recovery efforts, it might be critical to reexamine your need for support.

CHAPTER 14

Looking into the Mirror

CONDITION
Self-delusion

ALTERNATIVE
Self-revelation

We deluded ourselves that our lives worked. "Everyone has problems," we told ourselves. Our solution to these problems, both large and small, was substances or compulsive behavior. A major crisis occurred: health failed, employment or finances gave out, relationships ended, or litigation forced us to see that our lives were falling apart not because of the problems but because of our solution. We found ourselves marching down the road to total destruction shoulder to shoulder with dishonesty and self-delusion.

Looking at what is instead of what isn't, reality-testing the experience of our lives as sexual minorities, is essential for recovery. At group therapy sessions, Twelve Step meetings, and/or one-on-one sessions, we learn that our awful-terribles are not so awful-terrible when someone else speaks them. When we look with compassion and understanding into the mirror of human experience, we see ourselves!

Step 4

Made a searching and fearless moral inventory of ourselves.

Our thinking processes are carefully evolved and developed over the years of our lives. Just because we stop using or acting out doesn't mean that the influence of compulsive behavior on how we think and act is ended forever. The way we think about ourselves and about the world today is deeply affected by what we have experienced in the past. This is true for everyone in recovery.

Masks and Criticism

Many sexual minorities have grown up and lived under conditions that severely inhibit healthy mental and emotional development. The experience of lying to others, wearing masks—removing one, putting on another, whenever the occasion calls for it (and sometimes even when the occasion doesn't)—is very familiar to us. Mask changing is a habit that becomes so natural we rarely acknowledge we are doing it. Having grown up in nongay households, we developed a common-sense understanding of what it takes to go incognito among the people who care about us as well as those who don't. We do what we think will work for as long as we think necessary. In the presence of others, we are talented performers. When we stand alone in front of the mirror, we are often harsh critics of ourselves.

Sexual minorities, as a group, may be the largest "critical mass" in society. The expertise derived from self-criticism has honed this ability so sharply that it functions with little or no restraint under any and all circumstances. For some, being hypercritical is a source of humor and delight. For others, it is the cause of deep dissatisfaction with family, friends, and strangers, as well as the basis of their unhappiness. The critical voices inside their heads never stop for a moment.

How else is it possible to be "the best little girl" or "the best little boy" in the house, the neighborhood, the school, the town, the WORLD? Unless they work at self-criticism every waking hour, the possibility of reaching this goal of imagined perfection is unobtainable. This kind of thinking, both on the conscious as well as the unconscious level, is vivid and familiar to sexual minorities. Individuals use substances and/or act out over it constantly.

Many gays, lesbians, and bisexuals have particular difficulty activating the "pause" button on their own hypercritical attitudes and self-contempt. The distorted rules of survival sexual minorities have learned have made them feel even less acceptable as human beings. Thinking in this mode is often so natural that the mere suggestion to examine it usually meets with powerful resistance. For us, showing up in life—participating completely—has always meant being criticized or else criticizing everything, everybody, and especially ourselves.

Using substances, at first, was the only means many of us knew for anesthetizing the pain we felt over not being perfect. Some of us translated not being perfect into meaning that we were not lovable. With substances and compulsive behavior, we tried to deaden the pain of being unloved and the suffering that comes from having a poor self-concept, a distorted self-image because of internalized homophobia, and low self-esteem. Escaping into fantasy and self-delusion was a welcome relief from the barrage of criticism that continually battered us. For a period of time, the silence we achieved with substances even sounded like sanity—until madness of compulsive/dependent behavior took over.

When this happened, strident voices were added to the chorus of self-destruction. If it was bad before, our self-criticism intensified, along with the criticism we got from others. What appeared to be escape turned into a head-on collision with unmanageability.

Compulsive/dependent behavior feeds on criticism because its message is always clear and consistent: "YOU CAN'T DO ANYTHING WITHOUT ME!" Individuals who are still using substances or acting out cannot allow themselves to believe in support for handling life WITHOUT substances. Recognizing the need for support from others is one of the first indications that we are getting ready to begin implementing the change process.

It often takes a long time to reach this awareness. Even when we do, this does not recast the mold in which we have trained our minds to think. If we have carefully taken the first three steps of this journey into recovery, we have achieved some new and valuable understanding about ourselves along the way. We have been able to observe how often our minds make everything far more complicated than it actually is. No matter what data or circumstance is presented, our minds seem to complicate it. And if nothing except silence is offered, this same mind will function to make the individual a victim. The pattern of thinking in this fashion generates suffering. We generate our secrets out of this same pattern.

Our Secrets

During Hal's earliest days in recovery, one of the first slogans he learned was "We're only as sick as our secrets." With that reminder, he knew he was *very* sick because of the thousands of secrets seeded through his life. There was no area free of them. A shocking realization came to him as he listened while others shared their stories: these people were telling intimate details he never believed could be told! For him, this was the beginning of actually understanding what change would be like in his life. For him to be able to do what those people were doing, he knew he would have to change. But at that time, he didn't know how, or if he even wanted to make such a change.

When Hal shared this, the people in the room reminded him that they were just like him when they started. The only reason they were doing what they did was because each person truly wanted to recover. If that was what he wanted, then he'd just have to find the way to dump all of his "precious" secrets. Hal had never thought of them as "precious," and it certainly startled him when they were referred to like that.

The truth has an unusual way of reaching into our lives. Indeed, our secrets are precious to us whether or not they are to anybody else. For most of us, one or two secrets outweigh all the rest and are the cause of the greatest suffering: being gay, or lesbian, or bisexual, and afraid someone will find out. Damn right that's a "precious" secret! Damn right we've got to suffer over it! That, at least, is what many of us think in the beginning of recovery.

Over the past decade, many gays, lesbians, and bisexuals have told how difficult recovery was for them as long as they kept homosexuality their secret. The deep-seated fear of discovery—of not being accepted, of being thrown out of a group or a Twelve Step meeting—continues to inhibit gays, lesbians, and bisexuals from sharing major problems they are facing. At the least, it often motivates them to change gender pronouns when referring to loved ones. Hiding or lying about sexual orientation is the route chosen commonly rather than honestly revealing sexual orientation to others—if those others are not gay or lesbian.

In spite of the insistence that all chemically dependent individuals are alike, most sexual minorities experience a deep sense of uniqueness that makes them feel different from everyone else at nongay meetings. Denying the validity of the experience of being gay in the midst of a heterosexist society results in additional harm instead of much-needed support. Many of us have endured this painful confrontation. But that is precisely what many sexual minorities have done: endured it by hiding behind phony masks or by lying.

Using what happens (or doesn't happen) for us in recovery as the justification for returning to compulsive/dependent behavior is more self-delusion. Support groups of every kind exist everywhere. We have to find the circle in which we get the help we need for our recovery. It is up to us to seek out and discover where to find this support.

Those of us who find our way into special interest meetings for sexual minorities are fortunate because we can more easily let go of the secret of our homosexuality which is most often the cause of relapse for individuals who are gay, lesbian, and bisexual. In cities and towns where such special interest Twelve Step meetings are not available, sharing these secrets with a gay, lesbian, or bisexual sponsor is very helpful. Even when sponsors don't live in the same town or state, there is always a telephone handy to call them.[1] When sobriety comes first, letting go of the burden of our secrets will definitely improve the chances of not picking up the first drink or drug again.

"Who Wants to Know?"

Relapse is common, and the triggers for relapse are myriad. Some of the triggers are the compulsive habits we have formed before entering recovery; some habits were begun in childhood. These habits do not fall away from us easily or by magic. It is as if our minds have been programmed with these patterns of thinking. Holding on to our deepest, darkest secrets about our sexuality has been a way of life for many of us. The prospect of living without this secret is beyond anything many have ever hoped, and the suggestion that we share the truth about ourselves with someone else can cause tremendous anxiety. What would it be like to live *without* our secret?

That answer waits behind another question: "Who wants to know?" When we stop using or acting out, everything around us changes. If *we* do not change, it will not be too long before we will resume using some substance or behavior in order to endure what we perceive to be the intolerable experience of living. But if we wish to recover, if we choose to live in sobriety, we have the choice of coming forward with the answer to that question. We need to want recovery enough, however, in order to speak out with a voice that affirms this commitment.

How often have we heard someone comment on how badly so-and-so needs to get into a recovery program? None of the Twelve Step programs are for people who *just* need them; they are for gays, lesbians, and bisexuals who WANT them. When we become clear about that, we begin to understand in a very practical way how the program of recovery works. These programs work because the individual makes a commitment to change that is independent of the transitory desires and temptations of the moment.

Very slowly, as a result of the efforts we make, we are changed. Patterns of thinking are modified gradually by the effect of the process of recovery in our lives and the new habits, attitudes, and beliefs that we develop. Our actions reflect the changes. Even if the compulsion to drink or to use or to act out may not have left us, we do not yield to it. We have begun the work of altering our old ways of thinking with reasonable and self-nurturing ideas.

Once we have taken the first steps of our ascent out of the darkness, we are ready to put our foot on the next step. At this time, it is essential for us to reassure ourselves that the way forward is by taking it.

Making Our List

We begin by looking at ourselves not for the old and familiar purpose of suffering and self-destruction but for the positive reason that our continued progress depends on *honesty*. Instead of hiding behind masks, we need to look at ourselves and acknowledge what we see.

To some, this suggestion seems like an invitation to create a catalog of disasters. In recovery, however, there is no need for any bills of indictment. Step Four encourages us to inventory our strengths—our assets—as well as the areas for improvement in our lives. Unless we include both areas, the list is too likely to foster additional feelings of worthlessness, low self-esteem, shame, and demoralization.

As human beings, as sexual minorities, it is quite easy to have a distorted sense of ourselves. Sometimes we may overemphasize the positive or the negative or see assets as weaknesses or vice versa. We need to bear this in mind. The fact that any of us have survived long enough to begin the process of recovery is sufficient evidence of strengths. These strengths, like courage and determination, absolutely belong on the plus side of the ledger.

Not by burying our misconceptions and distortions under more lies but by revealing them to ourselves in an honest and conscientious manner we continue our progress in recovery. Our secrets will continue to control us unless we get rid of them! Health depends on the willingness to undertake this effort at self-disclosure.

It will come as no surprise that most of us have monumental resistance to writing this inventory. This resistance is closely linked with the habit of denial, and is intimately related to our dependence on self-delusion or avoidance. Confronting self-delusion is the only way through it.

With Step Four, we have the unusual opportunity to see ourselves as no longer being the frightened and confused children who were forced to make up our own unique rules. We remember the rules we created in order to survive:

- "Be perfect!"
- "Be a rescuer!"
- "Be silent and unnoticed!"
- "Be funny!"
- "Don't look like a queer!"
- "Pretend you're not: gay, lesbian, bisexual!"

Those rules got us through childhood in our dysfunctional families and in our schools and neighborhoods. Unless we are willing to look at ourselves, at who we are now and how we do things now, we will continue to act as if we were still children. We can make honest and meaningful choices about how we wish to be and act during the rest of our lives only *after* we have seen ourselves the way we are and the way we have been. The journey out of self-delusion is through self-revelation.

For years, we have lived in the midst of an arena bombarded with criticism about ourselves and all the things we have done, as well as the way we have done them; about how our orientation has been the cause of so much suffering and unhappiness to others; about how badly we have mistreated others; about how justly we deserve the punishment—the disgrace—that has fallen on our plate, etc., etc. Each of us has our own code words to unlock the door to suffering and guilt over the past. It's amazing how well they always work! We carry with us the burden of criticism—our own and others—wherever we go, even though we pretended we were leaving it behind. We escaped into fantasy and, in our fantasy, we found our way into chemical dependency and compulsive behavior.

We do well to remember an ancient story about a weary Chinese traveler on the road to a city he had never visited before. He had journeyed a long distance and lost his way many times. Finally, he saw a man sitting on a fence beside the road, and his burden of discouragement seemed to melt into the air. "Please, sir, can you tell me how far it is to the city of Chang An?" he asked the man sitting on the fence. The man answered with the utmost seriousness, "It is only six miles, sir, but it is better not to start from here."

"Here" is the place that we MUST start from, because this is where we find ourselves now in our journey into recovery. Facing the unfaceable. Our secrets form an integral part of the way we think about others and ourselves. Living with them as we have done over the years, we are imprisoned in the past. Many people have found out the hard way that unless they are freed from the need to hide their secrets by disclosure they will again and again return to compulsive/dependent behavior. Secrets support this behavior; each one of our precious secrets lies ready and waiting for us or others to say the code words that release them into action.

To those who begin working on the inventory in Step Four, some of these darkest secrets are often a great surprise. As we begin on ones we knew were there, we discover many others crawling around beneath the first rock. Pursuing the effort to develop the list further, we find ourselves able to reach far back into childhood and the secrets we had buried there. One secret is tied to another, and that one to still another. Secrets we never even knew existed appear as we patiently go about developing the list.

Let us remember that we are not making a perfect, exhaustive list. We are merely identifying those aspects of our lives that wait in hiding and pounce on us when we are most vulnerable, when we think we have escaped from the wreckage of our past. In this list, we are also identifying the patient, courageous, loving parts of ourselves that have helped us to sustain our lives through the darkest moments.

It is important to write only what comes up for us now. Later on in recovery, other secrets will reveal themselves. We do well to use this Step as one of our first opportunities in recovery NOT to be perfect.

Because of low self-esteem, or other sources of negativity aimed toward the self, many individuals look on the task of completing the inventory as an obstacle instead of as exactly what is needed to overcome the roadblocks standing in the way of recovery. This is particularly perilous for sexual minorities who often harbor even greater negative thoughts about themselves and use this Step as another opportunity to beat up on themselves about their sexual orientation and how they've responded to it in a homophobic society.

Many beginners work through the first three Steps and then avoid Steps Four and Five for these reasons. It is only later, when they are baffled and cannot understand why recovery is such a dead end for them, that they discover the cause is quite simple. Their secrets and shame sentence them to live under conditions identical to those they have known prior to entering recovery.

Discovering what we are like, what we have done, what we have not done, and what our assets and liabilities are is an astounding revelation. Developing this inventory is the first time that many of us move out from behind the shadow of criticism of ourselves. Our thoughts about ourselves and our actions have actually been the source for much negativity in our lives, and it is possible to see and understand this as we go through the process of developing the list of these secrets.

What others share in therapy groups and meetings may provide us with support and encouragement when we sit down to write an inventory. Some of us, indeed, discovered only after we began writing how much we have in common with other sexual minorities. But someone else's secrets do not keep us locked in the past; only *our own* prevent us from being available to change our lives for the future.

The shift in perspective we create through making the inventory separates us from those obstacles. This is extremely valuable for our recovery. We can attempt this by observing

a. ourselves as the source and support of the obstacles;

b. the obstacles themselves that we have created and supported; and that

c. we are capable of standing apart from both a and b.

When we do this, we begin to appreciate the magnitude of our potential for living a new and different life in recovery. We may even discover that we no longer have to choose to be the same obstacle maker, nor continue to hold on to those obstacles that are standing in the way of our recovery.

Until now, we have lived as prisoners and our minds became accustomed to this manner of thinking. That is why it is so important in early recovery to experience the possibility of a different perspective, one that is free of this kind of victimization. Through developing the inventory, we create the opportunity for changing the way we think by revealing ourselves to ourselves from the perspective of this moment, now. The fear of looking at ourselves in the present as objectively as possible has kept many of us stuck on the "fix." We have allowed fear to control our lives through our secrets from the past. Step Four offers us the chance to move beyond this extremist way of thinking into the present.

Developing an Inventory

When we look in the mirror each day, we see what we choose to see. Today, we may have an "attack of the uglies," and see ourselves as ugly. But tomorrow or the day after, when this feeling passes, we see different things about ourselves. The truth is that there are certain features we like about ourselves, and others we don't. Observing what is there *within* ourselves, as honestly as we are able, and allowing ourselves to list what we see, is the task we undertake in the Fourth Step.

Extensive guidance is available for developing our inventories. Some general publications may be helpful for gays, lesbians, and bisexuals.[2] Remember however, these guides are merely suggestions. Before following through with your inventory, consider the following carefully:

1. Discuss your intention to write a Fourth Step inventory with your sponsor or counselor.

2. Develop an outline that will cover the areas you need to focus on the most. (The general Fourth Step guides may be exactly what you need. You may also find you need greater depth in certain areas, such as your childhood, violence, incest, internalized homophobia, or health issues.)

3. Target a date by which you will complete the inventory, and develop a plan to accomplish this. Set aside time to write and make it a priority in your daily schedule.

4. Use your own words instead of language that may sound better after you edit it. (Your own words have special meaning for you, and it is important to connect this meaning with your feelings.)

5. Write whatever comes up for you, and then go on to the next thing; don't get stuck in any one area.

6. Stay in close touch with others via telephone and meetings; don't get out on a limb all by yourself just because you're writing your inventory.

7. Share your experience—what it's like for you—with others one-on-one and in group sessions; you will support others who are doing a Fourth Step and, at the same time, receive support for yourself.

8. Don't minimize your efforts or your feelings. This is a unique opportunity for you to see yourself as you are.

9. Allow others to support and love you in your process of getting better. No matter what you discover about yourself, you are taking the action that is needed to change.

10. Keep in mind that Step Four is a vital part of the process of helping you feel better—not worse—about yourself. It is a step toward recovery and not backward into compulsive/dependent behavior.

We need to identify our strengths along with the areas for improvement in our lives. Listing "faults" or "defects of character" can easily pander to the victim who cannot get enough of suffering. When the founders of Alcoholics Anonymous wrote "The Big Book" and other guidance material, they used language appropriate to their experience. Today, instead of using words like "faults," "defects of character," and "shortcomings," we know that "survival tactics" can often be closer to the mark when it comes to revealing what we did in order to get through our lives. (Regardless of the words chosen, it is important to look for the meaning and not get lost in the semantics.)

The guidance and support of someone who has already done this Step can be invaluable for everyone engaged in writing an inventory. We need to learn to use this important tool because sponsors can be a significant part of our recovery. No longer do we have to be alone. Working with a sponsor can be an excellent way of developing a new model of relationship, a new framework for intimacy, that does not confuse love with sex. Gay men and lesbians are wise to use this opportunity to discover what a relationship with another person who cares about them can mean—without sex.

A gay or lesbian sponsor of the other sex, with several years of recovery in Twelve Step programs, who has worked through his or her own issues related to homosexuality, can be of help through the major ordeal of owning homosexuality. For others, it will be more appropriate to work this through with the help of a therapist. Having made a secret of it all of our lives, having created hundreds and even thousands of lies and secrets behind it as well, the prospect of bringing it into the light may seem too formidable for the thimbleful of recovery we have so far been able to accumulate. Postponing the day, however, may create another delusion— that there is "an easier, softer way." We should look at the possibility that our progress in recovery can be greatly advanced if we will let go of this secret—and all the rest—instead of holding on to them. It is our way of thinking that makes us believe otherwise.

Nongay men and women do not write "heterosexuality" as a character defect on their Fourth Step inventories. Many gays, lesbians, and bisexuals begin their inventories with "homosexuality" at the top of this list—or would do so if they were truly honest about their feelings. This is a symptom of a pattern of thinking that thrives on criticism. Being gay, or lesbian, or bisexual, is as much a "defect of character" as having blue eyes when 90 percent of the population has brown eyes. If we think of this list either in terms of *survival tactics* or *obstacles to recovery,* we understand that our sexual orientation doesn't belong on it. We are who we are!

Pretending to be what we are NOT is precisely what we are striving to put behind us. That some of us have basically negative thoughts about ourselves as a result of incorporating a tremendous amount of homophobia from society is the truth. Admitting this truth is the beginning of the end to shame and low self-esteem. Letting go of this shame is as essential to our progress in recovery as breathing fresh air, exercising, and eating nutritious food.

Facing ourselves, acknowledging how seriously self-hatred has influenced our lives, dismantles one of our basic obstacles. All the rest of our obstacles must take second, third, fourth, fifth . . . place behind it.

So many of us have deluded ourselves into thinking that we were born with our hypercritical attitude. When we write "homosexuality" on the inventory, we know this is a lie. And we know, at the same moment, that we have survived *in spite of* the lie. Once we discover that we have survived something that almost killed us, what should we do? In the Book of Exodus, we are told that the children of Israel sang a great song when they escaped the pharaoh's army and reached the other shore of the Red Sea. We, too, can celebrate our survival by continuing to develop the inventory of our secrets, our obstacles, as well as the strengths that supported us to get us through.

Unless we can own ourselves, we are nothing. No matter what secrets we have kept about ourselves, we can write them on the page and acknowledge them. In the privacy of this safe room of our house, we can take off the mask and look at what "is" instead of continuing with the pretense of what "isn't." As gay men, as lesbians, as bisexuals, this is a reality-testing of our lives as we have lived them. "Mirror, mirror, on the wall. . . ." In the reflection of this inventory, we see who we are, and we discover we dare not turn away. Nor does the world implode when we become honest. Our thinking processes can now receive encouragement to evolve in a healthier environment that supports recovery instead of addiction.

❋　　❋　　❋

The next time you catch yourself saying you're doing the best you can, say instead that you're doing *what* you can. Is it true that you always felt you could do better, no matter how well you did? Make an effort to "lighten up" on yourself, and discover what happens.

※　　　※　　　※

Before you start to do a Fourth Step inventory, spend some time looking at honesty and what it feels like to be honest in your life. Is there any benefit to you from honesty? Record these benefits in your journal. Are there any risks? Record the risks in your journal.

※　　　※　　　※

You have already made a special effort to identify old ideas and how these function in your life. As all of us progress in recovery, this process will continue. Because of these old ideas, it is natural for many of us to feel daunted by the enormity of Step Four: developing a fearless and thorough moral inventory.

1. When you use the word "inventory" it means:

   _____

   _____

   _____

2. And a "*moral* inventory" means:

   _____

   _____

   _____

3. Write the dictionary definitions of "moral" and "inventory."

   _____

   _____

   _____

How do these definitions add to your understanding of these terms?

_____

_____

_____

4. What needs to be included in your present definition of "moral inventory" to reshape it? In addition to "areas for improvement," does the opportunity to identify "strengths" figure in your conception? If not, why not?

_____

_____

_____

5. "If I can't do something perfectly, I don't want to do it at all!" This attitude is not at all uncommon for people in recovery. How relevant is this attitude to how you feel doing Step Four? *(Check one of the following)*

    ☐ a. completely

    ☐ b. moderately

    ☐ c. not at all

6. If neither of these old ideas—a limited definition of the term "moral inventory" or an attitude toward perfectionism—is at the heart of your resistance to working on Step Four, identify any other reasons.

_____

_____

_____

7. For getting these secrets out in the open, say something positive to yourself like "Good job!" or "Way to go!" and then write it down to make it even more real to you. How does it feel to write this?

_____

_____

_____

We need to be clear about the "new ideas" that are developed in Step Four. First, this Step is about ending self-delusion by using *self-revelation* and NOT self-destruction. Second, because our honesty is the foundation on which recovery is built, we cannot construct a solid house on a precarious foundation. Third, no matter what we may know about ourselves today, we can be certain that by working on change, MORE will be revealed tomorrow as we are changed by this process. The inventory we make today is only for what we understand about ourselves *today*. We will have all the time we need for more self-revelation as we progress. Fourth, whatever we did, or did not do, before entering recovery is past. It is already done, or not done. For many of us, recovery provides the opportunity to get closure on the past, make peace with ourselves, and stop avoiding and start facing the past instead of leaving it as "unfinished business." Without making peace or closure, or facing ourselves and our histories, it is all too likely that the past will continue to influence our present in often unacknowledged and destructive ways.

Because this commitment to change creates such profound differences, it is very helpful, before even considering what to write in any inventory of our lives, to look at some of the masks we have worn and to examine what we find there in the mirror. Step Four provides us with a unique opportunity to examine both the masks we wear in our lives and the critical voices that provide the acoustical background (and sometimes the foreground) of our lives.

8. In addition to wearing the mask of *Hero, Clown,* or *Victim,* what are some other masks in your life? *(Add the names of your other masks in the first column to the list below.)*

Catalog of Masks:	When I wore the Mask:	I wore the Mask… A = before recovery R = in recovery
_____	_____	_____
_____	_____	_____
_____	_____	_____
_____	_____	_____
_____	_____	_____

9. Now, on this list under question number 8, in the second column write *"Today"* beside each mask you have worn today. And then write *"Yesterday,"* or *"Last weekend,"* or any other time to indicate when you have worn each mask.

10. In the third column under question 8, identify the masks you wore *before entering recovery* with an *A* and those *in recovery* with an *R*. (This will provide you with a list of some of the masks in your repertoire. Perhaps additional masks will occur to you as you begin to do some of the other exercises. Add them to your list.)

11. Using the ovals below. briefly sketch the facial characteristics of five of your favorite masks. *(Use colored pencils, be creative, and give each of them a name.)*

Example

Poor Me

| Mask 1 | Mask 2 | Mask 3 | Mask 4 | Mask 5 |

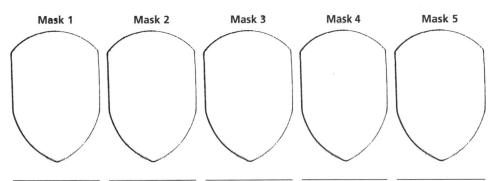

12. For each mask you have identified, name the person or the situation you faced when you wore the mask. Then, write how you felt at the time.

	Person/Situation I faced	*How I felt*
Mask 1	_____	_____
Mask 2	_____	_____
Mask 3	_____	_____
Mask 4	_____	_____
Mask 5	_____	_____

13. On the top two lines for each mask listed below, describe in your own words the characteristics of each of the five masks.

Mask 1: _____

_____

_____

_____

Mask 2: _____

_____

_____

_____

Mask 3: _____

_____

_____

_____

Mask 4: _____

_____

_____

_____

Mask 5: _____

_____

_____

_____

The masks you wear are related to the kind of response (both positive and negative) you'd like to get from others. It's no accident that all of us put them on. Being "the best" (or the "worst") in the family, the neighborhood, the school, the town, the *world* takes lots of effort. Our masks have often helped us compensate for our frustrations in obtaining certain kinds of responses or getting our needs met.

14. On the bottom two lines for each mask (in the above list), identify the kind of criticism you want to avoid or diminish by wearing your mask.

15. Below, list the kinds of criticism from others that you'd like to silence or avoid.

16. Associate this criticism with specific voices you most often hear sounding inside your own head. Connect these voices with real people you know or have known in your life. (Parents, relatives, teachers, schoolmates, friends, lovers, etc.)

_____   _____

_____   _____

_____   _____

_____   _____

_____   _____

_____   _____

_____   _____

17. Using colored pencils, draw lines to attach the names of the people with the criticism they make/made about you.

18. Below, write what you wish each person would say about you instead.

_____

_____

_____

_____

_____

_____

19. Use a colored pencil to circle the key word in each statement above.

20. List these key words below.

_____

_____

_____

21 Describe how you *feel* when others use these words in reference to you or the things you do.

_____

_____

_____

22. How often do *you* use these words when you refer to others? *(Check one.)*

☐ Very often

☐ Sometimes

☐ Seldom

☐ Never

23. Which of your "secrets" are revealed in the responses you've just written? Write one of them.

_____

_____

_____

24. How do you feel now that you've written it down?

_____

_____

_____

25. In making your secret explicit for yourself, to what degree are you currently able to confront any of your worst fears? Identify some of your fears.

_____

_____

_____

26. List any other secrets that you find in your responses to the questions in this chapter. Then, look back over your responses in the earlier chapters to discover additional secrets in them. Add these on a sheet you can insert below.

_____

_____

_____

After putting your secrets on the table, step back and observe yourself as separate from them. You have lived as if these secrets are who you are; but, by putting them out there, you can see them on their own, apart from you. Now that you are in recovery, you no longer need to hold onto your secrets and thereby support the conditions of your life that kept you a prisoner. By revealing these secrets to yourself, you take a major step forward into a new way of living in which you no longer need to use your secrets, or your weaknesses, to beat up on yourself.

27. Ask yourself: "What will it be like to live without my secrets?" Record your answer.

_____

_____

_____

28. Steps One, Two, and Three have helped you to get ready to do an inventory. Take this opportunity to assess your readiness. Do you feel you've made progress moving

   a. from denial toward acceptance: ☐ Yes ☐ No

   b. from isolation & fear toward confidence/faith in recovery: ☐ Yes ☐ No

   c. from *willful powerlessness* to positive action: ☐ Yes ☐ No

29. What additional tools of a Twelve Step recovery program are you using?

_____

_____

_____

30. What has the discussion with your sponsor or therapist about your intention to write a Fourth Step inventory produced?

_____

_____

_____

31. Who is your support person/group to offer you encouragement through the period of writing the inventory?

_____

_____

_____

32. Have you examined the Twelve Step guidance material on writing inventories that is available to support your effort?

☐ Yes ☐ No

33. What are your motives for making this inventory to support your progress in recovery at this time? Explore this.

_____

_____

_____

34. If you have not yet answered the previous questions, what action(s) are you taking to become ready to address these issues?

_____

_____

_____

35. If you are ready to proceed, take some time, without any interruptions, and lay out in your journal the areas of your life you'd like to cover in your inventory. After you have done this brainstorming exercise, put it aside for a day or so. Then examine it and create an outline from it. Discuss your outline with your therapist or sponsor. Also, set up a schedule for completing your inventory. Some people find it helpful to set aside a specific time of the day to work on this project. Customize your Action Plan to help keep you on track based on what level of detail fits your style.

CHAPTER 15

Catharsis

CONDITION	ALTERNATIVE
Regression/stagnation	**Cleansing/renewal**

Our lives have been filled with pain and suffering; but salty tears have become sweet to us. We've learned to accept suffering as the norm. This pattern accompanies us into recovery when we experience the terror of revealing ourselves to another human being. "If someone knows me, knows everything about me, then I can't go on doing crazy things. *I'll have to change!"* Or, "If they really knew what I was like, they wouldn't have anything to do with me!" Fear of losing what we already have, no matter how little it may be, causes us to dig in our heels. We find ourselves slipping back into our old ways.

We suspend the habit of suffering by sharing the inventory of our secrets with another human being. Clearing out the wreckage of the past begins with inventorying it, along with our strengths, and going on from there. We make a fresh start when we clean house.

Step 5

Admitted to God, to ourselves, and to another human being the exact nature of our wrongs.

Living in a maze of obstacles generated by our secrets has been a test of ingenuity as well as a constant drain on our energy. We tell ourselves: "With him and her and him (but *not* him), I can be honest; with her and her and him, I can't; with X and Y, we know the score about each other and can play the game; but with the rest, no way!"

It takes infinite skill to remember who knows what about whom. Now and then, we have made devastating mistakes by sharing something with someone we didn't want him or her to know. Secrets complicate and fragment our lives into a kaleidoscope of suffering and misery, and we pay a high price for keeping them.

Before entering recovery, a few rare moments may surface in which we have the experience of just not giving a damn. We wish the whole labyrinth of lies would collapse. What a tremendous burden to be relieved of! But then, the thought slips away somehow, and we are back again locked in the compartments our secrets had fabricated.

Addiction to Suffering

There is very little chemically dependent individuals can hold on to except their commitment to their secrets. Consider the reason for this: substance dependency is supported by secrets, and secrets are supported by dependence on substances/ behavior. Together, with all the rest of our secrets, what we are doing becomes but another monumental secret to extend the maze. In this confusion, the idea of recovery can slip away from us with a high probability of getting lost entirely.

Gay men, lesbians, and bisexuals often feel caught in a maze created by guilt and shame. They see the world through an ugly oppressive grid. The contempt, anger, and fear that others exhibit toward them is something they never chose. Nor did they choose to become dependent on substances or behavior either! And they certainly did *not* choose to be homosexual, or choose the vast array of secrets to hide their shame, their guilt, and their rage over their powerlessness to change those who harass and persecute them. These secrets forced on them for survival have turned them into prisoners. What they did choose are the individualized survival tactics that now, all too often, become their obstacles.

If you have ever visited anyone in jail, you have experienced, for a brief time, the overwhelming sense of frustration and wasted opportunity that penetrates the lives of inmates every hour of the day and night. Individuals with dependent/compulsive behavior live in a similar mental and emotional environment. Their secrets incarcerate them in such a way that they react like prisoners condemned to cells that grow smaller and smaller as their problems intensify. Soon, they come to depend on their cages in order to survive. Accepting the fact that each of us has chosen the obstacles that will keep us in this cage, many have changed "cages"—

from alcohol to pot, from pot to speed, from speed to heroin, or from drugs to food or sex or gambling—rather than face anything that threatens this existence.

This is the paradox: the secrets we create to protect ourselves become the bars of our prison! Instead of the safety we thought we had found hiding behind our secrets, at this point in our journey, we find they are major obstacles in our path. Pretending they will go away on their own, or that they really do not affect our recovery, is a step backward into denial. Too many of us have found this out the hard way.

Because we have lived as if our lives depended on our secrets, we need to be encouraged to understand that our secrets depend on *us* for their existence. Without us to support them, they vanish. The belief that they are so precious to our survival keeps us stuck in them. Recognizing that we are stuck, however, is a sign of progress. Since childhood, the habit of lying has helped us survive. How difficult it is to speak the truth, for often we don't know it. Often we don't know honestly how we feel! Unless we experience these lies, we do not become willing to do what we must to change this condition.

Looking into the mirror at ourselves, at our lives as we have lived them, is a great deal to ask in early recovery. For those who are terrified of what they may find, it might even be too much. "Haven't I suffered enough? Why do I need to continue beating up on myself in recovery?" We support our commitment to recovery through the willingness to trust the process of implementing the Steps in our lives. If we are patient, it will work. We are worth the time.

In Step Four, we created an inventory that for many has been the source of great anxiety. They spent weeks and even months developing this list, and their inner turmoil reached towering proportions. For the first time, in a very vivid and dramatic way, they recognized themselves looking at the world through all of their problems. They understood how much everything in their lives was colored and influenced by their secrets, their habits of lying, their survival tactics and the ironclad rules they learned to live with in their families and in the world.

Secrets act like substances and compulsive behavior—to dull the senses and to drown wishes that might develop potential for growth and change. When people are lost to their problems, they have neither the time, the energy, nor the inclination to make any efforts to work on themselves. Step Four is a task that vigorously confronts this familiar pattern of behavior while, at the same time, encouraging individuals to see themselves exactly as they are.

After years of hiding and pretending, after years of burying feelings beneath the facade of secrets and lies, we can be amazed to discover that we have survived such an insidious campaign of self-sabotage. What we find hidden in the midst of all the emotional rubble is not the awful-terrible we thought was there. Instead, we find ourselves—sensitive, caring, kind—waiting to be nurtured and healed. What a find!

But what a heavy price we have paid for our deception! Our secrets, our obstacles, have, over the years, completely taken over the entire focus of our feelings. In addiction, we have had little or nothing left over for spontaneity or creativity. Most of us are astounded to discover that our patterns of dishonesty are so ingrained that we barely hesitate lying about things we have no reason to. We lie sooner than we tell the truth because that is what we have learned to do.

Sexual minorities protect themselves under a far heavier mantle of secrets than heterosexuals. Taking Step Four contradicts everything we have learned about survival. It is especially difficult for us to accept that continued survival and progress in recovery depend on taking this Step. Because it was an effort at private self-disclosure, many were willing to begin to work on an inventory; since no one *else* except ourselves was involved, our fears were under control.

Step Four was difficult; but Step Five can loom even larger over us in recovery. It is a frontal assault on the never-never land of telling anyone else who we really are. Revealing our secrets to another human being can arouse the very feelings of inadequacy we have been tormented by in society, along with the fear and mistrust of others with which we often fueled our compulsive behaviors! "How can you ask us to do such a thing?"

Into the Light

Unless we become willing to share our secrets with another person, we will continue to use them in the same manner as in the past. Sooner or later, the moment will come when we will reach for the support of our "fix" to make it bearable to live with them. Making the list of our survival tactics is only the beginning of the process of stepping out from behind the shadows into the light.

We think we can just put the inventory in the drawer and blithely go on from there because we fail to assess the power our secrets have over us. These secrets helped us justify the way we lived in the past. Revealing them to another human being will change our lives in the present and in the future.

In the past, we faced our lives through both the weaknesses and the strengths identified in our inventories. We saw our obstacles as the very survival tactics that became the source of our secrets and deceptions. It is all there: what we have lived through in the past is now vividly revealed in the words we have written. And is nothing changed? Are we not the same as we have always been?

There are important differences, some we can recognize and others we cannot. The most obvious change is that we have stopped using mood-altering substances and/or compulsive behavior. Unless we have done this, we are still deceiving ourselves about the meaning of recovery. Next, the effects of taking Step One, Step Two, Step Three, and Step Four are continuing, day by day, to penetrate our patterns of behavior. It is often the case that while we can observe the changes these

Steps have made in others, we cannot clearly see them in ourselves. Possibly others have shared their observations of the changes they have seen in us, and we have been surprised to learn such good news. Indeed, something is happening within us and a brief spot check will reveal this. For example:

- we have stopped isolating ourselves and begun relating with others;
- we have begun to take care of our bodies with nutritious food, exercise, and rest;
- we have stabilized our sleeping patterns;
- some of us have begun to read again or return to interests or hobbies we'd abandoned;
- some of us have begun to pray or meditate on a regular basis.

Taking a good look at all of the positive things we are doing in our lives provides us with information we need to know. And as small as these changes are, they are significant to acknowledge.

It is not uncommon to hear recovery spoken of as a "gift." For those of us who have been through the hell of addictive/compulsive behavior, beginning recovery has been the most precious gift we've ever received, and to continue in recovery is a source of daily gratitude. Maintaining and extending recovery a day at a time is, perhaps, the dearest wish of all. Hanging on to our secrets will prevent us from experiencing the benefits of these gifts. Living differently for us means living without secrets.

Facing Our Fears

At some stage in early recovery, it is not at all uncommon for us to begin to think that we do not deserve recovery and good health, especially after the kind of lives we have lived. Even after having begun the process, many of us fear it is all a mistake and it will not be long before we wake up to discover we were only dreaming. This temptation to destroy the benefits already received is central to the role of playing the victim. Believing that the other shoe must fall, or waiting for tragedy to strike, some will unknowingly devise the crisis and the tragedy that will bring everything crashing down on their heads.

When we are fearful, we focus on that which will frighten us. When we expect "bad" things to happen, the inevitable "bad" things that occur as a part of life will take on greater significance and we will zero in on them. As long as our self-esteem is in shambles because of what we have done or how we view ourselves, we are like magnets for negative messages about ourselves.

It is not uncommon for individuals with substance dependency problems to habitually indulge in thoughts and actions harmful to themselves and to others. To change these thinking habits, to act in positive ways, we must have room to move into a different place in ourselves—into a healthier space. When we are filled with guilt and shame and rage over the past, there is no alternative except to continue to live with old behavior. Saturated with guilt and shame, we cannot fail to respond guilty and ashamed; seething with rage, we will seek and find ways to act out this anger. Through the effort to clear away the inventory of all the baggage we have collected in the past we can begin to experience the possibility of living in today without such negativity.

We cannot put the past behind us by pretending it does not exist, nor by minimizing it, nor by convincing ourselves we will never live that way again. We must take positive action to deal with our negativity. We must confront it. We must go through the experience of feeling what has gone on before, of living through it not as a recitation of "ancient history" but for the experience of observing what it is like to act and think negatively. Most of us have been in deep denial about our role in what has happened to us. We need to see this and put it into a truer perspective. Unless we understand our role, we have no responsibility for changing our thoughts and actions in the future.

Feeling Our Feelings

We are creatures of feeling. Through our feelings, we come to understand ourselves, and others. We can change our habitual behavior by deciding that we no longer wish to have the feelings arising from these actions. We reach this decision after we are clear that we do not value those actions but, instead, choose to value very different ones.

Our minds, alone, do not change us. Our feelings, our emotions tell us they do not wish to continue in the same pain. While our minds can support our choice once we make it, remember that this mind has been seriously affected by what we have endured. And it may also be influenced, as well, by growing up as a child of parents with substance dependency. We have also damaged our bodies. Fortunately, many of us still have unusual restorative capabilities, and both the mind and the body can spring back in amazing ways. In order to change, instead of being in conflict, the mind and the body must be linked together with the same intention instead of going off in different directions.

It is possible that many of us made the decision in our minds to make a change, to stop using addictive/compulsive behavior. We know what happened with these decisions. Our bodies may have been chemically dependent, and it was not long before our minds and emotions sought the refuge they knew could be found in the behaviors we had promised ourselves to give up.

In therapy groups, in Twelve Step meetings, we found for the first time the help essential to get our bodies and our minds to join forces instead of working against each other. Our self-help efforts have focused on our own responsible action. This action restores our minds, our emotions, and our bodies. Instead of using substances or compulsive behaviors, in recovery we can use our energy to develop equilibrium through the tools of recovery programs.

Through information about these programs, we were challenged to begin to believe that we are capable of recovery. Around us, replacing the physicians in white coats, other survivors reinforced in us the belief that we do not need to depend on something or someone to fix us, or that our health and recovery is *outside* our capability. Recovery programs carry the message of self-renewal and peer support as we find our way through the wreckage of the past.

And all of us have a past. What we do about our past is very significant at this point in our journey. By the time we have come to Step Five, we will honestly wish to turn our lives around and change our negative patterns of thought and action into a positive direction. To do this, we use our lives, as we have come to understand them through the inventory we completed, as the basis for this change. Instead of burying this list in the same way we have always done with our secrets, we need to share it with someone else. The act of sharing the entire inventory with another person is a totally different approach than we have ever taken and, in itself, marks a break with the past.

In admitting to another person what we have done and what we have left undone, we hear our own voice in our ears. Now, the basic idea of taking action—the key to recovery—takes on new meaning. With meaningful action, we suspend our role of victim, of being acted on, of being incapable of handling life. By taking this kind of positive action, we continue to make progress on our journey.

Sharing our secrets with another human being is an affirmation of ourselves *by* ourselves. "Yes, I am the one who did this, and this, and that. I own it; this is the way I have lived my life. *And* I can go on from here." We began our journey in denial—"I'm *not* an alcoholic; I'm *not* dependent on substances or behavior; I'm *not* gay; I'm *not* lesbian; I'm *not* bisexual." We now progress to the place that is new and different for us. When we are willing to take this step, we experience an unfamiliar burst of self-esteem by saying who we *are* instead of who we aren't. For some of us, it may be the first time in life we discover that the earth does not split open and swallow us! Facing the unfaceable takes courage.

The basis of our denial has been self-delusion, and through self-revelation we reverse this process. A step at a time, instead of escaping into fantasy, we have had first to confront ourselves. Next, we need to share this with someone else, a witness, someone outside ourselves. The act takes courage because the honesty we bring to it unlocks the door that we have sealed shut: responsibility for ourselves. By accepting responsibility for our secrets as we share them with another, we step into the present. Because we have revealed ourselves as we are, we no longer have to live imprisoned by our secrets. We can begin to use our energy for positive thinking and action.

Admitting our secrets gets them out into the open and creates some space between ourselves and them. This space is exactly what we need to begin to understand that we have a choice in deciding how we will act or think. In recovery, we always have a choice; dependent on substances, we have lost sight of our choices and think only about our next fix. Yes, that is the way we have lived in the past. That was one of our secrets. And we have learned that others have hidden the same thing from everyone else. Now, in recovery, we do not have to hide, and because of this, addictive/compulsive behavior no longer controls our lives. It is quite difficult to permanently change anything for today unless we understand the way we have been yesterday. Taking Step Five acknowledges to ourselves and to someone else our old patterns of thought and action. If we no longer value the way we have lived in the past, we now have the opportunity to make different choices.

Processing Our Own Material

With the help of others like ourselves, we find encouragement to begin to process our own material. For those who are able to avail themselves of the benefits of group therapy, in the presence of others, it is possible to get some new insights into how we have done things in the past, and new ways in which we can look at our lives with a different perspective. Whether in formal groups or in individual therapy or in contact with a sponsor or friend, we can begin to initiate healthy approaches to living and working. We need to process our material—to identify it, to understand it, to clear it out, to make way for new information. It is particularly difficult to do this because we have become so used to living with the wreckage of the past. We have structured our houses and the furnishings of each day with it, and we count on it for support. When we begin recovery, it is as if we have moved into a new "house" bringing with us all of the old "furniture." This is hard to see with any clarity, except through others. Other people's habits and priorities are much easier to discern and evaluate than our own.

Using Step Five, we take direct action to end the stagnation that frequently sets in after the "pink cloud" of early recovery has vanished and we are once again facing "the same ol' same ol'"—our daily lives. When we share with another person our habits, our priorities, our obstacles, these appear in sharp relief to us, and provide us with a new perspective on living one day at a time.

There is no right way to take this Step. A few suggestions for going about it may be helpful:

1. The person you choose to listen to your inventory should be someone with whom you can be as vulnerable and as safe as possible.

2. With someone you can trust in this way, give yourself permission to honestly review your life.

3. Schedule enough time, several hours at least, in which to go over the inventory. Don't rush through it.

4. Choose a place in which you have a sense of privacy. Some public places, like a park bench or a quiet restaurant, may also provide an excellent setting.

5. Begin with what you have written, and, as you speak, add new things that occur to you. Talk about your thoughts and feelings as you proceed.

6. Feel your feelings: let them be okay with you.

7. Accept whatever comments are offered to you at the time instead of negating them with "Yes, but. . . ."

8. Remember this is not a perfect inventory. (Some people take the Fifth Step annually to review unfinished business from their past that surfaces in ongoing recovery.)

9. Bear in mind nothing is too terrible or impossible to share; your recovery depends on sharing everything you can.

10. Allow yourself to trust in the process, and go on from there.

Many sexual minorities have little or no experience with such a privilege. For some of us, it is the first time in our lives that we have an opportunity like this, and the element of threat is very real. "You'll hate me once you know what I'm really like." "How can I go on living my old ways once you know all about me?" The fear of rejection and the fear of change, losing the little we think we've got, are powerful inhibitions for us. By doing the Fifth Step, we learn that it is safe to tell our secrets, and that we will not be rejected because of them. With this experience behind us, we can move on to share honestly at the group level and to know a broader acceptance.

During our lifetime, prior to entering recovery, many of us have made foolish choices regarding the people in whom we confided. It seems that, with a few exceptions, we have turned to those we could absolutely count on to criticize, punish (in some way), and reject us. We have chosen the ones who were the least able to accept us as we are, and who never failed to rush in to change us, "fix" us, make us some other way. If this is not a pattern for you, then you have been very fortunate and will have no difficulty deciding with whom you will take Step Five. Others will have to consider carefully the people who are available.

In many cases, the obvious choice is your therapist or sponsor. Or you may prefer a different person, an individual who is outside the daily routine of life, or even a complete stranger. Whomever we choose, this individual is one who will support us at this point in our recovery simply by listening.

Many gays, lesbians, and bisexuals avoid getting a sponsor or a counselor because of deeply rooted fears of intimacy. The possibility of rejection is so intense that they avoid using this valuable tool to aid their recovery. Instead, they rely entirely on literature, meetings, and telephone calls to a vast array of friends with whom they can share a piece here and a piece there, but never the whole story in one place. It is important to take Step Five with one other person, and, if the question of intimacy hasn't arisen before this, it will certainly come up now.

There is no way around it; we cannot take this Step alone. That is why the Step is introduced at this place in our journey. Until this time, we could work on any of the first four Steps on our own, and for many of us, working in isolation was a basic part of our pattern. Now, however, we need another person to review our inventory with, and this changes everything. It is a risk that we *must* take and it tests the limits of our recovery to their fullest.

It is not a good idea to rely entirely on our intellect to make this decision about whom to ask. In recovery, we are able to tune in to our intuition more and more as time goes on. Until now, no one was home to listen; in recovery, we can become available to the good counsel that we have stored away and may now be able to give ourselves. We can begin to listen to and develop trust in our own counsel the longer we are abstinent. This is one of the most heartening rewards of our new way of living in recovery.

With help from our intuition, we can make the decision regarding the sharing of our inventory. It may, indeed, be someone outside of a Twelve Step program. Whether it is with a therapist, a sponsor, a stranger, or a member of the clergy, the point is that we actually choose to reveal ourselves to another—and to God/H.P.—instead of burying our past.

If we are ready to be supported in other issues, like intimacy, fear of rejection, fear of the consequences, then we will choose someone to listen who can support us in our efforts to face the inventory of our obstacles.

Taking this Step with an appropriate person neutralizes our own negativity. No matter what we thought of our actions, in revealing them a certain kind of dilution occurs. Perhaps our listener shares something from his or her past that is similar to something in our own inventories, or else acknowledges our courage for being willing to make such a revelation. In place of the void that always seemed waiting, there is a connection with the world that we hadn't experienced before. Nothing is too bad or too terrible to be told to another human being, but we never would have believed this until we actually did it ourselves!

The catharsis that is possible is of vital importance to recovery. Our secrets have functioned exclusively in the void of our imagination without any larger frame of reference. In revealing our secrets to another, we set up a scale against which we can balance the worst that we believed with the entire gamut of human actions.

We experience the movement of life through *all* actions, and instead of being "the worst culprits in the world" (i.e., "the center of the universe"), we discover who we really are. We lose our uniqueness in the discovery that we are more *like* others than we are different from them.

Instead of living as if we were separate and special and without any share in the chain of humanity, gays, lesbians, and bisexuals in recovery can come to understand, through taking this Step, that we are human, just like everyone else. We can choose to use our energy in a positive way just as we made the choice to use it negatively in the past. This is the decision we must make now. In this Step in which we reveal to another what our lives have been, we clear space in which we can begin to think and act positively. In a swirling storm of negativity, it is not possible to find our way through the maze of secrets and dishonesty. If we will allow Step Five to set our foot on cleared and solid ground, we will find our way out of the labyrinth.

❋   ❋   ❋

In working through the material presented in Step Four, you assessed how ready you were to write an inventory of strengths and areas for improvement. Whether or not you have written the Fourth Step inventory, working through the material in this chapter will support your efforts to progress in your recovery. Use it to overcome obstacles standing in your path.

Step Four, like the previous three Steps, required only yourself for completion. When you come to Step Five, you are faced with the prospect of involving someone besides yourself in your efforts. For this reason, it is likely that some issues will arise that may not have surfaced before this time. It will be important to examine them and learn as much as you can about yourself in the process. Before addressing these issues, consider Step Five as the natural sequel to Step Four, and check that the necessary foundation has been prepared.

1. If you believe you are *still not yet ready* to develop the inventory for Step Four, what are the reasons for this?

    _____

    _____

    _____

2. If you are ready, and have developed the inventory, how do you feel now that you've written it?

    _____

    _____

    _____

3. Are there areas of your life you plan to reconsider at a later date? If so, what are they?

    _____

    _____

    _____

4. What are our reasons for looking at them later, instead of now?

    _____

    _____

    _____

5. Have these reasons been discussed with your sponsor/therapist?

    ☐ Yes   ☐ No

The experience of doing something is often very different from the way you pictured or anticipated it. Putting together, side by side, what you imagined and what actually happened when you began writing an inventory of your life will be helpful for the future. (For anyone who has not yet done the inventory, consider only the list on the left.)

6. **What I Expect(ed)**	**What Actually Happened**

7. In comparing the two lists, did you observe anything that will help you in the future?

_____

_____

_____

8. As you worked through the inventory and confronted some of your fears, which of your strengths were you able to rely on?

_____

_____

_____

9. Check your inventory to make certain these strengths appear in it.

10. At the same time you are doing that, review the inventory and allow whatever appears there to stand on its own. Separate the act from the actor. Use this space to write whatever surfaces for you.

_____

_____

_____

_____

_____

_____

_____

_____

At the heart of both Step Four and Step Five is the need for honesty. Honesty is, in fact, the cornerstone of recovery. You were able to become aware of this when considering the masks you wear and the secrets you keep. For many of us, because of the devastating experiences we have been through in our lives, being honest takes practice. The following exercise may help you to begin the effort.

11. For five to ten minutes at a time, instead of speaking quickly, or thinking only about what it is you want to say to another person, *listen and hear every word that comes out of your mouth.* Practice this exercise several times a day for a few days; then write what happens for you when you do it.

12. What are some things you can do to work on these outcomes?

_____

_____

_____

13. Whom can you ask to support your efforts and what can this person do to assist you?

_____

_____

_____

14. What do you fear most about being honest with another person?

_____

_____

_____

15. In the past, with whom have you shared your secrets, and what were the circumstances that prompted you to do this?

_____

_____

_____

16. What were the results of these previous disclosures?

_____

_____

_____

17. When others have shared fears and secrets with you, how have you felt about them?

_____

_____

_____

18. Have you used what others have shared with you to harm them?

☐ Yes   ☐ No

How do you feel about this?

_____

_____

_____

19. What other experiences have led you to mistrust others? Write those that currently influence your willingness to take this Step.

_____

_____

_____

20. If someone has taken advantage of your trust, have an imaginary conversation with that person. Give yourself permission to say everything you have held back. Allow yourself your feelings, and then write them below. *(Insert a sheet of paper here if you need more space.)*

_____

_____

_____

21. If relationships with other people have caused you disappointment, distress, or pain, how have you handled these feelings?

_____

_____

_____

Instead of burying the pain, or pretending that whatever has happened is okay, consider Step Five as implementing positive action to change the way you treat yourself and others. Taking Step Five breaks all of the old rules. It means you are going to find someone you are willing to reveal yourself to (to the extent you have been able to be honest with yourself). Whatever you have seen reflected in the mirror of the Fourth Step inventory, you are going to share this revelation with another human being—not as a punishment, but as an *affirmation* of your own efforts to progress in your recovery.

22. List the people you could share the inventory with and the reasons for choosing him or her.

_____

_____

_____

23. It may be a good idea to choose your therapist or sponsor for Step Five, with whom you have already discussed Step Four and the outline you developed for your inventory. If, for some reason, you do not choose the same person for Step Five as for Step Four, choose one of the other people on your list. Arrange to meet with him or her, and explain that you'd like to go over the Fourth Step inventory. Be certain that the person is available to do this with you. Because you have chosen this individual does not mean he or she is obliged to do a Fifth Step with you. Take this excellent opportunity to practice honesty, and be prepared to ask someone else in case the person recommends it. Identify the other people with whom you would consider sharing your inventory.

_____

_____

_____

24. Because there is no right way to take this Step, list your concerns about sharing your inventory.

_____

_____

_____

25. Take the Fifth Step and at the conclusion of the conversation(s) about your inventory, consider how you plan to reward yourself for completing this difficult task.

_____

_____

_____

26. Make a journal entry of your Fifth Step experience and how you feel, now that you've done it.

27. Reward yourself for a difficult task done with commitment and courage. Find a healthy and renewing activity to reward yourself with after you've completed your Fifth Step. Find something special that works for you as a way to celebrate your achievement *(e.g., take a bubble bath, listen to your favorite music).* Now celebrate your accomplishment with the reward that you have planned.

CHAPTER 16

That's How I Am!

CONDITION
Inflexibility

When it comes to people pleasing, individuals suffering from addictive/compulsive behavior are expert doormats; and they are as rigid as a brick regarding old rules, attempting new approaches to living, or relinquishing the role of victim. Security depends on hanging on to inflexibility. They never have permission to make mistakes. It is weakness to flinch from this position, and only the strong survive. Life is a struggle that grows more and more unmanageable.

ALTERNATIVE
Flexibility

Manipulation, that fine art in which many of us are skilled, does not make us winners in recovery. Changing staterooms on the last voyage of the Titanic did not get any passenger off the ship that was already under way. We implement real change by putting into practice what we have assimilated through the first five Steps. By giving ourselves permission *not* to have the answers and to make as many mistakes as we need to, we begin to live on life's terms.

Step 6

Were entirely ready to have God remove all these defects of character.

Continuing this journey into recovery, we discover we no longer see ourselves solely from the perspective of substance-dependent gays, lesbians, and bisexuals living lost lives. We are beginning to take a different look at the society in whose midst we have experienced our closeted or uncloseted lives. The efforts we have made, so far, have provided us with new understanding of ourselves. Life in the wilderness of early recovery has helped us to appreciate that it is one thing to *live* in the desert and another to *be*, inside ourselves, a desert.

We lose all perspective in the desert. Every grain of sand blazes and the fire of the sun is everywhere. Those courageous ones who decide to examine themselves in this desert have discovered things about themselves and others they never considered possible. The most incredible discovery of all, perhaps, is that even in this blazing furnace, love *of* and *for* others and *oneself* can exist, and that no degree of torment or persecution can destroy this love.

As we worked first to identify, and then to begin to accept our lives and how we have lived them in the past, we learned a great deal about the individual we are *not*. In this process, we observed many things we were critical about in ourselves and others. While none of this changes anything about the past, we established a conscious link *with* the past. This link is very important if we wish to work on changing ourselves in the present. By identifying what we need to work at, we can develop abilities to handle these areas. When we discover we do not have the necessary skills or knowledge, we can find others who do and then make efforts to learn about these areas.

Understanding Our Obstacles

Unfortunately, the opposite can also happen. We may discover things about ourselves that we believed we knew or understood but, in fact, did not. Our refusal to accept these can provide us with insight about additional obstacles in our path. But remember, we do not learn what we do not accept as important for us. That is why writing down the inventory of our obstacles, our "secrets," was so important. It documented what we presently know and understand about ourselves. From this inventory, we understand the basis for our rigidity, our inflexibility. This list is exactly what we were referring to when we said in the past to others, "This is how I am. Take it or leave it!" Let's take a closer look now at some of the obstacles that shape us the way we are.

We conceive of obstacles from our own limited, personal focus, our private habits of thinking. What may seem significant to us, because of our unique perspective as gays, lesbians, and bisexuals, can frequently be insignificant to others, and *vice versa*. Understanding obstacles in all of their dimensions is the key to using them to help us instead of to thwart us. Instead of seeing them as walling us off from the future, preventing our growth and happiness, it is important that we begin to see them as opportunities waiting for us, like fields, to till and plant for the harvest of tomorrow. When we approach them with this attitude, we also change the perspective in which they appear.

Consider the example of waves crashing on a beach. Instead of conceiving of them as attacking and overrunning the land, think of them as a wall of force that holds the ocean back from the land. At times, a greater force breaks through the wall from the ocean depths, and, when this happens, there is a flood. But seen from the perspective of a wall, the waves that ring the shoreline *contain* the ocean. Our obstacles contain us for as long as we exert no effort to pass beyond them.

What we now see as our obstacles are the result of our present level of understanding about ourselves. We have created the walls through which we must pass by our own concepts of limitation or capability. Instead of seeing them as permanent and absolute, "for ever and ever," we can begin to allow ourselves to consider them as "qualities," like colors that in a different light may appear to be entirely different hues. Obstacles—and opportunities—are the products of our understanding. We have been given the opportunities we now have in early recovery to assist our understanding to go beyond itself—to pass beyond our obstacles.

There are no obstacles too difficult for us to overcome. When we become willing to assess the effort and energy it requires to work on them, we reach a different understanding of the nature of these obstacles. Before recovery, we endured and suffered with them rather than launch any kind of action to change them. When we do begin to act, however, many of us are shocked to discover that it is not the first time we have encountered these same obstacles. They have always stood in the way of a deeper level of self-understanding. When an obstacle is put behind us, that level on which we stood is also, miraculously, behind us. We learn this only after we have attained the new perspective.

As a result of addictive/compulsive behavior, we were held hostage by our obstacles. Our progress so far on the journey in recovery has made us keenly aware of this condition. Until this time, we have accepted our predicament as gays, lesbians, and bisexuals who have been killing ourselves in a dungeon of our own construction. Many of us now come face to face with a desperate dilemma: in all of our pain and our suffering, can we remove our shackles now that we have the choice?

Prison is a predictable place for those who have become accustomed to it. Freedom can be terrifying unless we are prepared to face life with new and healthy patterns of behavior that support recovery. With the realization that we need to learn these new ways, we begin to understand that this opportunity is present for us when we begin work on Step Six.

Our Old Rules

For sexual minorities, it is quite easy to experience life as happening to us without a sense of urgency to alter the course of our lives. This makes it an easy step to see ourselves as victims. Before this time, as we have already observed, this attitude of victimhood was merely intensified and made more indelible. In order to understand change in recovery from a totally different perspective, we need to work at changing our idea of ourselves as victims. This basic attitude is at the very center of the way we have conceived of—and lived—our lives.

From the time we were children, we developed life skills crucial for our survival. We began developing these skills when we first discovered we responded in different ways from others. We may have noticed that other children were not attracted by the things that attracted us, or perhaps we experienced roles that did not seem to fit us. Or it is even possible that some of us were aware of feelings of interest in or attraction for someone of the same sex. No matter what the cause, we felt there was something different, something unique about us that needed to be protected from others.

The next step in the process of victimization was the development of rules that made it possible to hide our feelings. We never did this, or that, in front of others, because it would give us away. We always pretended that we liked to do X when the truth was that we really wanted to do Y. We hid our feelings and tried never to expose them to ridicule or punishment. We learned not to share who we really were, or what we really felt, with others.

These rules helped us to survive as children and as adolescents in our homes, and as adults in the larger (and homophobic) world. Even when we ventured out of the closet, our basic rules still worked the rest of the time. By sticking with our rules, we continued to set ourselves up to suffer as victims for the rest of our lives—even in recovery! The process of healing involves the willingness to revise these rules that no longer work, even though we do not know the consequences of such radical action on our lives. In addition to the external sources of oppression and victimization that a homophobic culture engenders, our rules have helped to make us victims. Change requires that we become willing to change these rules.

Rigidity—"This is how I do this"; "This is the way it is done"—is actually a behavior pattern that supports stagnation. Instead of attempting to suppress these realizations, we need to examine them. The distress that these rules bring is further indication that things are out of balance. For example, disturbing physical symptoms are often the signs that motivate us to get help for physical ailments. Psychological distress is a similar sign that intervention is needed.

In recovery, it makes an enormous difference how we look at and evaluate our survival tactics, which, in the terminology of Step Six, are our "defects of character." Recognizing these symptoms as ripe for study instead of being afraid of them is of the greatest help in healing ourselves. Every entry we have made in our inventory marks the way forward on our journey. This, unfortunately, is NOT how most people read their list.

We have survived because of our rules, and we have suffered from them as well. Our rules supported and sustained our survival tactics, and our survival tactics carried out the instructions from the rules. Support for living any differently has never been part of our experience. Now we stand looking back at years of wreckage strewn with the heavy burden of the rules and survival tactics we have collected along the way. We see that none of it will fit through the new doorway of recovery. At the same time that we may feel angry that we've carried this baggage around for so long, we are fearful of what will happen when we leave it behind. Anger, fear, and hurt; the story of our lives! A sense of sadness overwhelms us when we see the time and energy we have wasted only to come to this moment in which we understand that our lives can't work in the old way. This can be truly painful—if we will allow ourselves to feel it!

Let us openly acknowledge how disloyal we have been to ourselves all these years, how we have denied our feelings. Somehow, the terrible emptiness inside coalesces when we do this, and some little murmur of support for ourselves living honestly filters up. We are children learning to become adults. Our illusions have backed a step away from us and we have a little space in which we can see them for what they are. We need to go on from here either with them—or without them. We may honestly have no idea what it would mean to be loyal to ourselves, and that is okay. We can learn.

A man in Chicago spoke about this place we reach in ourselves. "Yo' mamma ain't comin'!" is the refrain he used over and over again as he told his story. As you think about Step Six, allow it to reverberate inside. "No one but me can do anything about *my* obstacles; no one but me can change *my* rules. I'm the only one who can become willing to be different. But this won't happen unless I am willing to assert my right to a healthy, happy life as a valuable member—a valuable gay, lesbian, bisexual member—of society! My mamma ain't comin', but I don't need her to rescue me anymore or give me permission! I can do it myself, together with you. We can help each other."

Heterosexuals in recovery are intrinsically assumed, to some degree, to be acceptable members of society. Gays, lesbians, and bisexuals have the difficult task of asserting for themselves their own acceptability as full members of the general community without knowing what this feeling of membership is like. Becoming ready to work on eradicating "defects of character" entails insisting that these limitations are not related to sexual orientation, but the kind of shortcomings of *every* human being who has become dependent on substances or behavior. The obstacles of nongay addicted individuals are neither greater nor smaller than ours. Healing ourselves means believing this. Healing ourselves means becoming flexible about changing our rules for survival.

Valuing Recovery

Before beginning recovery, when all we were capable of truly valuing was drugs, or alcohol, or compulsive sex, or compulsive eating, etc., we filled our lives with these. When we begin to value our abstinence, we begin to choose support for the freedom from the conditions that wrecked our lives.

It is important to ask ourselves, what have we come to value in the wilderness of early recovery through which we have journeyed? Considering the question carefully, we may discover that we have mistakenly compared our experience of today with our lives before we began in recovery. Our minds have set up the comparisons, and we have experienced recovery in the reflection of these images from the past. Even in the wilderness, the values from our dead-ended lives have been our baggage. Didn't we begin recovery in order to end the despair, the isolation, the bondage of compulsive behavior? If we truly wish for a new beginning, we must work on ending the comparisons with what has been, even though we have no idea what life will be like when we do this. We must now be willing to change even though we do not completely understand what this means.

In the wilderness, we live in the desert of our dreams, the tangle of cross-purposes, the paradox of life as we thought it would be in comparison with life as it actually is. We are in a crucible in which forces that appear to be beyond our control pummel us from all sides. In it, we seek a place to begin laying the foundation for our future. In the past, we may have believed we knew where we were going, and how we were going to get there, even if we never admitted it to ourselves. In the wilderness, we face the truth that in order to change, we do not know where we are going or how to find the way. This is the opposite extreme from knowing the answers.

Our Survival

Allowing ourselves to examine our former goals and our approaches to them without any delusions, we understand that we must have help if we are to find our path to a new way of living. This is an opportunity for us to observe, once again, our ability to effect change with appropriate assistance. At the same time we see this, we understand much more clearly than before that accessing our power means that we will have to make ourselves available to assistance from sources deep within, as well as beyond ourselves. Only after we have come to believe that such help, such support, exists are we able to allow ourselves to receive it.

As children, we were powerless in the midst of parents and grown-ups who exerted their influence on us. Many of us have tasted the bitterness that comes from expecting more from these power sources than they were able, or had adequate intellectual or emotional resources, to provide. Nevertheless, we survived. But now none of us are powerless children at the mercy of parents or caregivers. We are adults who can become empowered to make great changes; we can choose to seek out people with the resources to be of assistance to us.

In the wilderness, we experience the failure, the bankruptcy of our own power as we have used it in the past, and come to the realization that others can help us find a new way to proceed. Whether or not we wish to identify this power as God, "good orderly direction," H.P., our therapy group, or our therapist, it has been possible to recognize that this new self we discover within us *can* allow others to help. Even the most unbelieving of us has lived through some experiences in childhood where we needed outside help and received it. And this experience of living through it now as adults is invaluable to the gay, the lesbian, the bisexual in recovery. We have already encountered others we know who have helped us and who can be of further help if we let them.

Whatever isolation and despair we have felt, now and in the past, have been linked with the isolation and despair that these others have shared with us. Because they have been able to survive, we have connected with the hope that we, too, can survive. Even now, they support us in the belief that we can continue to survive. For some of us, it may be possible to observe in them a Higher Power working in their lives. Identifying with them, we can admit the possibility of change entering their lives, and with this admission, ours as well. If others have been able to make themselves available to help after all that has happened to them, then it is possible we may be able to do the same.

We certainly have every reason to be afraid. We have lived without expectation of help for so long that we do not know how to act now or what its effect on us will be. That is why this period is so valuable! In it, we begin to learn the basics; we learn that we are beginners again, and that it is okay to be as children: teachable. In adulthood, it is all too easy to deceive ourselves either that we have the answers already or that we *should* have the answers. We are in denial about *not* having the answers. In early recovery, we are no longer able to deceive ourselves about this.

It is terribly important to remember not to be in a hurry to leave this vulnerable state. When we leave it without adequate preparation, the old habits quickly return. If we are concerned with change, real change, we need to know that the greatest changes of all are made *in* the wilderness. The question, then, is how much do we wish to change? Here, in this place, we can confront this question in our most teachable mode.

Being alone here is only an illusion. This has become clearer and clearer as we journey on. Our past isolation was the result of the way in which we used our energy, the things that we chose to value, and the secrets we hid from others and ourselves. Acknowledging that we need help to change these, and witnessing these changes in other people's lives, we have begun to understand that this help is available. We have come to accept this even as we observe it, and the infusion of it in our lives provides us with convincing evidence that we are not alone.

Even more help has come to us in our observation of it flowing to others: we are like them; they are like us. Our self-esteem takes an enthusiastic leap upward when we discover, to our amazement, that we can be the source of help to others who are just beginning the journey. After the ordeals we have been through, that we are now capable of helping others seems miraculous.

Many people in early recovery throw themselves wholeheartedly into helping other newcomers, and they are quite surprised to discover themselves caught up in old patterns of thinking and acting. Giving other people advice, or "taking their inventory" as it is called (making judgments about others), is much easier than working on changing oneself! Having taken Steps Four and Five, we have provided ourselves with exactly what we need in order to change ourselves: *our own inventories.* Instead of directing our efforts toward other people's failings—indulging in the critical habits from our past—we need to focus on our own.

As experts on ourselves, we need to use our inventories as advice to ourselves on what we need to do in order to change. Reviewing our inventories with another person, as we have done, has brought our secrets out of the darkness of denial and into a new light; now we have the opportunity to begin working on the substance of our own material in a new space. We understand, at last, that this is no longer someone else's blueprint for recovery but our own. This is our own prescription for change.

Is there another word more threatening than "change"? Even for those of us who believe we truly want it, the idea of change is limited by what we already know and rarely, if ever, completely open-ended. When we think about what our lives could be like, we use as a frame of reference our lives *before* we became substance abusers. For some, this "before" period goes back as far as childhood or adolescence; nevertheless, as unrealistic as it may seem, these memories are often the only basis we have for the comparison.

Most of us realize that, as adults, we cannot live as we did in childhood or adolescence. But because we do not yet know other alternatives, we may struggle with grave uncertainties and an inexplicable sense of misgiving about the future. These disturbing feelings frequently remind us of living with addictive/compulsive behavior, and many people find themselves questioning the value of being clean and sober when tormented by these fears.

Unless encouraged to do otherwise, we will continue to respond with old patterns of behavior. The pull of old associations with people, places, and things from the past will exert powerful influence on us in our new surroundings. Having gone for years without the support of families, professional associations, and the acceptance of society in general, many bisexuals, gays, and lesbians in recovery often suffer deeply from the loss of those friends and lovers who are still acting out compulsive behaviors. This can help foster the feeling that, even in recovery, we continue to be victims. This time, we are victims of change. For us, change has always meant we have nowhere to go and no one to go with. This is how it may feel to some, even though the opposite is true.

Living in recovery is not easy. We have learned, as far as we have come, that the only way to do it is through action. It is not possible to stand still: we move either toward or away from the fix on which we became dependent. The kernel of all Twelve Step programs is action. The action we are willing to take to let go of old patterns of addictive behavior supports our recovery efforts.

The Two-Way Street

Our efforts so far have helped us to understand that we are surrounded with help on all sides if we stand in the right place. Nothing has occurred to alter this understanding, not even taking Step Five, the sharing of our inventories with another person. Most of us, after taking this Step, have experienced a taste of freedom previously unknown to us. We have shared this with others. We have also been willing to lend our support to newcomers. Whether we have gone to gay or nongay Twelve Step meetings, or counseling groups, a deeper understanding of our value as recovering individuals has dawned on us.

Each step we have taken has increased the value of others for us and, by the same mathematics, of ourselves to them. As we have become more and more willing to change, we have become more and more valuable in supporting others in their efforts to change. Recovery, unlike the dead end of addiction, has become a two-way thoroughfare on which we all may journey together.

In Twelve Step programs, one of the experiences people often speak about is the incredible feeling of love and gratitude they experience when they first walk into the rooms. "It is so real; you can almost reach out and touch it!" someone once said. When we begin to participate in this, we begin the process of change that makes us available to working all of the Steps in our lives. Not one of us has done it alone; help has come to us all along the way. It would be a mistake for us now to forget that. Just as we have received this support for the first five steps of the journey, it is there for us, as well, for Step Six. We no longer have to do anything by ourselves—in isolation. That is one of the promises of the programs. Therefore, becoming "entirely ready" is a task we can work on with the support of a counselor, a sponsor, our friends in and out of the programs, the literature we read, and our prayers and meditations. When we are willing to honestly say who we are and what we need, and when we are available to receive it, we are no longer victims either of compulsive behaviors or of the society in which we live.

❋   ❋   ❋

❄ ❄ ❄

It is much easier to see the changes that occur in others than in ourselves. One of the best ways of identifying change within ourselves is through keeping an account of our feelings and reactions to what goes on around us, day by day. Keeping a daily journal helps us stay in touch with the places we've been in our journey.

❄ ❄ ❄

A Creative Visualization Exercise

Creative visualization is an opportunity to explore your imagination and, at the same time, to get in touch with some feelings and thoughts. Begin by choosing a comfortable chair with lots of support for your back. Now, sit with both feet on the floor, and rest your hands comfortably, palms down, on your legs. Then, close your eyes and take several deep breaths. Allow your body to feel the change when your breath is inhaled, and then feel what happens when it is released. Observe how your internal weight and density shift and then come together several times as you breathe in and out. Feel your body in all of its parts: your right arm, right leg, left leg, left arm, torso, neck, and head.

After you have gone around this circle a few times, with your eyes closed, in your mind's eye look off in the distance and observe someone journeying on a road, far away against the horizon. The figure is moving very slowly. On the traveler's back is a very large and heavy sack. It's a very heavy load, and it takes the traveler an enormous amount of effort to make any progress under the weight of it. Let yourself feel the burden; feel how exhausting it is even to watch the traveler. Let yourself feel the weariness.

Slowly, very slowly, allow the traveler to approach. There is something vaguely familiar about the traveler. Allow yourself to see specific details of the traveler's body, and now observe the strain on the face before you. Imagine what the sack is filled with. As the traveler comes closer to you, observe the words "Old Baggage" written on the sack. Suddenly, as if by magic, your eyes can see right through the material of the sack. You discover heaps and jumbles of things—like boxes of disappointment, parcels of jealousy, and stacks of dishonesty. The containers resemble the work you inventoried in Step Four and shared with another person in Step Five.

All the containers are labeled; read the labels but allow the contents of the boxes to remain under the lids. After you've completed your survey, look now at the face of the traveler and recognize yourself. After you are sure you are the traveler, walk for a few minutes along the road with the pack on your own back. Feel the burden of it. Let yourself stagger under the weight. What does this weight do to you? How do you see the world with this sack on your back? How does it affect your life? Then stop for a moment. Slide the pack off your back and allow it to sit on the ground beside you.

Ask yourself: what is in this sack that I truly need for my happiness? Answer the question. *Then ask:* what's in this sack that I can live without? Answer the question. *Then ask:* if given the opportunity to continue my journey without these things, would I choose them? After answering the question, take a few steps away from the sack. Observe how this feels. Walk about ten steps away from the sack, and observe how this feels. Then take another ten steps even farther from it.

Now, consider whether you can leave the sack exactly where it is, or if you need to go back to collect a few things to take with you on your journey. Decide this. If you can, use this opportunity to leave the sack, the whole sack, where it is. If not, go back and take only what you think you cannot do without. Put these inside the small sack you have folded up inside your pocket.

You are now ready to walk down this road into your own life. Feel the difference in the burden you no longer carry. Allow yourself to feel the joy of it; allow yourself to run, or skip—whatever way you wish to move along the journey. Feel your breath as it enters your body now and then leaves it: how much lighter you feel! How much more alive your heart and lungs and organs feel. How much easier it is to walk on your legs and swing your arms in the present, and move into the future without all that baggage! Feel the breeze in your hair and around your ears. As you go, put your arms around you and embrace yourself for the work you have done. Take a few more deep breaths and experience lightness and freedom in every part of you.

And now, we are going to take five steps forward from this place where we have been in our imagination and return to where we are sitting at this moment: one step, two steps, three steps . . . we're almost here . . . four steps, five steps. We're back again. Gradually open your eyes, and bring as much of that feeling of lightness and freedom with you into this moment.

1. What surfaced for you as you visualized this experience?

_____

_____

_____

(Suggestion: Over the next few weeks, do the visualization several times and record what happens for you when you follow it through. Record your experiences in your journal.)

2. Have you experienced any resistance to leaving behind the sack filled with old baggage? What might be the source of this resistance?

_____

_____

_____

_____

_____

3. When you encountered this kind of resistance in the past, what were the circumstances?

_____

_____

_____

4. What connection can you make between this feeling and the idea of *change* in your life? Describe it.

_____

_____

_____

5. What has been your experience in handling this resistance?

_____

_____

_____

6. What happened in the past when you worked to change something about the way you live?

_____

_____

_____

7. Are there particular aspects, or items, of your inventory that you feel stuck with or stuck in? Identify them in the first column below.

Obstacle:	My Feelings:	Time Stuck:
_____	_____	_____
_____	_____	_____
_____	_____	_____
_____	_____	_____
_____	_____	_____
_____	_____	_____
_____	_____	_____
_____	_____	_____

8. After each entry, describe in the second column above what each one feels like to experience as an obstacle in your path.

9. Focus on each obstacle, and estimate the length of time you have found yourself stuck behind it. *(Write this in the third column above.)*

10. Consider how much longer you are willing to allow each one to stand in your way. Allow yourself to be as flexible as possible. *(Write about this here.)*

_____

_____

_____

_____

_____

_____

11. When you think of the word "rigidity," what comes to your mind? What does it look like when you draw it?

12. What about the way you live your life is connected with being rigid?

_____

_____

_____

13. What, if any, childhood memories do you have in which you observe your own rigid thinking? Give yourself a few days to write in your journal about these memories. Write as many as you can remember.

_____

_____

_____

_____

_____

14. What "survival tactics" have you used

(1) to deal with other people?

_____

_____

(2) to deal with disappointment?

_____

_____

(3) to handle money issues?

_____

_____

(4) to make life a little easier on yourself instead of facing your problems?

_____

_____

15. Which of your old rules maintain these "survival tactics"?

_____

_____

_____

16. How rigid would you estimate you are about hanging on to these old rules?

| Very Rigid | Rigid | Flexible | Very Flexible |

17. Which of your developing values, attitudes, or priorites are being denied, or neglected, because of your rigidity? Discuss.

_____

_____

_____

18. If you value something, yet are unable to have this in your life, consider reasons for this.

_____

_____

_____

19. To have these things in your life, identify for yourself

(1) the efforts you can make

_____

_____

(2) the support you need from others

_____

_____

(3) how your Higher Power can assist you

_____

_____

20. List all the things you need to do to get ready for an important event in your life.

_____

_____

_____

_____

_____

21. Review your list to discover the similarity/difference between the preparation on this list and the preparation you need to make in order to take Step Six: were entirely ready to have these shortcomings removed.

_____

_____

_____

_____

_____

22. How will you know when you are ready? What will be the signs of readiness?

_____

_____

_____

_____

_____

23. What will be your timetable?

_____

_____

_____

24. _Take the Step!_

CHAPTER 17

The Paradox of Arrogance

CONDITION

Arrogance

Having all the answers is a way of life. This attitude is one of the few ways we know to protect ourselves. Arrogance, grandiosity, unapproachability all encourage isolation and self-doubt. Hiding behind our audacity lurks the constant fear of being found out and losing everything.

ALTERNATIVE

Humility

Instead of self-centeredness—"self-caringness." We begin to observe the effects of this shift in other people's lives and gradually experience this in our own.

Real humility is quite different from false humility. We can choose now to take pride in being a member of the human race and gay and bisexual. We are available to accept the invitation to live a new life, and experience the power of being part of the fellowship in recovery that exceeds any single individual. We learn that we can call on this power for help in removing the very obstacles that sustained arrogance.

Step 7

Humbly asked [God] to remove our shortcomings.

We did not become dependent on substances or behavior in a day; everything in our lives has taken place over time. It takes time to change the way we think and act, and this is true in recovery as well. The first six Steps have prepared the way, as well as being themselves the path of change. We have encountered many distractions and tangents so far, and we can be certain that there will be many more ahead. Expecting them is helpful because our progress depends on our willingness to face these difficulties and setbacks in recovery.

Change Agents

Finding other lesbians, bisexuals, and gays to make the journey with us has been very supportive. The discovery of ourselves as important to others in their progress introduced a major change in our understanding of how to begin to relate with adults in recovery. Many of us hadn't a clue as to how to act with anyone unless we had substances or compulsive behavior to depend on. No matter what our chronological age, in recovery we often feel like children or, at best, adolescents in social settings. Through the efforts we have been making to implement the first six Steps in our lives, we have begun to develop some of the interpersonal skills we lacked or struggled with in the past. As awkward as we have felt, we learned that others sense this same awkwardness in themselves, and the mutual support we experienced did great things for our self-esteem.

At some point further down the road, when we look back at this period, we will be able to better understand what we have come through. Now, it may appear only strange and confusing. Later on, we may appreciate the courage it took to confront such a wilderness. By then, we will have discarded more of our "disguises" and we will be wearing our own faces and our own clothes. When we are dressed in our own clothes, we appear as we truly are. This is of great help in the evolution of our recovery. Now, we are passing from who-we-have-been-in-the-past into who-we-will-be-in-the-future. It takes time to discover what fits and what doesn't, and it also takes time to stop feeling awkward and uncomfortable.

This happens slowly. Small revelations sometimes appear when we least expect them, and these will grow in significance as a new perspective develops. These experiences bear comparison with sitting in a planetarium with life projected on the ceiling. From time to time, as if with a touch of a button, moments from the past or the present suddenly move millions of light-years closer. Our journeys have been a process of looking at ourselves, but what we have observed is still so far off that we cannot appreciate all that is there. Day by day, we have been moving out into an adventure with ourselves that knows no limit. It can be astonishing to experience and share with others the excitement we feel about no longer living lost in our secrets.

Such a change! Being excited about life instead of about our next fix! We even look different, if we will believe what others have told us. Some of us are startled and amazed at the extent our physical condition has improved. What we eat and drink actually tastes different now, and our bodies even move differently when we stand or walk. Tremors, if we suffered from them, have diminished. Our work appears to go forward in all areas. Our bodies, along with our emotions and our minds, are being transformed.

When we change how we live and what we do with our energy, we modify our own structure. If we act no differently today from the way we acted yesterday, there is no basis for change. But through our efforts at working on recovery, if we perform in new ways and think new thoughts, we become the catalysts of change. The modifications that set in make it more possible to continue in these and even newer ways. The basic economy in nature regulates this process. We are changed by what we do, and others see these changes in us.

It is a grave temptation to stop here, to settle for this as the limit to recovery. "If it works, don't fix it" is a comment often used to justify this decision. If so, this is a choice straight out of our old habit of denial, and we need to be honest about this. We are accustomed to settling for the least most of our lives. Early recovery is a long way up from the bottom—so why not get off here? Many of those who have done this have discovered how fragile and vulnerable they are, and the power the old patterns of behavior still have on them. Unless we continually use our energy and attention to work on recovery, we slip back again before we even realize it.

Only if we are willing to face the truth about our fear of change do we get back on track. Without any answers for ourselves or for others, without any pretense about our ability to manage our own lives entirely on our own, without any drugs or alcohol or other substances or compulsive habits to escape into, we can take a look at ourselves and experience, perhaps for the first time, what it means to be humble.

Humility was rarely a trait others associated with us. Besides being intensely egocentric, most of us were frequently grandiose and very demanding—especially when it came to the way we felt others should behave toward us. Even when we hit bottom, we had vivid moments of righteous indignation about how miserably we were treated.

For most of us, humility has meant "humiliation" and "degradation," and we have had more than our share of this. Whether we had a low bottom or a high bottom, the experience of humiliation usually shocked us into doing something about our condition. Pride, if nothing else, was the lifeline that propelled many of us into seeking help. Many people in recovery have shared the same reaction: "I couldn't stand myself any longer." "I got sick and tired of being sick and tired." "When I found myself doing something I swore never to do, I knew I needed help!" "I might as well be dead—if I was going to live like that!" "I wasn't human anymore; I hated myself for being such an animal."

Pride has saved many lives. If "humility" meant only the opposite of "pride," many of us would be unable to survive. With our chin on the floor, we'd never make our way even in recovery! Let's accept that being humble means *much more* than acting the opposite of proud.

When we talk with others who came into recovery about the same time we did, or those who have come in afterwards, we often sense something we cannot put our finger on. When we listen to gay men, lesbians, and bisexuals share some of the incredible hardships they have endured in their lives as children, adolescents, and adults, we can be touched with something that is different from sympathy even though we don't know exactly what to call it. When we see hundreds of people marching in the streets behind the banners "SOBER AND GAY" in the Gay Pride parades and the national demonstrations advocating gay rights, we can feel something else riding the wave of pride that lifts our own hearts. And when thousands of recovering sexual minorities gather at the regional, national, or international conferences of Twelve Step programs, we can be overwhelmed with gratitude for the experience of participating in such an exhilarating response to life.

None of us has done it alone. All of us can feel humble in the presence of something at work far beyond any single individual's capability. In the past, many of us have lived our lives lost to the shame of being gay or bisexual, as well as being dependent on substances. In the midst of these public experiences in which tens, hundreds, and thousands of us show up to take pride in ourselves and in our recovery, we can also feel deep humility before the power that has brought about such a miracle for all of us—and society—to experience.

"No Pain; No Gain"

Where did we start from? "Keeping it green," as it is called, reminds us of the lives we have lived. Unless we remember this, it is easy to lose the perspective we have reached. Without a point of reference, we slip into comparisons with others that often prove dangerous and even destructive. Identifying ourselves as being in recovery is a way of touching base with our own progress. These words acknowledge the efforts we are making to change our lives. They also help to remind us about what may still be waiting for us should we decide to turn back in our journey. "Pain is inevitable; suffering is optional." This is one of the slogans repeated at meetings. Another slogan is "No pain; no gain." Both slogans remind us of truths vital to our recovery—that we are only human, that we are vulnerable even in our sobriety, that we must go through our obstacles if we are to overcome them.

Pain deflates everyone's ego. It is the great leveler. Goliaths and Amazons have been humbled by pain. A significant part of our expertise about ourselves relates directly to the pain we have known prior to, as well as in, early recovery. The Twelve Steps encourage us to learn new ways to deal with pain instead of relying on old habits of self-medicating. These are some of the ways people in recovery manage pain:

1. Make a list of basic needs, expectations, and goals at this moment.

2. Use the Serenity Prayer and other prayers or meditations.

3. Work the Twelve Steps of recovery.

4. Share the pain with someone else either through face to face contact or over the telephone.

5. Listen to the "places" inside ourselves that call out for support and comfort; acknowledge them.

6. Dispel any guilt or shame over feeling pain; pain is the sound of an alarm system going off and we are wise to heed it.

7. Avoid activities, physical/emotional/mental, that will result in intensifying or extending the pain.

8. Instead of rejecting ourselves for being in pain, embrace ourselves, lovingly, like children who are hurt and need attention.

9. Strive to remember that the pain will pass, that it is not forever, and that rest and care *do* have an effect.

10. Recognize that recovery from pain is a process, and that instant results are often short-lived and rarely permanent.

11. Make certain that what we feel is actually pain, and that we are not, once again, creating new pain because of ingrained patterns or habits.

12. Instead of collapsing into helplessness, actively seek help from the sources that have supported our recovery. We have not come this far only to get dumped now! (Unless we dump ourselves!)

13. Don't wait too long before visiting a trusted physician.

Until we have taken the first six Steps of the journey into recovery, it is very difficult—if not impossible—to attempt to use these measures. They are indices of change, the effect of beginning a new way of living instead of relying on old ways.

After we have taken Steps One through Six, we begin to have a far deeper understanding of the magnitude of the gift of recovery we have received. The gift has to be experienced, lived through, before we can become humble about receiving it.

And, just as the experience of pain is itself very humbling, so is the release from pain. Many people in early recovery, including Dr. Bob, the cofounder of AA, go through days, weeks, months, and even, in some cases, years of living with addictive/compulsive behavior after beginning abstinence! Some of us have thought we couldn't survive; but by using the tools of recovery and the help of others, we made it. It is a nightmare that can still evoke horrifying memories. None of us wish to live through it again, and it is often this memory that keeps our feet on the path through the wilderness.

On this journey, we are not victims. Not because we no longer feel pain, but because we no longer suffer from the compulsion. The humiliation from that is over; humility in the face of recovery is ours to acknowledge. That is why Step Seven is placed in our way at this juncture. Unless we consciously become humble about our recovery, there is significant danger we might take it for granted. "Victims will be victims," someone not very famous once said. We fall back so easily into suffering, and in suffering we deprive ourselves of self-esteem.

Developing Self-esteem

The development of self-esteem is intimately linked with experiencing humility. Humility, not arrogance, is the key to adjusting the balance that has been missing in our lives. Most of us have lived at either one extreme of grandiosity or the other, either in triumph or in humiliation, either the brightest angel or the wickedest monster. We have never known how to sustain ourselves in the middle ground. Step Seven, appearing in the middle of the Twelve Steps, proposes an idea that may never have occurred to us: humility creates balance in life once we begin to rid ourselves of our obstacles.

Because of the lifetime it has taken us to accumulate our secrets, our obstacles, our "defects of character," are not simply going to vanish overnight. We need to take some kind of consistent action in order to have them leave us. At the center of recovery is our willingness to deal with our obstacles, and all Twelve Step programs focus on this central activity in the journey into recovery.

Humility is essential. Because we cannot change entirely on our own, we need to learn to ask for help. For some of us, this is the most difficult effort of all. During our lives, most of us have been willing to squander many of our resources, sometimes without even having them. We learned to be people pleasers instead of letting others know what they could have from us and what they couldn't. It was never possible, however, to say what *we* needed and what we didn't. When we were children, at a time when we had to trust our parents, many of us were unable to do this because they told us that we were not entitled to our feelings or our thoughts. Their criticism established the rule of "Don't trust!" This rule lies at the heart of our difficulty in receiving the love and support others may have wanted to give us. Not trusting leads to isolation and feeling different. In recovery, in working the Steps, we break down this isolation and establish a connection, a communion with others.

We have already experienced, in Step Three, the effects of turning over our will and our lives to the care of God/HP as we understood God/HP. In Step Seven, we add our survival tactics to this and ask for help in getting rid of these obstacles standing in the way of our recovery. The willingness to ask for the help to do this opens the way to a new freedom. Never have we asked for anything like this before. Operating always with the fear of being rejected, we usually tried to get what we wanted by either stealth or manipulation. Or, rather than be turned down, we did without. This effort of asking for help marks a milestone in our recovery.

In the past, if we did force ourselves to ask someone for something, it was often from those who were unable or unwilling to give it. This was one of the ways we, as victims, used to reinforce our lack of self-esteem and to confirm the fact that the only way to survive in this world was by manipulation and dishonesty. When we can ask for what we need with the hope of receiving it, from healthy people, we are saying that we are worth it. Whether or not they can give us what we ask, we raise our self-esteem and sense of self-worth.

These are a few suggestions to remember about implementing this Step:

1. Remember to be careful what you ask for. You might get it!

2. Remember not to ask for something you don't really want.

3. Remember you are not making a deal, or manipulating just to get your way. You are asking for what you need.

4. Remember to be grateful for what you already have; everything else will rest on this foundation.

5. Remember that your words are important for you to hear in your own ears; you need to listen as you say them.

6. Remember, if you value your recovery, there is no shame in asking for what you need!

7. Remember to be patient after you ask; there is one thing you can be certain of—you have no control over time.

8. Remember that the list of obstacles is usually quite long; ask for help in removing them one at a time instead of all at once. It is progress, not perfection, that makes the difference in recovery.

9. Remember to ask for help joyously; children are sad only after they have been rejected—not before!

10. Remember to say, "Thanks!"

Relating with Higher Power

Guilt and shame over everything that has happened in our past stand in the way of accepting ourselves as children of the Higher Power. This is the same Higher Power who loves us. "If HP loves me, why don't I feel it?" Indeed it may take some time, years even, for us to understand that the obstacles standing in the way of our future are the same ones in the way of a different relationship with a Higher Power. Once we do face this, however, we comprehend that these obstacles make us unlovable.

Believing that, as homosexuals or bisexuals, HP could love everyone except us has the effect of excluding God from our love—and our lives. In the process of canceling out HP from life, we feel isolated from everyone because of our own uniqueness. This is the perfect precondition for spiritual bankruptcy.

An aspect of the depth and breadth of wisdom found in the Twelve Steps is the acknowledgment of a Higher Power not as conceived in our past—our childhood, or during our use of addictive/compulsive behavior—but "as we understand" this power now, at this time. For many of us, we do not easily leave behind our old ideas about God. This takes as long as it takes; it is left to each individual. Nevertheless, hanging on to old ideas keeps us stuck in the past; embracing new ones opens us to change.

Step Seven, "Humbly asked God to remove our shortcomings," is an active way of entering into a new and different relationship with a Higher Power. Some have referred to it as a "resting step," but it is actually a very active and pragmatic approach to dealing with what is optional in our lives: suffering.

Until we can understand we are in charge of developing a relationship with HP *different from* that in the past, we will continue to suffer over the kind of relationship we have always had. Here is another paradox for us in recovery: by humbly asking for help to remove our shortcomings, we enter a new relationship with life that is based on asking for, and believing in, the possibility of receiving help. This goes far beyond identifying and acknowledging our obstacles. It is a giant step away from our past and into the present; it is change in its most basic form.

For many sexual minorities in recovery, it is a profound revelation to discover that God, or HP, loves them. This revelation is at the heart of the "spiritual awakening" referred to in Twelve Step programs. For many, this awakening begins from the first day we hear the words "Keep coming back!" No one ever asked us to come back—not even the drug dealers! (They knew we *had* to come back because we were hooked.) The caring and the unconditional love we have felt from others in recovery have opened us to the possibility of trusting a Power greater than our own.

Did we believe we were worth it back at the beginning of our journey? Given the way we thought about ourselves, this does not seem likely. But a day at a time, we gradually came to believe that we were indeed worth it. Our choice kept us coming back, and it will continue to be our choice. We can take pride in this, because that is the part we have played: choosing recovery. Parades and demonstrations for gay causes express support for our rights and our dignity as gay brothers and lesbian sisters and bisexual brothers and sisters. Our abstinence celebrates, each day, our new lives as the valuable free spirits we are.

Recovery is something all of us do together, no matter what our beliefs or unbeliefs. The process of recovering has no time schedule, and there are as many ways as there are individuals who work at it. Of course, we can complain about this whenever we wish. We can also be humble about it as well. Like everyone else, we are human beings. Working on Step Seven, if we haven't already appreciated the slogan "God doesn't make garbage," we can now. We can also be grateful that it is always our choice to take these steps of the journey into recovery.

※　　※　　※

❋   ❋   ❋

When you attend a meeting or a counseling session, listen to the words that others share without comparing yourself with them. Don't compare your recovery with anyone else's, or even with your own from an earlier period. Whatever it takes to get on with your journey, that is the prescription you need for your own recovery. Add an entry to your journal about your personal prescription for recovery—for yourself.

❋   ❋   ❋

Having the answers has often been the source of great pride in our lives. Whether it was for someone in our families—a parent, spouse, child, relative—or for our boss or a coworker, or for anyone who asked (or started to ask), we felt good about ourselves when we could solve the problem they faced. The satisfaction this provided was frequently the brightest moment of our day. We lived from one of these moments until the next; in between came lots of other things.

1. Remember back in your life what the experience of helping other people solve their problems meant to you. Who were some of these people? In what ways did you help them?

_____

_____

_____

_____

2. How did you feel when you were unable to help them?

_____

_____

_____

3. Relate this with your realization about how deeply you had lost yourself in compulsive behavior and didn't have the answer for *yourself.*

_____

_____

_____

4. In recovery, what do you do when people ask you for help?

_____

_____

_____

5. In what ways is it similar to or different from before?

Similar	Different
_____	_____
_____	_____
_____	_____
_____	_____
_____	_____
_____	_____

6. All of us have known arrogant or insecure people in our lives. Think about a few of them and list some things about the way they deal with others.

_____

_____

_____

7. How do you feel when they deal this way with you?

_____

_____

_____

8. What connection, if any, do you see between "change," "arrogance," and "insecurity"?

_____

_____

_____

9. Have you ever thought of yourself as arrogant? as insecure? If so, about what?

_____

_____

_____

10. Draw a picture of a humble person. *(Use colors.)* Below it, describe your picture in a few phrases.

Description:_____

_____

_____

_____

11. What are things humble people do?

_____

_____

_____

12. Contrast a few of your survival tactics with the behavior of a humble person.

_____

_____

_____

13. Is "humiliation" or "degradation" associated with humility in your thinking? Explore any "messages" you received growing up about this way of thinking.

_____

_____

_____

14. What patterns of behavior did you use in your past to avoid being humiliated by others?

_____

_____

_____

15. Can a person be proud *and* humble at the same time? Explore what this would mean and how it would be possible in terms of your own life.

_____

_____

_____

16. When you think about the efforts you are making in recovery, what feelings of pride surface for you?

_____

_____

_____

17. When you think about the efforts you are making in recovery, what feelings of humility surface for you?

_____

_____

_____

18. When you now consider asking Higher Power for help, what concerns come up for you?

_____

_____

_____

19. When you asked Higher Power for help in the past, how ready were you to part with your own shortcomings?

_____

_____

_____

20. Enlisting Higher Power support for removing your shortcomings isn't a topic for debate but a suggestion for action. What particular obstacles come up for you when you think of taking this action?

_____

_____

_____

21. Prioritize your shortcomings in terms of your need to have them removed.

Top Priority	Medium Priority	Low Priority
_____	_____	_____
_____	_____	_____
_____	_____	_____
_____	_____	_____

22. What efforts have you made to develop a connection with HP to deal with these fears? In what way is the relationship different from the past?

_____

_____

_____

23. Identify any concerns you may have regarding your life after these shortcomings have been removed.

_____

_____

_____

24. Discuss these concerns with your therapist or sponsor to assist you to move beyond your fears.

Putting ME into Perspective

The work we have been doing on the past four Steps has been different from anything we have ever previously attempted. No matter what we have been told or asked to do before this time, working at discovering WHO we are is more rigorous than any assignment we were ever given. And we did it because we chose to do it—for ourselves! We did it in order to continue on our journey. This willingness is in itself a significant change!

It is helpful to look back over both our efforts and what has resulted from them. The time we spend doing this is important. We have been learning new things, as well as new ways of doing things. And in this process, we are affirming for ourselves that we are able to get results. "But they are not perfect!" you insist. Right you are. And this is the best evidence that you are making progress in recovery. Unlike the impetus to perfectionism that before stymied all efforts even before we could undertake them, we have become willing to allow ourselves the opportunity to become realistic about what we can accomplish today.

A New Model

This is an entirely new model of behavior for us. Considering that the old patterns of behavior didn't work for us, we need to understand that we are creating out of our own material a new way of doing things. No one else can do this for us. We must work with our own material in order to alter the process we have used.

Unlike the fantasy we have lived in about what we were going to be, have, or do, we have looked into the mirror of reality and seen who we have been, what we have had, and the things that we have done. With the help of others around us, we have resisted the habit to be critical about what has been revealed and, instead, replaced it with honesty. Our fears have deceived us; we did not disintegrate. A few of our strengths began to emerge from the shadows of our secrets, and as we shared our findings with another human being and our Higher Power we were amazed to find ourselves no longer lost in the abyss of self-destruction but finding our way through the wilderness.

Learning that we were teachable, that we no longer had to live by our old rules but could create new ones and still survive, and that there is always help for us to deal with our obstacles has all worked to reconfigure the foundation of a life that had been built on self-delusion, inflexibility, and arrogance. The first faint blush of self-esteem has appeared to replace the "pickled" pallor of our cheeks. No matter what we have done in the past, we are facing our lives today. Instead of the powerless victim, we are members of a community of men and women, gay and lesbian and bisexual, who are in recovery. This is a powerful admission. This is a whole new perspective of our lives—one that sets each of us in right size and prepares us for putting the rest of our lives in balance.

Looking back at our journey, we can observe the process: Step Four created an inventory and forced our secrets out of hiding; Step Five shared them with another human being (along with a Higher Power); Step Six encouraged our willingness to have them removed; and now Step Seven encourages us to ask for help in dumping them. Linking the four Steps together adds up to consistent action to change the conditions of life in recovery.

Working on our own obstacles introduces a consistent approach to achieving equilibrium in our lives. These are the survival tactics that have unbalanced us—in thought and action—and by working on them, we can make the changes that will influence our lives. Embodied in the Twelve Steps is the wisdom that self-renewal depends on the unusual combination of individual effort *and* asking for help from others—the group or the source of power beyond us. Personal effort, in Twelve Step programs, does not mean recovering on one's own without outside assistance.

❀   ❀   ❀

1. Many sexual minorities have experienced how fears and secrets isolate us from others. Taking these Steps marks a change from this pattern. How willing are you to use these Steps to work directly on changing the way you relate to other people—gays and nongays—in your life? *(Circle your estimate.)*

Entirely Willing		**Moderately**		**Completely Unwilling**
1	2	3	4	5

2. If you are dissatisfied with your answer to the previous question, whom can you turn to for help to become more willing to change how you relate to others?

_____

_____

_____

3. Asking for support from others—sponsors, therapists, and others in recovery—can often put you in an unfamiliar place in yourself. Knowing that recovery depends on receiving help from others, how easy or difficult is it for you to do this? *(Circle your estimate.)*

Easy				**Difficult**
1	2	3	4	5

4. How often have you asked for help from those who couldn't or wouldn't give it? Identify those individuals you asked.

_____

_____

_____

5. What are some of the things you asked for and the words you used to ask for help?

_____

_____

_____

6. How often did you manipulate others into giving you what you wanted? *(Circle your estimate.)*

Rarely   **All the Time**

| 1 | 2 | 3 | 4 | 5 |

7. What role does this play in asking for help now?

_____

_____

_____

8. Now in your recovery, are there any differences when you ask others for help? Identify the differences.

_____

_____

_____

9. If there are "defects" that you're not ready to let go of yet, what's their hold on you?

_____

_____

_____

10. Are you holding on to some defects for just a while? for a longer time? forever? What's this about?

_____

_____

_____

11. If you've already made efforts to let go of some defects, what has happened? How do you feel about this?

_____

_____

_____

12. What are you learning about your strengths as you work to let go of your defects?

_____

_____

_____

13. What is happening to your sense of equilibrium and balance?

_____

_____

_____

14. How important are Steps Four through Seven for your ongoing efforts to change?

_____

_____

_____

15. Imagine that all the changes that you have asked to occur have happened overnight, as if by magic. What is now different about you? about your attitudes, thoughts, and behaviors?

_____

_____

_____

_____

_____

_____

_____

16. In what way do these changes in you alter your present? your future?

_____

_____

_____

_____

17. What are the implications for your relationships with others?

_____

_____

_____

18. How have your efforts to change affected your sense of self-esteem? What has already changed? What is changing now? What is staying the same?

_____

_____

_____

_____

_____

_____

_____

_____

19. How have your expectations of the results of your efforts met with your experiences?

_____

_____

_____

20. What is your perspective now about yourself and your sense of worth and value as a bisexual, lesbian, or gay man?

_____

_____

_____

21. How have you been coping with any disappointments, setbacks, or discouragements you have experienced as a result of taking these Steps on your own?

_____

_____

_____

22. Anything less than perfect, or the need for instant results may tempt some to think that "Change is impossible," "I am worthless," "It will never work for me," or some other variation on negative, extremist thinking. Is this the case for you? What thoughts are getting in your way?

_____

_____

_____

_____

_____

_____

_____

23. If you are encountering such thoughts, which can generate a self-defeating spiral, what type of help will you seek to assist you to get back on track?

_____

_____

_____

CHAPTER 19

The Gift of Responsibility

CONDITION

Irresponsibility

We have been caught in the quicksand of desperation in which one day is identical with the next, and the one after that. We slipped deeper into despair and destruction. We lost all sense of responsibility for our lives and what happened to us.

ALTERNATIVE

Responsibility

Most of the wreckage of the past is in human lives—our own and others. Owning our actions advances recovery because it involves confronting ourselves about what change actually means. Real change means treating ourselves *and others* differently. Setting the record straight is an important way to make this correction.

Accepting responsibility for our actions breaks down self-delusion and fantasy. From this point we can go on to be responsible for living a healthy and productive life in recovery instead of only reliving the past. "Look back, but don't stare!"

Step 8

*Made a list of all persons we had harmed,
and became willing to make amends to them all.*

Vivid images and fantasies from the past flourish in our newly experienced recovery. These powerful impressions often disturb us as we attempt to make our way into new territory. "Somehow, no matter where I go, I always find that I bring myself with me." This may strike a familiar chord because all of us have thought and acted in the past in ways that continue to affect us. No matter where we journey, we bring with us the memory of where we have been.

Extending the Focus

Until this point, we have been working within the boundaries and limitations of our own thoughts and actions and their impact on our lives. As unsure as we may have been in early recovery, we still felt reasonably safe because we were encouraged to keep the focus completely on ourselves. Even the person we chose as a therapist, sponsor, or the one to listen to our Fifth Step was someone we felt could help guarantee our safety. All this while, we have been tunneling through our personal histories to create the foundation for a different kind of life. The time has come to extend our focus.

It is natural to resist doing this. Our old pattern of isolating is always there waiting for us, and we recognize the temptation. Do we yield to it, or not? This is always our choice in recovery. We live in today with our choices.

If we truly value this new life we have begun in recovery, choices must be made to support it. Valuing recovery means taking an active role in living it. This, then, *is* our new life; choosing recovery instead of living with compulsive/dependent behavior is entirely our own responsibility.

For some of us, this word "responsibility" is loaded with guilt over what we have failed to do with our lives, as well as blame for the mountains of things we have already done. For many, this word recalls old debts that have been left unpaid and that have accrued staggering interest. Individuals who have become dependent on compulsive behavior, in general, are not famous for taking responsibility for their lives, apart from securing the next fix. In recovery, taking responsibility is one of the changes that we never thought possible to make, and we make it with the loving support of others just like ourselves whom we never believed were out there.

This is not the only change. Work is already in progress on another major area of concern: pain. In Step Seven, we identified some effective ways in which to handle pain, to play an active role in dealing with it. Wasn't this a different kind of role from the one we have been used to? In the past, our expertise has been in *suffering.* During our addiction, we assumed complete responsibility for living with suffering. Now, in recovery, we begin to assume responsibility for abandoning suffering. Acknowledging this shift in perspective is further progress in the process of recovery.

When we shed our status as life's victims, we no longer need to look through eyes that search only for opportunities to suffer. How strange and remarkable the world appears when we stop setting ourselves up for a life of suffering!

This may take us awhile, but gradually, we will begin to notice that, as sexual minorities, we have typically acted in ways that have ensured our victimhood. We have invited others to prey on and mistreat us. It may be very difficult to accept this realization. The most important thing, at this time, is that we understand we have played a key role in this. We need to understand that many of us have been active agents and not the passive victims we have thought ourselves to be. We have not simply been "done to." We have, instead, consistently performed in ways to make it appear as if we had no responsibility for the disasters that found us.

Recovery, at this stage in our journey, invites us to take an honest look at our role in relation to others. If we cannot see what we have done and the way we have done it, we remain completely in the dark about changing it. Observing these important patterns and events in our lives is the beginning of becoming responsible for ourselves.

In the past, we often made poor choices; in recovery, we can make different (and, we hope, better) choices. Acknowledging what our role has been in the past helps us to understand how we can begin to make other kinds of choices in the present. We do not change without seeing ourselves. The task always begins with us.

It is essential to understand how we have acted, the roles we have played that have often helped to provoke or invite others to victimize or oppress us. This will help us create a conscious connection with the source of our power and make it possible to refuse to continue to act in ways that invite or tolerate oppression. If we have been able to influence others' actions with negative results (as a result of low self-esteem, feelings of worthlessness, or internalized homophobia), we understand that we can become responsible for doing what *we* now need to do for *ourselves* in order to recover! The role we have played in the past with others provides us with important clues for today.

In Steps Four, Five, Six, and Seven, we embarked on exploring the continents of our secrets, our mountain ranges of obstacles, our deserts of shortcomings. With Step Eight, we add to the map of our experience the names of the people we encountered along the way who are now an integral part of who we are in this moment. This Step introduces into our recovery everyone who has appeared in our lives before and during recovery.

Naming Names

Many of the disturbing fantasies that have intruded on our recovery have involved the people in our past: parents, siblings, other relatives, childhood playmates and grown-up friends, lovers and partners, husbands or wives, employers and co-workers, as well as strangers. The list goes on and on. Some of them are no longer alive, but that doesn't matter. Each of them lives in our memories, and we reincarnate them and whatever they did or did not do to us every time we fantasize about them.

For many of us, the people from our past march like a parade of phantoms always ready and willing to pass before our reviewing stand. They go in circles around us, and we go on and on experiencing what we did or didn't do with them. For some inexplicable reason, even in recovery, they have some kind of special power over us as long as we avoid dealing with them. If we avoid addressing our "unfinished business" with these people, phantoms in our minds will continue to haunt us.

In the past, we were unable to escape from our secrets or stop using our survival tactics. Now, we will never be able to do away with our fears of those who have this kind of power over our lives unless we take that power away. These fears stand in the way of our recovery. Didn't we discover a new kind of freedom when we inventoried and faced our secrets? Now, we will find a different way to live with the host of people from our past if we face our fears by bringing their names out of the shadows and into the light.

The actual process of developing a list can be like this:

1. Begin by identifying situations in which you experience guilt and blame, both in addiction and in recovery.

2. Recall as many of the participants in these situations as you can and call them by name.

3. Instead of hiding from them, write their names on the list.

4. Let the feelings these names evoke surface.

5. Allow these feelings to reverberate in your memory and connect with identical situations in which different people were involved.

6. Write their names on the list.

7. Don't attempt to write a complete list of names the first day you begin.

8. Put the list in a safe place; plan to look briefly at it each day during the period you are working the Step.

9. Discuss the process of developing the list, and whatever it calls up for you, with your sponsor, your therapist, and so on.

10. *Do not consider taking any kind of action at this time.*

On the page, they are only names, but what memories they evoke! Summoning their names into the present, we often discover that our fears of many of these people have matured in our memory into a vintage brew of considerable proof! Over the years, guilt and shame have fermented the events we have experienced in the past into a concoction that may even taste strangely familiar, like something bubbling up from our past. Perhaps we are even abstinent enough to appreciate that we have used the fantasies about these people stored in our imagination in the same way we have used substances or compulsive behavior—to get high or low over them.

Naming names is not an exercise in abstraction. When we name any individual from our past, we experience reverberations that penetrate our mental, emotional, and physical existence. We may find ourselves wishing to run and hide. But having come this far in our journey, we are aware that getting in touch with these feelings is crucial to our recovery.

We have denied our feelings about what we have done, or not done, to and with other people, just as we have denied the effects of the substances/behavior we abused. In working Step Eight, we make a conscious effort to end this denial and admit the truth. In recovery, denial about anything or anyone stands in the way of progress.

We do not have to start from scratch; we can use the inventory we wrote in Step Four. Each of our secrets, each of our survival tactics, has involved other people. Not one of them is sealed away in a vacuum separated from human interaction. Unless we end our denial about this, we will go on watching that parade of phantoms circle in our imaginations. This is the choice we must make: whether or not to call a halt to this kind of suffering.

Regretting the Past

Even in recovery, regret over the past is one of the surest ways to perpetuate it. Because of the efforts we have already made on our journey, we now understand that we can live in the present only when we become willing to face the past instead of hiding or running from it.

The shrill voice from the loudest member of the committee inside our heads calls out to object: "That's all very well for you to say! You don't know what I've done to my mother/father/brother/sister/lover/spouse!"

Haven't we all done something to someone? Everyone shares this fate with everyone else, and no one is unique in this respect. Even though what each of us has done may be different, and there is, perhaps, some shred of uniqueness in the actions themselves, nevertheless, they all have something in common. They have already been done; they are facts. Not one person among us can change anything that has already happened. In recovery, it helps to be very clear about this.

As strange as it may seem, people may understand but still be unwilling to think or act on this understanding. They persist in acting and thinking as if they can change what has happened in the past. For this reason, the past fetters and subdues their lives. They do not live in today with today's *actual* opportunities but remain stuck, throttled, with yesterdays' and yesteryears' *lost* opportunities. Is it any wonder they live under such a burden of suffering? Too many of us take this burden of suffering for granted and allow it to destroy every opportunity we have for happiness.

We cannot do this if we are committed to progress on our journey into recovery. No matter what other people do with their lives, we need to learn to live without suffering. Many gay men, lesbians, and bisexuals have a particularly difficult time accepting this and living it because of the distortions and lies they have allowed themselves to believe. Being homosexual or bisexual does not require living in the closet, or in a ghetto, or with hardship, misery, and failure. We have the same entitlements in life that every heterosexual has! But we must claim them for ourselves. No one else can claim them for us.

This was even more difficult to do in the past because substances and compulsive behavior controlled our lives. In recovery, we can begin to work at the task of claiming happiness, love, success, and freedom for ourselves. Step Eight is crucial in providing the foundation for accomplishing this. Let us understand the reason.

In our lives before beginning recovery, we put on different disguises for other people. Not the least familiar of these disguises was the invisible "halo" of shame that some of us wore in the presence of heterosexuals. From the time we were children, our sense of feeling different encouraged us to believe that something must be "wrong" with us, and therefore we had to deal with people in certain ways—some of them acceptable, others unacceptable. It is easy to understand that if something is "wrong" with us, then something must be "right" with other people. With this as the basis for our thinking and action, we have been responsible for giving away most of our power because they are "right" and we are not. So many of the things we have done or not done in the past have been motivated by this mistaken conviction.

This is a basic premise on which many of us have operated in our lives. Other premises include: "If they are going to do *that* to me, then I'm going to do this to *them*." There is no doubt we have suffered, and we have caused others to suffer, by living this way. The wreckage of our past is the best evidence for what can happen to us.

Most of this wreckage has been in human lives, our own and others. Call them what you like—"mistakes," "errors in judgment," "whatever." Perhaps they involved stealing money from an employer, or going to bed with our lover's best friend, or never being there for others when they needed us, or failing to do what we promised. These create a battlefield on which we will continue to bleed until we are willing to confront our actions instead of covering our heads with regret and shame.

Taking responsibility for what we have already done is real change. Indeed it *is* possible to treat ourselves and act with others differently in recovery. It means the end to our familiar ritual of suffering over the way we have acted in the past. Taking this responsibility on ourselves gets us into the present.

With that, another know-it-all voice from the committee in our heads pipes up: "If that means I have no past, how is it possible for me to have a future?" No one is suggesting that we can erase the past; everything that has happened has already happened. But regretting the past steals our energy, and taking responsibility for our actions in the past restores it. It is possible to observe this as we go about setting down the list of names of individuals who interacted with us in our lives over the years.

This list of names we make is for ourselves. At this place now in our journey, we can see only as far as our vision at this moment permits. Just as with all the other Steps, progress and not perfection is the goal. The clearer our minds become, the more names we will remember. And there may always be those we will never remember to put on this list. Our honest willingness to undertake this task is more important than any of the names we write—except one: our own.

At the Top of the List

Of all the people we have injured in our lives, we have harmed ourselves most in harming others. The backlash of the harm we have done to others has devastated our own lives. We have deprived ourselves of the happiness that comes from healthy relationships and self-realization. We have wasted our gifts and lost touch with our value as feeling, thinking, loving human beings. We have put ourselves through hell. No matter what anyone else has done to us, we have harmed ourselves worse. Taking responsibility for this is an enormous step!

It takes many of us a long time to be able to comprehend this because of our deep-rooted sense of worthlessness and lack of self-esteem. Our addictive/compulsive behavior has intensified all the feelings of inadequacy, incompetence, guilt, and shame we have known as gay men, lesbians, and bisexuals. No matter how low we have ever been before, compulsive behavior has brought us lower. It is only through consistent and loving encouragement that we can restore balance in our lives. We need to take each opportunity to acknowledge ourselves that recovery provides. Therefore, in working Step Eight, we need to place our own names at the top of the list of the people we have harmed.

Taking this initiative for the first time, perhaps, we make a list of the names of those who have waved the banners of our darkest secrets as they marched through our imagination in our phantom parades. Mother, father, brothers, sisters, husbands, wives, lovers, children, friends, enemies, employers, employees, friends, strangers. The Step encourages us to name as many as we can remember.

For many of us, when we do this, something unusual happens, and it is important to notice it. There is now a difference when any of the individuals on our list appear before our imagination. *We* have summoned them; they have not sprung out at us from nowhere, the way they usually do! By writing their names, we introduce a new element into whatever relationship we ever had with them. This may be the first inkling of what taking responsibility for ourselves means.

Many of our past relationships have been completely out of balance. Our secrets, our dishonesty, and our lack of trust for others have affected us deeply whenever we tried to connect with others. We have suffered over what we attempted to hide, as well as from the dishonest relationships that resulted from these efforts. The others have suffered too. Dishonesty and duplicity have diminished us. We have not been the person we appeared to be. How many times have we offered this as the reason for using or acting out?

Step Eight is not about fault or blame. It is another opportunity to examine the survival tactics we developed and that, by now, have become obstacles. By identifying the events of our past, we are acknowledging the role we have played in them. About one thing, we should be very clear. Acting as if it is possible to hide from any of those we have harmed is as threatening to our recovery as attempting to hide from our secrets. It ensures us against change; it supports addictive patterns. If we can believe this, we will overcome our natural reluctance to disturb old memories and, instead, concentrate our efforts on this task.

Many of us, in this Step, encounter a deep sense of sorrow the moment we begin to work on it. How badly we have disappointed those we have loved and who have loved us! How cruelly we have rewarded those who have been kind to us! Perhaps we could not see this in the past, but we can certainly see it now. It is important to remind ourselves that when our blindness is ended, the very least we can do is to be grateful for the light. The restoration of our ability to feel gratitude is one of the most significant changes that occurs in recovery. We can accept it with joy instead of sorrow.

The people from our past provide us with a rich reservoir of images and memories in much the same way as our behavior provided us with a rich source of fantasies. We need to give ourselves the space in which to change by putting the past in its proper place. With all of our thoughts and feelings occupied with the past, it is little wonder that we have no room either to live in the present or to change in the future. When we understand that "responsibility" means we must take action about separating what was from what is, we change our concept of it.

Taking Responsibility for Recovery

We are constantly using our energy at cross-purposes when we insist on the past functioning in our lives as if it were the present. The task of separating past from present is an act of responsibility. It defines "This is mine *now*" and "This was mine *then.*" Getting into the present means identifying what cannot be changed and using our energy to handle, in whatever way we can, the business of today. Appreciating our possibilities for action, along with our limitations, establishes balance in our lives. We get very clear about what it is possible to do about the past as we begin to exercise this responsibility.

When memories and fantasies confuse what we can do with what we cannot do, we have no opportunity to act. Even in recovery, we may become so caught up in all the things we haven't been able to do, or things we have left undone, that we become paralyzed over doing anything. We create balance in the present with the attitudes we have about what we *can* do and what we *cannot* do. Staying stuck in our fantasies about and from the past, as well as the present, unbalances us.

A Step at a time, we have been learning how to take responsibility for our recovery. Living in the present, we assume an active role in creating balance that is completely different from our previous role of seeking escape. The process began with Step One, and Step Eight follows in a natural progression.

Now, we are no longer helpless; we are no longer victims; we are no longer lost to our addictive/compulsive behaviors. The choice we have been offered in recovery is no longer to wear any of the disguises we have worn in the past. Acknowledging who we have been and who we are now marks an end to irresponsibility.

As essential to this Step as writing our list of names is our willingness to make amends for our actions. Changing from the way we have been in the past takes more than a writing exercise. The person we have been has caused harm; accepting responsibility for this begins with the willingness to do what we can to make amends to alleviate it. Willingness, for many of us, may take considerable time to develop; nevertheless, we must make this effort because it provides us with a solid basis on which to create our lives in recovery.

We are no longer going to live in isolation, and we are no longer going to treat people the way we have treated them in the past. Step Eight provides us with a "declaration of independence" from the irresponsible individual we have been. It gives us the opportunity to act responsibly with everyone on our list as well as every new person who now comes into our lives. We extend the boundaries and limitations of our world as we become more able and willing to exercise this freedom.

With this gift of responsibility we have given ourselves, we can work on living healthy and productive lives in recovery instead of only reliving the past. That means we can no longer allow the past, or anyone from the past, to control our lives. In Step Eight, we make our first claim to being who we are now, and we allow the people whose names we have written on our list to emerge from our imagination and stand on their own. Living in the present depends on this.

❋   ❋   ❋

This Step is not about confrontation; it is about acknowledgment. It is an exercise in ego-deflation: recognizing the nature and extent of the harm you've done to others. No longer being "the worst offender" or "the tiniest trespasser"—this will help to put yourself into being the right size and to dump any old disguises.

❋   ❋   ❋

"Amends"—to change, to do something differently, to say "I'm sorry"—isn't at the heart of this Step: change is! *Lots of people have lived a lifetime saying, "I'm sorry." This is an opportunity to stand up to the realization and do something about it: changing what you are going to do NOW! Think about this and write your thoughts at this time in your journal.*

❋   ❋   ❋

1. Perhaps you will need assistance in addressing the phantoms from your past. Whom will you seek out to discuss your fears about this process?

   _____

   _____

   _____

2. If contemplating further action on this Step begins to feel overwhelming and threatens to paralyze your forward progress, review what you wrote in Step Six about your "defects of character" and "survival tactics." Also consider whether this task requires additional assistance from others such as sponsor, therapist, or clergy member.

3. For those prepared to move forward at this time, be sure to put your name first on the list. It is healing to know that you *belong* on this list and can accept responsibility for self-support. Now, look over Step Four. Select the names of people for this list already identified in your inventory; add the names of those who do not yet appear on the inventory. Write your list.

   _____

   _____

   _____

4. First, write your name in one of the circles below. Then, write the names of those in your Step Eight list in relationship to their "distance" from you. *(Feel free to add more circles.)*

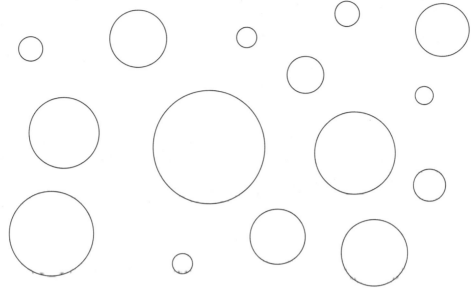

5. "Making amends" can be thought of as the process of altering or improving behavior patterns, or repairing something broken or damaged. How might this be relevant to you and your relationships?

    _____
    _____
    _____

6. How might this be different from saying "I'm sorry"?

    _____
    _____
    _____

7. What have your experiences been like in the past when you've tried to change things by saying "I'm sorry"?

    _____
    _____
    _____

8. What are your expectations about your ability to alter relationships now?

_____

_____

_____

9. What are your excuses to avoid making the efforts to alter such relationships? *(e.g., "I'm too old, or young, or poor, or sick" or "They're too . . .")*

_____

_____

_____

10. What do you have to lose by making these efforts?

_____

_____

_____

11. What do you stand to gain?

_____

_____

_____

12. Now that you've completed your first pass at this list, how did the experience match up with your expectations?

_____

_____

_____

13. What have you learned? What issues do you need to discuss with your supports?

_____

_____

_____

14. What differences have you observed between your value system and your actual behavior? (Discrepancies between the two often cause guilt feelings.)

_____

_____

_____

15. How do you learn to be up-front about your needs and your actions?

_____

_____

_____

16. These are some statements regarding the ways people treat others. Feel free to add your own to the list:

- The ends justify the means.
- Do unto others . . .
- Nice guys finish last.
- Intentions speak louder than words.
- Actions speak louder than words.
- Do as I say, not as I do.
- You can't take it with you.
- God will provide.
- Everybody else does the same thing.
- When I say this, I really mean . . .
- Can't you take a joke?
- I'm only doing this for your own good.
- This hurts me more than it does you.
- _____
- _____
- _____
- _____

17. Which of the statements describe your attitudes toward people on your list of amends?

_____

_____

_____

18. Identify the attitudes you are willing to alter at this time.

_____

_____

_____

19. What do you propose to do about the attitudes you are not yet willing to alter?

_____

_____

_____

20. Which people are you not prepared to make amends to at this time?

_____

_____

_____

21. How does the harm that others have done to you get in the way of considering making amends to them?

_____

_____

_____

22. What will it take for you to become willing to do this?

_____

_____

_____

23. How "entirely willing" are you to make amends to yourself?

_____

_____

_____

24. How does this mesh with your understanding of responsibility?

_____

_____

_____

❄   ❄   ❄

This Step appears deceptively easy until you actually begin to work it.
Instead of getting discouraged, seek help and support from others.

❄   ❄   ❄

CHAPTER 20

Fusing the Fragments

CONDITION	ALTERNATIVE
Suffering and fragmentation	**Healing and reconfiguration**

Our lives collapsed into smaller and smaller pieces. Even the tiniest decisions terrified us: we lost our coping skills. Fragmentation resulted from the growing inability to change this ever-worsening slide, and the disorder in our lives accelerated. We could not explain why we were falling apart. We suffered over everything.

Owning our past changes our direction in recovery. Making amends to those we had harmed extends the cleansing and healing activity of Step Five—as long as we are clear about the need to do it for *ourselves*. When we get rid of this debris accrued from old dysfunctional relationships, we find room for fulfilling, healthy relationships now and in the future.

Forgiving ourselves accelerates when others we have wronged forgive us. But whether they do or not, we have made the effort and have taken responsibility for our lives today. This effort fuses together our brokenness into a new configuration in which we can live a new life.

Step 9

Made direct amends to such people wherever possible,
except when to do so would injure them or others.

Living in the present is different from what we think it will be. As we continue to work the Steps, an orderly routine begins to emerge out of the chaos of our unmanageable lives. Now, we wake up, we get washed, we have breakfast, we do the dishes, we meditate, we go to work, we go to our group meeting; our health improves. As the months continue, we find the opportunity in the space created by our routine to make important connections with the past. These connections help us begin to live in a new way.

"More shall be revealed." Each of the Twelve Step programs stresses the effect of time on recovery. No matter what we understand today, each new day provides the opportunity to understand even more about ourselves. A pivotal incident from childhood can reveal staggering insights about events that have triggered patterns of a lifetime.

The following is from the journal of a man in his fifties. He writes about what it was like being in the body of the three-year-old who actually had the experience:

> Standing at the top and looking down, he stared at the flight of stairs before him and hesitated. They seemed too long and too steep for him ever to make it to the bottom. His small hand reached up to touch the banister above his head for support. It was smooth and firm.
>
> He had been wakened from a nap and dressed in short white starched pants and a white starched shirt with big buttons on it. His feet hurt in the new shoes which pinched. From the living room below, he could hear strange voices. The sound frightened him although he didn't know why. He could remember nothing from before his nap, neither his excitement at the arrival of guests who were coming to celebrate Thanksgiving at his house, nor any of the pleasure he had helping to fold napkins for the big table in the busy dining room. At this moment, all he felt was terror, as if he were coming apart in many pieces.
>
> From behind, his mother reached down to touch his shoulder, and he began his descent. The pitch of the voices grew louder and louder. His progress slowed; his three-year-old legs did not want to bend. With each step, the feeling grew larger and larger within him—if only he could become INVISIBLE! Then, as he reached the bottom of the stairs, completely surrounded by faces which circled the room high above him, he suddenly burst into tears. "That's how he is sometimes," he heard his mother say behind him. From behind her explanation, he felt a part of himself actually become invisible.

Remembering this incident from the past connected the writer with a place he had started from: it revealed to him the moment when he first wished to be invisible.

Without ever realizing it, this moment became the basis for interacting with other people from then on.

Over the years of our journey into recovery, we will spend a great deal of time getting in touch with the little child inside us. And if we are willing to face the way we have lived during our years of growing up, amazing revelations will occur. This means, of course, lots of space clearing, mind uncluttering, letting go, and, at the same time, the consistent effort to live in the present. The effect of this helps us to make new connections. These insights help us to care about ourselves and others in new ways. As we make the journey, we will become clearer and clearer about the fact that the Twelve Steps are about becoming an adult instead of continuing to live as a child or an adolescent. Perhaps the key is that in order to grow up, we need to show up in our lives.

The three-year-old descending the staircase refused to enter that people-filled room because it meant revealing how different from them he felt. That was the last thing he wanted to do! Because he desperately wished to fit in, to be a member of the family, he chose invisibility instead. He held back a dimension of himself from everyone else, and this was the beginning of the pattern of never being "all there" for anyone—not even for himself! Whatever the underlying cause of that three-year-old's initial response to others, his orientation to the world was so deeply affected that he was unable to live in it any other way except "invisibly."

The Invisible Person

Because we are homosexual, or bisexual, many of us have chosen invisible lives rather than be exposed to rejection, punishment, abandonment, or worse. Others of us have chosen very demanding roles as heroes, or clowns, or mascots, while still others become scapegoats or rebels. All of us have experienced a great deal of suffering and despair over these roles. How many times have we used our fix to isolate ourselves and bury the feelings that kept coming up because we were hiding who we really were? Let's be certain about this: we did not choose any of these roles because of our honesty. We isolated ourselves to keep other people from knowing how guilty we felt and to protect our dishonesty.

The effect of this was fragmentation. We broke ourselves into hundreds of thousands of pieces that neither "all the king's horses and all the king's men" *nor compulsive/dependent behavior* could put back together again. No matter what the occasion, there were always certain "invisible" pieces of our lives that appeared at the most unexpected moments. These never fit in with the rest of the puzzle. It was never possible to get the whole thing to work together. Dishonesty consistently shielded some of the parts while it exaggerated or minimized at different moments the importance of other fragments. We could never be "all there" because there were just too many vanishing pieces to be there with. Our daily lives have been infinitely more complicated because of the need to keep our homosexuality invisible.

Perhaps this may sound too harsh. If it does, then remember the periodic interrogations by parents concerning the people we were dating, and how long it would be before they could meet these prospective sons-in-law or daughters-in-law. Remember the constant pressure we felt in conversations to be on guard about changing the personal pronoun from "he" to "she," or vice versa. And the fear of being seen by a brother or a sister, or some other relative, with a friend who was so obviously gay or lesbian we'd never be able to explain it. If this ever happened, and it inevitably did, how we danced around the endless questions that never failed to come up each time we met this relative. Perhaps some of us even married, and then, to our amazement, we met someone of our own sex—and fell head over heels in love for the first time. Remember the confusion and despair we felt as well as created?

Living invisible lives creates devastating bad faith that influences every relationship we have. In addition to the havoc this wreaks on other people's lives, it utterly fragments our own! No matter how long we get away with it, and actually succeed in deceiving others, our own self-esteem is eaten away by the mistrust we naturally begin to feel for ourselves. Because we *know* the truth, we can never get away with the lie to ourselves. We spawn repulsive monsters—at least as large as the ones we were told stories about as children—in the realms of deceit in which our invisible selves hide their being.

We never escape from these monsters. Unless we become willing to face them, and then actually follow through with it, they will always be there to torture us. The process of becoming willing to do this takes time, patience, courage, and the deepest wish to continue on the journey of recovery. We need to consistently remind ourselves of this wish if we are going to work at changing our old rules for living.

For years, we have lived with rules that allowed us to preserve our invisibility through manipulating facts, events, and other people in ways that we believed would ensure we would get what we needed. We became experts at manipulation. Victims are always experts at manipulation. It should come as no surprise that many of us, along our journey into recovery, have tried to use these old rules in this new life we are beginning. Perhaps others have pointed this out, and that observation has irritated us. How lucky we are now to have friends who care enough about us to tell us things we need to hear about ourselves!

Nevertheless, we do not change because we know better. The truth is that for most of our lives we have known much better than we have ever done. Now, in recovery, the issue is what will we do about it? Each of the Steps requires us to act in a new way, and we need to take the action they suggest if we are to progress on the journey.

Careful thought has certainly been involved, and with it we developed the basic inventories in Steps Four and Eight. But we have not written these lists to lose them in the drawer. We wrote them in order to begin to change the way we acted in the past. To accomplish this, we must get rid of some of our old rules, and one of the basic ones relates to the manner in which we deal with others.

Creating a New History

The willingness to change old rules is essential even if we do not understand what the new rules might be. When we first began our journey with Step One, few if any of us started out with very much understanding—let alone intention—of becoming responsible for our lives. All that most of us wanted to do was to stop the pain and suffering, and surrender our claim to managing the mess our lives had become. No one said anything about responsibility. No one said anything, either, about manipulation. Our willingness to follow the directions suggested in the Steps has lead us into territory some of us never considered worth the time or the effort. "How did I ever end up here?"

In recovery, we direct our attention to the previous way we have lived so that we see what we must do to change how we will live now and in the future. Rather than learn from the past, however, many who participate actively in Twelve Step programs choose to go on living in the *story* of what happened to them instead of becoming willing to create a new history in recovery. They rave on and on in Twelve Step meetings about people, places, and things from long ago. They live in their stories about them as if today *were* yesterday. The miracle is that we are alive today *in spite of* our stories, and we need to remember this.

From the moment we start to work on Step One, even though we do not understand why, we have the chance to create a sober, abstinent history, and we add to this account each day we use our energy to work on our recovery. Showing up in our lives as the individual we are now, instead of the person we have been in the past, we own what we have done. We recognize that denying it is the surest way of finding ourselves back in old patterns.

A step at a time, we have gone about reclaiming our lives for ourselves. New understanding of ourselves has come with patience and willingness; we do not suddenly find ourselves "struck" responsible! Our journey prepares us as we go. Gradually, we discover that a major difference has set in. Instead of focusing on what other people have done, we begin looking at *our* role in whatever has happened in our lives. Along with what we see about ourselves, we are also aware that the value of recovery, in which we are no longer victims but the source of change, has shifted many of our priorities. In Step Nine, the time has come for us to live through with others the experience of being who we are now, instead of who we have been in the past.

Working at recovery has helped us to see that we cannot be rescued from life. Exactly as it is, and exactly as we are, we have learned that we have the opportunity to live through our experiences. This does not mean merely to suffer through and survive them, for that is closer to "dying-through" than living-through. Living-through means that we have the ability to be the man or the woman we are—to show up with our own strength and weakness, our own power and our own vulnerability—instead of being invisible. Showing up in our lives and living through them, experiencing an authentic relationship with everything and everyone in the world, especially ourselves, is a vital affirmation that supports our recovery.

Each Step encourages us to act in a new way instead of continuing in the old ways with the old rules. Step Eight began the process of going beyond ourselves to consider our relationships with others. No matter what we may have done in the past, we were encouraged to become willing to make amends to the people we have harmed. This is a major change for us. If and when we ever said we were sorry about anything we had done to someone in the past, it was usually because we wanted something from them. In our recovery, when we make amends to parents, family members, friends, lovers, it is because we understand that our lives as abstinent gay and bisexual people depend on it.

Showing up for ourselves makes it possible for us to live through who we really are, as well as provides us with the surprising experience of who others really are. For many of us, it is a first. Whether others accept it or not, it is an invitation for all parties to show up. When we arrive here in this new space together, we can begin to learn about emotional intimacy. In our new honesty, in learning to talk about how we really feel, about who we really are, our fears, our hopes, sadness and joys, we become authentic. Coming home to ourselves with authenticity makes us whole.

The fragmentation we created because of our need to hide from others reached its furthest limits in our previous behavior. In contrast with this, every effort we have been making to recover has been centered on developing a wholeness, a core of identity, that can be known by everyone and nurtured with honesty and self-esteem. Invisibility supports neither. We are aware that we no longer need deceit and invisibility for protection because we are developing a new way to live by working the Steps.

Fear, Guilt, and Resentments

Throughout most of our lives, the fear and guilt that being homosexual or bisexual created in us have been the basis for the way we related with other people. If we examine our work from Step Eight, we will be startled to count how many people on our list have been harmed not because we intended it but because of this source of fear and guilt. Whether they were gay or nongay, our interactions with them have often been influenced by the protection we sought in invisibility instead of honesty. Terrified of ever being totally ourselves, we have said and done things that cheated both them and us of authenticity. When we cheat others, the effect on us is that we must always suffer the consequences in some kind of inner loss.

Along with losing others' trust, we have lost our own self-esteem as well as our own power to create happiness and satisfaction in our lives. In our fear and guilt, we have given away to others the power to approve of us or to deny us approval. In this process, we have become people pleasers, manipulators, victims, and escape artists. Much of the harm we have done has been in wearing these disguises. It is mind-boggling to realize that all we really have to do to change this is get in touch with our feelings, and trust those we love to talk with about these feelings!

Instead of continuing to live invisibly or behind disguises, we need to live-through the experience of acknowledging the roles we have played in the lives of the people whose names we wrote on our lists. Journeying further into recovery means that we face them with our honesty and accept responsibility for our actions because that is how we restore our self-esteem and our power to live our lives completely and spontaneously.

In taking Step Nine, we have to find words that seem right to us. There is no accepted formula for making amends. Face to face, on the telephone, in letters, some people go into great detail about all the harm they have done in the past. Others keep it as simple as possible and say, "I'm sorry." Many have written letters to people who are no longer alive; sometimes they read these to a sponsor, and then burn them. We need to do what works for us in recovery and allow ourselves the opportunity of making mistakes. It is surprising how we seem to "accidentally" meet people to make amends to once we have become willing to do this!

What is it like to make amends? "I never thought you'd have the courage." "You must have been a very unhappy person." "It seemed as if you were oblivious to anyone except yourself." "Wow! I've never met anyone before who would take responsibility for something he could have gotten away with." "It sounds to me as if you've been through hell and back." "What a shock! So much is explained, now that I know. Thank you." "I never understood you before, and I don't understand you now!" "It's too late; but I'm glad you told me." "I'm glad you finally found out who you are. Keep it up!" "Listen, I never want to see you again; and no matter what you say, I'll never forgive you."

Not everyone we make amends to can accept them. Some of the people we have harmed are unwilling to let go of the deep resentments they have over the way we have treated them. There is nothing we can do but accept it. The new rules we are learning to live with in recovery no longer include fixing other people. Their resentments belong to them, and we must allow those who choose to hold on to resentments to stick with them.

What is important for us to be aware of is that the control these people had over our lives has been rooted in the power we have given them. They have used it like a club over us and it is not surprising that they are unwilling to loosen the grip that it gave them. That we will no longer be victims is a loss certain people do not easily accept. We threaten the precarious balance of every unhealthy relationship when we insist on getting well.

Unfortunately, even before as well as during our use of compulsive/dependent behavior, we have been in relationships with some people we would not have chosen had we been healthier. In addition to these people who have become our friends and our lovers, many of us have families who have been deeply affected by the same dysfunctional environments in which we grew up as children or lived in as adults. Dependence on substances has affected every family member because it never functions in isolation. Many of these family members are themselves still drinking and using, and that is their choice. Nevertheless, we can still make amends to them for what *we* have done and go on from there.

Our recovery depends on the efforts we are willing to make to get rid of our resentments, and nothing supports resentment like guilt and shame. Clearing out the wreckage of our past can only be accomplished through:

- the willingness to deal with these resentments;
- the acceptance of responsibility for what we have done to create them;
- taking action by making amends to those we have harmed.

We became prisoners of the harm we have done to others, and we have harmed ourselves by it. When we ask others to accept our amends for what we have done to them, we release ourselves from the prison in which we have lived our lives.

It is a risk few of us considered taking. "What if they refuse even to talk to me, let alone forgive me?" "Is this some kind of religious ritual that everyone has to undergo in order to work the Twelve Steps?" "What about the advice we've been given: 'What anybody else thinks of me is none of my business'?" The resistance to taking Step Nine takes many forms, and people in recovery frequently balk at it. There is no turning back from it, however, because we change our rules for living by actually living in a different way from the past! Where we used to run from confrontations, where we buried or numbed our feelings with substances and compulsive behavior, now we deal with life head-on and discover we will be okay.

By putting ourselves at the top of the list, which is one way to begin our inventories in Step Eight, we can gain some valuable experience when we begin work on Step Nine. Forgiving ourselves is a process that goes to the heart of recovery because we know, perhaps better than anyone else, all that we did to wreck our lives in the past. To begin to forgive ourselves for this, to be willing to give up the shame and guilt we have stockpiled over the years, to face ourselves with the facts instead of the fantasies, is a momentous task.

This Step also takes a great deal of time. It is not possible to complete in weeks, or months, or even years. We find ourselves remembering more and more about the past and the people who lived it with us as we continue our journey in recovery. Over the years, no matter how long it takes, we discover that no one can rescue us from the work that must be done on the obstacles that fear, shame, and guilt create in our lives. The only way forward is to live-through them—to show up and experience ourselves as we are, as we have become, and to let that be a positive moment in our lives instead of a source for punishment and harm for ourselves. We learn to love ourselves as we are when we forgive ourselves our past.

One of the most precious things we have to learn is that when we confront the obstacle, whatever or whoever it is, we do not collapse. Instead of our worst scenarios, usually something occurs far better than we ever expected. This will no doubt have a major impact on changing the way we relate as adults with everyone. The little boy descending the staircase, who was certain he was going to come apart when he confronted the world, discovered through Step Nine that invisibility was no longer an alternative to showing up.

All of us have told ourselves many things about the way we must live our lives as gay, lesbian, and bisexual people. We have been afraid of doing and not doing at the same time. We have been afraid of others and loved them at the same time. We have been afraid to discover, to reach out, to be who we wish to be, and, at the same time, we have discovered and reached out. But we have not been the person we wished to be; we have been afraid to live, and still went on living.

We have invited and allowed fears to be put there by others as well as ourselves. Many of these have had to do with images and ideas of ourselves as "me" and "not me": "Oh, I can't do that because it's not me!" It is easier to live in imagination than risk the real test: "I'd rather not know what they want than have to deal with the truth!" The list of fearful things we told ourselves is endless, and many of us may even be afraid of living *without* those fears! In recovery, we have the opportunity to change our rules and confront these fears. The test of our ability comes when we face first ourselves, and then other people, and push right on through the fears we have that we are *not* okay and *not* forgivable.

Showing Up in Our Lives

Instead of escaping as we have done in the past, we take every opportunity to become active participants instead of invisible players. The dreadful anxiety we have endured over what others will do when we make amends to them becomes dreadless when we actually do it. We live-through it, and each time we do, our self-esteem increases. Because we have the courage to ask, whether or not they grant it, we have taken the action that living responsibly requires. We have shown up in our lives, and head to head with others, we now have the possibility of honest interaction with them.

Through our efforts to make amends, we end the fragmentation that has always dispersed our lives. Having lived-through the encounters with people and relationships that have been riddled with survival behavior, we can begin to experience healthy responses to other people. Step Nine presents us with the opportunity to gain insights acquired through action. Each of us needs these insights in order to enter into a different relationship with our lives.

Working on this Step early in recovery brings great relief to the confusion of confronting other people from the past. Making amends today clears the way to change how they will behave in the future. Nevertheless, we should avoid rushing into other people's lives with our amends. The hurt we have brought to some of them is very deep, and our own healing process must be far enough along to support us through the confrontation. Remembering that we choose to take this Step not for them but for ourselves, we cannot expect more than they can give. And whatever they give will have to be enough. Forgiveness is a gift that healthy people can grant freely because it belongs entirely to them. It allows them to get on with the business of their lives, but they must discover this for themselves. For those with the courage to offer it, the healing it brings will help them begin to put the pieces of their lives back together again.

The act itself helps us to make amends to ourselves by celebrating a new way to live responsibly with the people who have been in our lives, the people from whom we have hidden through our invisibility, denial, and dishonesty. In recovery, we are entitled to our place at the family table of the human race, and we need to claim it.

❄︎　　❄︎　　❄︎

Owning your actions with others in the past restores a perspective of wholeness to your life. Fragmentation is the result of refusing to acknowledge responsibility for past actions. Fragmentation feeds on itself to create smaller and smaller pieces.

Making amends to others is a cleansing activity. Removing the debris from old relationships helps you to enter into a different, better, healthier relationship with yourself and others now and in the future. It is essential for this healing process to include self-forgiveness.

※　　※　　※

Write a journal entry about forgiving yourself. Do this exercise several days in a row, or perhaps once a week for the next three weeks.

※　　※　　※

Whether others forgive you or not, the fact that you are making the effort and are taking responsibility for your life in the past creates a new configuration in which to live a new life.

"To amend" means "to change," "to do something differently."

1. What does this mean to you now as you translate your willingness into specific action with individuals on your list?

    _____

    _____

    _____

2. Divide a page in your journal into two columns. Write at the top of the left column: *Past Actions;* at the top of the right column: *New Actions*. Then, begin with the first name on your list and complete the two columns as you consider:

    • How have I acted with this person in the past?

    • How might I act with this person in the future?

    • What specific actions will I undertake with this person?

    • Before you move on to the next person, note the ways these changes will affect your physical, emotional, and spiritual life.

3. Discuss your plans with your supports and record their suggestions. With your supports, role-play what you plan to say to others. Ask for feedback. Be sure to include in your journal what this experience is like for you.

_____

_____

_____

4. Making amends always entails altering attitudes and this precedes actions. What attitudes will you need to alter and monitor as you work to repair specific relationships?

_____

_____

_____

5. Rank numerically the order of difficulty that you expect to encounter as you interact with the individuals on your list.

_____

_____

_____

_____

_____

_____

6. Select someone on your list who you expect will present fewer difficulties for you to make amends to. *(Discuss this with your supports.)* When reasonably prepared, arrange to meet that person and begin the amends process.

7. Record your experience of initiating the amends process with this individual. Include what you learned, how you coped with your feelings, and how you coped with his or her feelings/reactions.

_____

_____

_____

_____

_____

8. While you were face to face with the other person, how "visible" did you experience yourself to be? How "visible" were you able to be with this person with regard to your sexual orientation, your vulnerability, your motivations, your concerns, and the meaning this relationship has for you?

_____

_____

_____

_____

_____

_____

_____

9. How did you cope with feelings of guilt, discomfort, and anxiety during this meeting?

_____

_____

_____

10. What past disguises were tempting for you to hide behind?

_____

_____

_____

11. What impact has this experience had on your ability to affirm yourself as a sexual minority?

_____

_____

_____

12. How has this experience impacted your confidence and motivation to continue to make further amends to people on your list?

_____

_____

_____

13. What additional work might you need to do on yourself in order to continue this amends process?

_____

_____

_____

This process of mending relationships will continue to help you move from irresponsibility to greater responsibility in interpersonal relationships. Getting started is a BIG STEP. Don't delay! Any roadblocks you may experience in this process may be signs that you need further assistance from your supports. If you find yourself unable to continue with the rest of the people on your list, this suggests that you require additional skills or support from different sources. Real progress lies in this direction.

CHAPTER 21

Putting OTHERS into Perspective

Acceptance of others, after all the victimization and oppression and other consequences of societal homophobia, is a process that requires attention and effort. This important work must be done if real balance is to be achieved. When we are ready for it, we need to accept responsibility for our actions with others in order to disperse the self-delusion, fantasy, and shame that disorders our lives.

The wreckage of the past does not simply disappear because we are now in recovery. What *is* changed is that we are honest with ourselves about our responsibility and are now treating others and ourselves differently. We have begun this by setting the record straight with our amends.

"If I have no past, is it possible for me to have a future?" The excesses in which we have squandered our lives add up to _____ (fill in the blank). But it is, nevertheless, the saga we have lived. As soon as we are ready, we take responsibility for what happened and go on from there, unlike in the past, when we merely lived in the desperation of the story, day after endless day. We have been given the opportunity to take responsibility for living a healthy and productive life in recovery instead of only reliving the past.

※　　※　　※

In this section, you are invited to return for another view of some of the issues raised earlier. Some of your answers to previous questions may have changed in the interim since you wrote them.

1. These are some statements regarding the ways you have treated others. *Feel free to add others to the list:*

   • We'll do it *my* way or not at all!

   • I'll cheat you before you can cheat me.

   • No one ever gave *me* a break!

   • I'm only doing this for your own good.

   • See if I care!

   • Life is so unfair.

   • Everyone is out to get me!

   • You know best.

   • _____

   • _____

   • _____

   • _____

2. Which of these statements describe any of your attitudes toward people on your list to whom you are making amends?

   _____

   _____

   _____

3. Which, if any, attitudes are you willing to alter at this time?

   _____

   _____

   _____

4. How does the harm that you have done to others get in the way of making amends to them?

_____

_____

_____

5. How does the harm they have done to you get in your way of mending your part of the relationship with them?

_____

_____

_____

6. What disguises do you imagine others were wearing in their relationship with you? Put yourself in their place and describe these disguises.

_____

_____

_____

7. How does this help you to understand others who are interested in you?

_____

_____

_____

8. What steps are you taking to learn compassion for your own internalized homophobia?

_____

_____

_____

9. What steps are you taking to learn compassion for others' homophobia?

_____

_____

_____

10. How has this learning process helped you to develop confidence as well as motivate you to make further efforts to change your relationships with others on your list?

_____

_____

_____

11. What additional work might you need to do on yourself in order to continue this amends process?

_____

_____

_____

12. What information about you might be helpful for others to learn as you work to relate differently with them?

_____

_____

_____

13. Draw a time line that begins from today and identify the dates in the next twelve to twenty-four months by which you would like to make efforts to mend the relationship with the people on your Step Eight list.

Today	**12 Months**	**24 Months**

14. If there are reasons why you cannot initiate this process with any of these people, write about these reasons in your journal.

15. We have often experienced how our fears and our secrets isolate us from others. Taking Step Nine marks a change from this pattern. Are you willing to use this Step to work directly on changing the way you relate to other people in your life?

☐ Yes   ☐ No

If the answer is no, whom can you turn to for help with this?

_____

_____

_____

CHAPTER 22

The Way Out of Cross-Purposes

CONDITION
Back-sliding

Fragmentation is the effect of cross-purposes on the individual's inner life. We disperse our energy in the conflicts that bombard us. This continues even in recovery. Addictive/compulsive behavior stymies performance; in recovery, energy is restored, and we still find ourselves at the mercy of competing desires and talents.

ALTERNATIVE
Self-discipline

Staying close to the mirror of observation, we come to understand ourselves through what we actually do and not what goes on in our imagination. Slipping into delusion is easy after the habits of a lifetime; staying in reality takes vigilance and daily effort. Unless we establish a list of priorities for action, our efforts at taking inventory seem to evaporate. We need to keep our list simple no matter how far along we are in the recovery process.

Step 10

Continued to take personal inventory and when we were wrong promptly admitted it.

Did any of us believe we would come this far in our journey into recovery? Not that we haven't been in unpredictable or risky places before as gays, lesbians, and bisexuals. But this is the first time we find ourselves so much more a part of, instead of apart from, the place we live in and the people we live with. Now, as active participants in the routine events that once bored or frightened us, we have stepped out of our fantasies, shared our secrets, and allowed ourselves our feelings instead of living only in our thoughts. We have observed the process at work and the effort required of us to make changes. This has meant that we show up now exactly as we are in our lives instead of wearing any disguises. Now, we can work at connecting our feelings with our thoughts instead of living as if their estrangement was as much a part of our recovery as it was of our past.

Becoming Part Of

Identifying the obstacles to recovery within ourselves as well as those outside ourselves has been very important. Only after we have done this can we begin to use our energy directly on the task of working through our problems instead of obsessing over the obstacles. Old patterns have, nevertheless, stuck with us. We have experienced considerable confusion over how to live in recovery, not to mention the vast uncertainty and vulnerability we still feel without the support of the substances and behavior we previously used for relieving our discomfort. Any one or all of these obstacles may get in the way and alarm us enough to wonder if we have made any progress at all in our journey.

For many of us, perhaps, it seems a long time ago that we set out on the road. We have begun to take for granted finding ourselves in today, alive and in recovery. This has even provoked in us an occasional response, "So what?" It is strange how so many of those "terrible" and "wonderful" things we did in the past may now seem much less terrible OR wonderful. Our perspective has definitely shifted away from such dramatic contrasts, for we no longer need to constantly create them on our own any longer. While none of this has been easy, we now consider all that behind us. "But isn't there something *more?*" we ask.

Once we have passed through the ordeal of withdrawal, our bodies responded with amazing changes that we have come to accept as natural. Since then, our minds have begun clearing slowly but surely. We can now remember where we parked the car, if we still have a car, and whether or not we ate or slept the night before. (Remember, also, that some of our difficulties/impairments may be a result of the normal aging process, or other trauma or injury in the past.) We no longer open our eyes in the morning to find ourselves in strange beds with people we have never seen before. "Is that all there is?"

One important discovery we have made about our new lives is that as sexual minorities we are a part of, instead of separate from, the human race; that we contribute to it every time we make the effort—even if we are only a witness to what happens. Witnessing life is, for us, as essential as an audience is to a performance in the theater. *Every one of us is necessary.* We have been invited to life, and the celebration is going on all the time. We understand that we must assert that we shall be welcome members of the troupe, the assemblage . . . the family. That's the meaning of the precious invitation we have accepted in recovery.

Along with this invitation has come the opportunity to enjoy life, to find happiness as we discover ourselves in it. We do this by sharing ourselves with others. Sharing what we feel and understand with others is something we have learned that we *can* do—with practice and support. The Twelve Steps have provided us with the unusual opportunity to be a friend, an ally in recovery, a sponsee or sponsor, and a witness to others who know nothing more than that they are suffering the calamity of addictive/compulsive behavior. When we choose to share our gift, it becomes an act of recovery.

Gratitude Is an Attitude

Most of the people we meet on the journey have felt deeply grateful at being given another chance at life. Think back to school days and a subject you weren't very good at. Remember being told: "You're going to do it until you get it right." At the time, that was a punishment. Getting it right, now, means something quite different from what it meant years ago. It's about living life without addictive substances and compulsive behavior. As bewildering as it seems, all of us have been given this chance in recovery, and we need to learn that just being alive means we deserve this chance. Gradually learning to love ourselves more each day, we come to realize without reservation that we deserve the best!

Gratitude can open the way to wonder. We may be filled with wonder about everything and everyone each day. Life is incredible. The feast it provides is always filled with surprises, from hearing words of gratitude we never thought would come from our mouths in the morning to closing our eyes without pain at night. All too many of us had never known what some of the basic experiences in life were like without our fix. What we did, whom we did it with, whether or not we enjoyed it was more or less a blur. For those who may need some reassurance, sex is a glorious new discovery in recovery! Now, just like adolescents, it can fill us with wonder for the first time.

Isn't it amazing that almost nothing is the way we have planned it? Usually, it's much *better.* We are filled with spontaneity instead of the deadening desire to manipulate results. We are able to decide what we wish to do in each day and to know we will not arrive drunk or "high" for it. Of course, we never know what actual events will happen, and that is exciting. In the beginning, this takes getting used to.

There are even more changes. Instead of our gnawing self-centeredness, many of the people in recovery we have met have become terribly important to us. Because they have gotten to know us and to let us know them, they have given us the opportunity for living in new ways. They have become the mirror in which we have been able to see ourselves without turning away. Through them, it has even been possible to love things in ourselves we never could have loved without them. Beginning to care about ourselves has helped us make the passage through some very difficult seas of self-discovery.

To our amazement, those new gay and nongay friends have been there for us when we least expected it. They have become loving companions, even when we have traveled to other cities on business or on a holiday. To our amazement, they did not abandon or desert us when we needed them. Many people who have gone to AA or other Twelve Step gatherings have heard, "Keep coming back," no matter what they'd shared at meetings. It is essential to have support from companions who can accompany us through some harrowing places. This will teach us it is possible to live a different way because of their concern and love. Instead of finding ourselves alone in early recovery, we can choose to surround ourselves by a great company of survivors who can live productive lives—with the support of each other. We can do this because we have already lived through this experience together.

The Need for Personal Inventory

Why, then, do we need to begin working on Step Ten? Isn't all that "old stuff" behind us? Haven't we proved we can live without substances as well as other addictive behavior? What is the point of stirring things up in lives that have finally settled down? Having already gone through an inventory of secrets and people, why do we need to begin working on a *daily* inventory of ourselves? Many of the people who find this suggestion most irritating also discover themselves taking recovery more and more for granted in their lives.

This Step is not an exercise for victims who need grist for their suffering mill. The effects of what we have been through do not all miraculously disappear in recovery: "Alcoholism is an '*ism*' not a '*was*m.'" But unless we understand how this applies to and operates in our lives with our own material, we begin to take it for granted. In time, we may even forget it. Forgetting, denial, and minimization are first cousins.

In Steps Four and Eight, the inventories we wrote revealed many things that otherwise would have continued to feed our patterns of denial. By bringing these crucial aspects of ourselves into the light, by confronting the past and the way we lived it, we have learned to live-through all we have done instead of needing to escape from it. In Step Ten, we begin applying the same technique to the present, to our daily lives just as we live them. We begin to see what we do, and how we interpret it, in today.

Each of the three inventory Steps deals directly with raising our level of consciousness about people, places, and things, and our relationship with them. Both as children and as compulsive/dependent grown-ups, we were oblivious to anything more than being carried away with what-happened-next and taking for granted that something "next" would happen. Some of us may still retain vivid memories of a great deal that went on then. In the past, however, many of us have been told about our blackouts in which we remember nothing about anything, or "brownouts" in which we have only blurred recollections we cannot be certain of. Recovery calls for developing a new manner of living, and taking a daily inventory of our lives is one way of accepting responsibility for continuing to grow instead of taking it for granted. This inventory provides us with a useful tool for showing up for our lives today with the person we are becoming.

Revealing ourselves *to* ourselves raises our level of consciousness. With the enhancement that this perspective of our lives gives us, we get many new insights about both recovery and the old habits we had developed. Among the first things we notice is that many of the same problems that beset us in the past are still with us in the present! Problems having to do with anger, envy, control, self-pity, and intimacy continue to come up for us, and they still throw us off balance. They can ruin our day and prevent us from sleeping at night, as well.

In recovery, we need to face these problems and learn to deal with them, because our journey continues *through* these confrontations and not around them. Does this voice sound familiar? "Is this what I got into recovery for?" "Why is it that when things get screwed up in my life, I'm always around?" "Back again to square one! Damn it!" "What a disappointment! What better reason to pick up and use again?" This is self-destructive thinking that pounds at us through that critical voice, and tries to push us back again into self-destructive behavior. For all of us, changing the critical voice to a loving one can be one of the biggest hurdles of recovery.

We did not use substances or behave compulsively over nothing. Whatever these reasons were, what we did to escape made every one of them worse. Through our efforts to work the Twelve Steps, we have discovered that we are able to live without the substances or behavior we used. Now, we need to prove to ourselves that we can survive our problems as well, no matter what they are. Finding ourselves back in the place we left off, however, we are thrown into confusion not only by starting to live our lives again but also by the effects of the condition that we left behind. Addictive/compulsive behavior is very disorienting. It is helpful to remind ourselves continually of this instead of dismissing it.

We have survived a major catastrophe and are now recuperating from it. Our attitude toward ourselves in the midst of this transition is important. We need to be loving and understanding. We need to learn new ways to help ourselves through dark passages and to appreciate our efforts and accomplishments even as we struggle with our obstacles. This takes being committed to ourselves and to our willingness to change. By loving ourselves and giving up being critical of ourselves, we begin to do this.

This new attitude of support is entirely different from the condition of self-pity we are familiar with. Supporting ourselves makes us a friend instead of an enemy. In the past, we have often been our own enemies when we have used our energy and the energy of others to fragment and destroy ourselves. Now, our challenge is to use this energy to grow and create a new life. And instead of making obstacles of ourselves, we have learned about the process of acceptance—of ourselves AND others—and what it means to live-through it.

Loving Ourselves

Many gays, lesbians, and bisexuals have years of experience withholding love from themselves and rejecting others as well. Becoming a friend to ourselves takes time. We have become abstinent, but that doesn't mean that either we or the world has become loving and nurturing. Because we are the source, we are the ones who must introduce this love through our own efforts—both with ourselves and with others.

Like a bellows from which a destructive perspective has been gradually emptied and then refilled with healthy ideas, our lives have breathed extremes. We have been learning and relearning how to be loving and patient, how to be our own friend. There is no protocol for doing this; in each situation it has to be created out of all the elements that are present.

One requirement, however, is basic: it is never possible to create a new life when we are our own enemies. Only through the integration of our conflicting wishes and abilities is it possible to live creatively in new ways. When we work on Step Ten, we discover a great deal of the information that we need to know about our wishes, abilities, and talents. These data form the basis on which to build a new inner relationship that is the foundation for positive self-caring.

We will be astonished, when we work on this Step, to discover how we have begun using our energy in so many different directions. Feeling healthier and better grounded emotionally than we ever did before, we have taken on many new responsibilities that make conflicting demands on our time and resources. We have gotten involved with new friends in recovery and some, perhaps, who have not had problems with substances or compulsive behavior. Many of us are back working at our old jobs, or new ones, and we have found ourselves once again in contact with family. Emerging from isolation, we have encountered people, places, and things that push our buttons in many of the same old ways as before. The effect of this is that we feel at cross-purposes some of the time—knowing what we should do, yet acting differently. It is good to know that the help we need to handle this is the help we get from working Step Ten.

By working Step Ten we prevent ourselves from being completely carried away by the cross-purposes that vie for our energy. Through a daily willingness to continually examine what is going on in our lives, it is possible to have some clearer perspective of ourselves. In recovery, many things happen to us and to others we care about, and we react. Instead of fastening ourselves to these events, to these reactions out of which we make obstacles, as if it were only by doing this that we had any reality, we can choose to separate from them. Listing them in our inventories, we may discover that we have halted before these obstacles only because it appears that we have reached our limit. The truth is that we have reached *their* limit and, with the efforts we have been learning to make, we can use our energy to pass through them.

In recovery, we have asked others to treat us differently and we must learn to do the same ourselves. Do we even have any idea how to do this? The daily inventory creates a dialogue with ourselves that encourages communication about what is going right and what is going wrong in our lives. Everything that is laid out in it helps reveal to us what works and what doesn't. In the past, we lived from disaster to disaster. Now, instead of waiting until disaster strikes, we can learn to recognize danger signals and self-defeating patterns early and to take the appropriate steps before these situations get out of hand.

Becoming our own friend is an active process in which we also stay honest with ourselves. We don't keep secrets any longer—not even from ourselves—and Step Ten provides us with a pattern of new behavior to accomplish this.

Without realizing it, we began developing this opportunity in Step Four. Whether we did it a long time ago or recently, most of us left out a great deal on the initial inventory. No one has ever taken Step Four perfectly. Nevertheless, what we wrote at that time in our journey was all we were capable of recording because of our limited awareness at that time. However, it was crucial for our recovery that we did it, for it cleared out space in which we could develop new and more adaptive patterns. If we will use Step Ten as it is intended, we can continue to have the benefit of more and more working space in which to grow.

Monitoring Perfectionism

As we look at ourselves each day from the perspective of what we need to do in order to grow, we get some major support in dealing with one of our major shortcomings: perfectionism. Individuals in recovery struggle with this problem no matter how long we are substance free. Even though we are constantly reminded not to take other people's inventories, we do it anyway. Perhaps it has caused resentment here and there, or even some serious rifts in new relationships. This is a pattern we have grown up with all of our lives, and it stays with us in recovery until we practice getting rid of it. When we take responsibility for ourselves, we don't have the energy or the same impetus to blame others.

Being as critical as we can of other people takes some of the heat off ourselves. We are constantly comparing ourselves with others even though we have been told how counterproductive this is. Who among us ever think we have progressed as far as we *should* have in our journey? Even though our index finger may point at times at others, three of the other fingers on our hand are always pointing back at ourselves. Most of us are even oblivious as to the frequency with which we do it, and that is one of the old habits Step Ten can reveal.

In recovery, we need to develop new behaviors to replace the old ones. As each of the other Steps before this has suggested, we have to use our own experience in order to progress beyond the limit we have reached. As each of us has learned through sharing with others in recovery, our experience *can* benefit others. In Step Ten, we can begin—in a very conscious manner—to allow this same experience to benefit *ourselves*. We can monitor our perfectionism by taking a daily inventory of it.

None of us is perfect nor could we be. Yet often we think of ourselves and criticize ourselves as if we were or should be perfect. It is no wonder that we continue to function at cross-purposes with ourselves. Completing a daily inventory grounds us with the evidence we need in order to continue our journey in recovery instead of turning off and getting lost again in self-defeating thinking. No matter how long we have abstained from the "cunning, baffling and powerful" substances and behavior we used, they still exist for us to use again. We can still let them affect our minds, and allow our thoughts to play tricks on us. It is all too easy for us to find ourselves going off on mental tangents that, if pursued far enough, would end in substance abuse or other equally self-destructive results all over again.

Instead of getting lost in these thoughts, we can look at the evidence that a daily inventory provides us:

- What have we done, and how are we reacting to it?
- What did we plan to do, and what have we put off doing?
- What problems as well as what solutions have we found in relating honestly with others?
- What new secrets, obstacles, and limitations have shown up in our lives?
- What can we be grateful for?

The answers to these questions provide us with the evidence we need to put the quest for perfectionism into proper perspective.

"And when we were wrong promptly admitted it," Step Ten concludes. The perfectionist in each of us needs this kind of direction. It highlights the fact that more important than being right is the value to us of admitting when we are wrong. The perfectionist attitude leaves us always with the terror of making mistakes, and the fear of failure as well as the fear of success. It is an unbearable burden to carry around for life. It is a root cause of inaction, escape, depression, and despair. In the past, the use of substances and compulsive behavior provided relief from these fears for a time because they deadened or anesthetized feelings. That relief ultimately ended; the fix stopped working. Like everything else we tried, using it turned into another mistake instead.

No one likes either to make or admit mistakes. In recovery, we need to change the rule that mistakes mean we have failed and that we are worthless human beings. In place of this, we can give ourselves permission to make as many mistakes as we need to every day of our lives—to be human. Only by changing our old rules in this way can we experience ourselves as imperfect beings. We can stop trying to live some dream of perfection that truly does not work in reality. We know that it does not work because we have tried it. No matter how high we managed to get, the escalator of reality was always there to take us back.

Being alive in recovery means we are going to make mistakes. Step Ten provides us with a safety net to prevent us from becoming overwhelmed by these mistakes. From our old secrets, we know that we *will* be overwhelmed unless we reveal them. Promptly admitting our mistakes, both to ourselves and to others, prevents us from being overwhelmed by them. Neither the world nor any one of us falls apart when we do it. That is recovery!

Action Instead of Reaction

The essential elements of the Twelve Steps can be encapsulated in these three simple sentences: "Things happen. I react to them. Life goes on." In recovery, we can learn to act on our behalf instead of merely reacting to others. There is a big change in us when we do this. We learn how to live in a new way through the efforts we make to act, rather than react, each day.

Often, we are confused by what goes on around us, and rarely can we see order in any of it. But we have lived long enough in our illusions to know that fantasy does not provide us with what we seek. Instead, the evidence that appears in our daily inventories points the way. Understanding and accepting the experience of our lives, as far as we are willing to be conscious of it, is the help we need in order to get on with the task. Confronting the things that happen to us, when they happen, and taking action to deal with the issues or problems created make it possible for us to go on with our lives in a healthy manner.

Many people are willing to work on all of the Steps except this one. Step Ten requires the kind of self-discipline and vigilance that we wish in others but which we excuse in ourselves. We need to realize that by doing Step Ten each day, many of our problems will no longer be problems. For some, this will involve actually writing down a list, or talking about their day with another. For others, it may mean some quiet time alone, with an unhurried look at the events of the day. It seems that many of us would rather suffer with our problems than make a daily inventory from which we could get some insight about solving these problems. The pattern of suffering is hardest of all to break, but it is not as difficult as we imagine.

A driver on a shuttle bus in Yosemite National Park suddenly announced to his passengers: "This bus is leaving Stop Eight, Yosemite Lodge, and will not be returning. This is the last bus tonight. Please deal with this fact *now;* do not wait until later!" Step Ten invites all of us to deal with what is going right and what is going wrong in our lives right now. Continuing on with our journey depends on creating this inventory.

We find ourselves back again at the question of priorities. Step Ten not only provides us with the assistance we need in order to set up these priorities for dealing with our problems, it also becomes a priority in our recovery when we make it one. The paradox is waiting for us: out of the disorder that shows up in our daily inventory, it is possible to begin to live in harmony with ourselves. We "keep it simple" when we establish priorities for dealing with our problems.

❈   ❈   ❈

The fragmentation in our external lives was *the effect of cross-purposes on our own inner lives.* The harm we caused others was often unintentional and rarely, if ever, did it penetrate the fantasy life we lived. So many ideas; so many projects; how could we help not being caught up in doing them at the expense of our relationships!

❄ ❄ ❄

It is essential to stay close to the mirror of observation. Change is possible because we come to understand ourselves through what we actually do day by day and not what we wish to do. Slipping into delusion is easy after a lifetime of doing it; staying in reality takes vigilance and daily effort. Taking pride in the efforts we have made assists us in not taking change for granted. Consider making several entries in your journal about some of the areas you wish to remember not to take for granted.

❄ ❄ ❄

1. Now that you have developed a different perspective of yourself (Steps Four through Seven) and others (Steps Eight and Nine), what is your revised definition of "change"? (Refer to your response in the exercise at the beginning of the workbook. See pages 68–69 and page 81.)

_____

_____

_____

2. What new perspective of recovery does this provide?

_____

_____

_____

3. Describe how this new perspective compares with your initial understanding of recovery.

_____

_____

_____

4. In what way have the inventories you have already developed provided you with opportunities for change?

_____

_____

_____

5. When you have encountered resistance in writing the inventories, what have you learned from the actual accomplishment of the tasks?

_____

_____

_____

6. How can you relate this to the need for doing a daily inventory?

_____

_____

_____

7. Of the three forms of taking this daily inventory—writing it down, sharing it with someone else, or including in your daily routine a "quiet time"—what are the advantages/disadvantages of each of them for you? Write them below:

	Advantages	**Disadvantages**
Writing:	_____	_____
	_____	_____
	_____	_____
	_____	_____
Sharing with someone:	_____	_____
	_____	_____
	_____	_____
	_____	_____
"Quiet time":	_____	_____
	_____	_____
	_____	_____
	_____	_____

8. What alternative approaches to these three would you consider?

   Writing:

   _____

   _____

   Sharing with someone:

   _____

   _____

   "Quiet time":

   _____

   _____

9. Which form will you use on a regular basis and why? *(Be sure to note this on your Action Plan.)*

   _____

   _____

   _____

10. This is an adaptation of the model for the daily inventory that appeared earlier in the chapter:

    - What have you done yesterday, and how are you reacting to it?
    - What did you plan to do, and what have you put off doing?
    - What problems as well as what solutions have you found in relating honestly with others?
    - What new secrets, obstacles, and limitations have shown up in your life?
    - What can you be grateful for?

    Write your answers in your journal to see what doing a daily inventory feels like.

11. What new issues or problems have surfaced recently that you need to work on during your daily inventory? What old issues or problems need to appear on your daily inventory?

    _____

    _____

    _____

12. What new (or old) secrets need to appear on the inventory?

_____

_____

_____

13. Those issues, problems, and secrets that continue to appear may require assistance from others. What are the obstacles in the way of getting help to manage them?

_____

_____

_____

14. Identify three of your major priorities in life.

#1 _____

_____

#2 _____

_____

#3 _____

_____

15. If you have done several daily inventories, what have you learned about how they relate to your priorities?

_____

_____

_____

16. How easy is it for you even now to admit you were wrong about something important to your progress?

Very Easy	Moderately Easy	Moderately Difficult	Difficult
1	2	3	4	5

17. What were the consequences of admitting you were wrong in the past?

_____

_____

_____

18. What does admitting you were wrong or mistaken about something now mean?

_____

_____

_____

19. What material from the exercises you completed on Step Six would be relevant to the work you may need to do when you undertake Step Ten?

_____

_____

_____

_____

20. How does perfectionism mesh with an admission of making a mistake?

_____

_____

_____

21. Identify ways to modify your perfectionism. Be specific. What will you say to yourself? How will you treat yourself? What will mistakes mean to you? How will you work to feel better about yourself when you fall short of perfection?

_____

_____

_____

_____

_____

_____

_____

_____

22. What are your fears about being less than perfect?

_____

_____

_____

23. In what ways can a daily inventory help you to monitor your perfectionism? procrastination? other characteristics? Fill in from your list of shortcomings.

_____

_____

_____

_____

_____

_____

_____

_____

24. How can you structure your time so that Step Ten becomes part of your life?

_____

_____

_____

Establishing priorities for action follows inventory taking. Keeping the focus clear is essential no matter how far along one is in the recovery process. If we ride too many of our wishes, they can take us on a tangent. When we set our sights clearly on specific, concrete changes to our thinking, feeling, and behaving, we move in those directions.

CHAPTER 23

Antidote to Egotism

CONDITION

Self-centeredness

Individuals with addictive/compulsive behavior are fruitlessly in search of self-satisfaction. They are self-seekers above all. Creating a bond with another human being is an impossibility as long as any "fix" inflates the ego with denial and the illusion of self-sufficiency.

ALTERNATIVE

Spiritual connection

Recovery opens the way to real intimacy with others through sharing instead of using, through appreciation instead of only gratification, and through self-revelation instead of dishonesty and secrecy.

Experiencing in our lives a power greater than ourselves, we understand that we did not create this presence on our own. We begin to strive for a deeper connection to ensure the continuation and extension of the benefits we have already received.

Step 11

*Sought through prayer and meditation
to improve our conscious contact with God as we understood [God],
praying only for knowledge of God's will for us and the power to carry that out.*

Our path through early recovery has rarely been easy in spite of the remarkably simple directions that the Steps have offered us. When we have been willing to follow these instructions, we have confronted and passed through major obstacles of our lives. The perfectionist in each of us and the victim, the isolator, the manipulator, and the people pleaser have all undergone major modifications. Getting honest with ourselves has raised our level of consciousness about who we are, what we do, and what happens when we take responsibility for our actions.

Creating Balance

Changing our relationship with ourselves and with other people is an ongoing process that shapes new developments every day of our lives. We may often feel as if the emotional swings we experience have landed us in risky, upsetting situations; nevertheless, we discover that we no longer remain stuck in them. There is movement, and there is space in which to make our way forward as well as to move in any direction. The longer we experience recovery, the more room we have in which to make choices that affirm us as responsible men and women.

As the years pass, we may from time to time encounter the I-who-was-compulsive/dependent. For some, this happens when feeling depressed or troubled; for others when feeling terrific, enthusiastic, or "high on life." However, the most puzzling appearance of this earlier aspect of ourselves is when no dark clouds sit on the horizon and when our focus is above the treetops delighting in the blue of the sky. When the phenomenon appears, we discover that it has stolen into our relaxed minds because of feeling safe enough to come out of hiding. Many in recovery have this experience and have shared the shock of it at a group level. What seems clear is that the space for growth that we have created in our lives will always be filled with something. Old patterns are ready to intrude when the possibility of any vacuum occurs.

Recovery is a different way to live. When we consider the way we lived in the past, we now have a great deal of new data to compare with it. In place of the fragmentation and isolation of our old lives, we understand that we can create balance through working on ourselves each day. Let's remember that extremes will always be waiting for us, and that our opportunity in recovery is to choose to create balance instead of hurling headlong in any direction.

In the beginning, we have no idea what balance means. Through the efforts we make working each of the Steps, we introduce our bodies, emotions, and intellects to this concept. For each of us, along with the efforts we need to make in order to experience it day by day, balance has a very personal meaning.

From deprivation and *im*balance, from being out of control and being swept away, we discover that the energy we create each day can be directed into action that affirms and supports our recovery. What seemed to be the impossible has gradually become reality. We have turned our lives around. Taking an honest look at ourselves, we find we have convincing evidence that tells us we will continue to make progress as long as we are willing to work on ourselves.

Acting AS-IF

All of us began without this evidence, and, at that time, we were encouraged to act AS-IF we had it. Journeying through the first ten Steps, we have accumulated a great deal of evidence of progress. Now, it is essential for us to begin to work through an area some of us either avoided or simply refused to confront earlier—our relationship with a power greater than ourselves, the dimension that begins where we leave off. Recovery does not depend on what we choose to call that source of energy, only that we acknowledge its presence in our lives.

Acting AS-IF required us to make a conscious decision. Even though we may have strongly resisted the idea of a power greater than ourselves, by acting as if it existed, we found ourselves relieved of the crushing burden of isolation. Freed from this burden, we were able to emerge from behind the barriers of bigotry and shame that religion uses to isolate and humiliate sexual minorities. No longer alone, we found ourselves standing in the midst of the multitude of men and women in recovery everywhere. We participated with all of them in the healing power of the group in action. For many of us, the spiritual dimension of our lives unfurled. To our amazement, some of us experienced the presence of a Higher Power in some of the most inaccessible areas of our being. Many of us neither understood how this happened nor gave a name to the source of it.

For those of us who were agnostics, atheists, or fallen-away members of some organized religion, this was something of a miracle! We found ourselves the beneficiaries of a healing power in our lives even though we may have been reluctant to do anything more than act AS-IF this energy were there to tap into. We saw, gradually, that our connection with this force had very little, if anything, to do with our old ideas about religion or God, ideas that had been nurtured and maintained by the homophobic society in which we grew up. That each one of us could experience his or her own connection with the spiritual dimension, apart from any church or doctrine, was a revelation waiting for us in recovery.

The conscious decision to act AS-IF brought results. We drank from a cup that seemed always to have been forbidden to us, and, unlike anything we had ever tasted before or after our entry into recovery, we did not find escape from life but *connection* with it. Something began to happen within us each time we relied on the Serenity Prayer or other prayer or other words we used. A brick at a time, we set in place a different kind of foundation in our lives that had not been there before—no matter how devout we might have thought ourselves to be in the past. We were preparing an availability within us that invited spiritual concerns and awareness to reinspire our old patterns of thought and action.

We began with little things and then, with larger ones, some of us found ourselves more available to spiritual ideas. The egocentricity of our lives began to undergo a modification. Instead of the fruitless pursuit after self-satisfaction and self-gratification, we discovered something happening to us in our own daily lives that was taking the place of self-seeking. When we made ourselves available for life in recovery, we found ourselves involved on a daily basis in caring for and loving ourselves and other people just because we were open to this and not because we were going to get some reward in return. In this process, we discovered that we had somehow gotten out of our own way and were connecting with life in a new way. This connection with ourselves and with others *is* the spiritual connection.

After a spiritual connection has been made in our lives, it is much more difficult to attempt to disguise ourselves as victims. We cannot get away with the old habits of self-pity and self-sabotage when we have forged links that, by their nature, indicate we are worthwhile human beings. Garbage doesn't have a Higher Power. Acting AS-IF we are worth receiving help, we received it, and no one among us could deny the evidence of recovery if we are honest.

Raising Our Consciousness

Steps Ten, Eleven, and Twelve are each concerned with raising our level of consciousness about the essential elements of our lives as gay men, lesbians, and bisexuals in the world of recovery. Step Ten focuses on ourselves, our personhood—who we are, how we are, and what it is like to live inside our bodies, emotions, and intellect on a day-to-day basis. Developing this higher level of consciousness of ourselves through a daily inventory, we have used our own experience to learn to live honestly and productively instead of ricocheting back and forth off the walls of our possibilities.

In Step Eleven, we direct our attention to raising our level of consciousness about a dimension that begins where we leave off—*"as we understand"* this power greater than ourselves. The italics appear in the text of the Step itself to remind us that we are to do this with the new understanding we have been developing in recovery and not the old ideas we operated with.

Just as we benefited earlier from making the conscious decision to act AS-IF this power existed, so will we progress much further in our journey by seeking "through prayer and meditation to improve our conscious contact" with this power. No matter how long we resist, through the experience of our recovery we will come to acknowledge and accept some kind of experience that can be called either a "spiritual awakening" or a spiritual connection within ourselves.

It is remarkable how many people, both gay and nongay, make the same comment after going to Twelve Step meetings for several months: "When I first walked through the door, if anyone would have told me that I was going to start to pray or meditate, I would have turned around and walked out!" Many of us can remember back to that time and admit we were unable to hear very much beyond the distinct message that we didn't have to go on killing ourselves with addictive/compulsive behavior. In what others said to us, we heard hope even if we weren't able to catch all the rest of the words, and we kept coming back. That is how we began the journey, and from that beginning we now find ourselves at Step Eleven.

No matter how often we may hear the Twelve Steps, or even read them ourselves, how many of us think they are meant not for someone else but specifically for ME? It is easy to make this mistake. However, as our minds become clearer and as we begin to do what is suggested in each Step, we may begin to realize that each one builds on previous progress and changes. Even more important than the sequence is the fact that we make conscious efforts to work the Steps.

Until we have spent time, effort, and energy on a Step, we may not be prepared to go on to the next one. When we reach a Step we are having particular difficulty with, one strategy can be to go back to the previous Step and work on it, in conjunction with the basics—Steps One, Two, and Three. A great deal of "unfinished business" can be cleared away by returning to an earlier Step. After we deal with some of these loose ends, unfinished business, we may discover ourselves able to continue forward with the Step that had been previously a stumbling block.

Because the progress of recovery depends on the individual, each of us must work on the Steps at our own speed. Recovery is not a race; it is a journey. We cannot get ahead of ourselves without running the risk of "slipping"—picking up and using old solutions that were part of our past. We need to remind ourselves, as well, not to compare our progress with anyone else's. In addition, it may be self-defeating to compare an earlier period in our own recovery with our present experience. By staying in the present with who we are now, it is possible to leave the past behind instead of living in it. We can give ourselves this support rather than fall back into the old self-defeating patterns (e.g., perfectionism, negative self-talk).

For those who are ready for it, for those who find themselves in recovery asking, "Isn't there something more?" Step Eleven provides direction to proceed on our journey forward.

The better we have come to know ourselves, to honestly reveal who we are to others and to ourselves, the better we have prepared ourselves to make new meaning of our existence in the world in our recovery. Without this knowledge and understanding of ourselves, we lack the connections essential for the development of new and healthy patterns of thought and action. Without them, we are unprepared for a major change in our availability to relate with all our potential for living creative lives.

The health that we, as well as others, observe returning to our bodies and emotions, our thoughts, our relationships has been obvious. What is far less obvious is that the development of our physical and emotional well-being creates a new capacity for spiritual growth along with it. The evidence of this is that we find ourselves no longer "shut down" but, instead, experiencing the wonder of living almost as though we were children once again.

The spiritual deprivation and abuse we experienced as sexual minorities should never be underestimated. The intense physical and emotional isolation, terror, guilt, and shame that we have known in the past was deepened because of our own spiritual void. Our self-seeking in relationships and jobs was rooted in survival, and our overwhelming fear of failure or need to be perfect tormented us in every area of our lives. Even though we had little or no self-esteem, we were still the center of the universe. And, at the end, there was absolutely no one to turn to—not even God! We were abandoned by everyone, including ourselves.

The first effort we had to make to change this was the acknowledgment of our predicament; we had to take Step One. Only after doing this was it possible for help to reach us. Until we were entirely convinced that compulsive/dependent behavior made our lives unmanageable, we stubbornly persisted in trying to manage our lives our own way. Many of us experienced what it was like to be truly vulnerable, in that early stage of recovery, and instead of feeling abandoned, we found ourselves nurtured and supported. Other people, just like ourselves, extended themselves to support us. What seemed at least as incredible as this at the time was that they needed *us* as much as we needed them. All of us found that we had something valuable to offer even as we received support from others.

From the knowledge and understanding we have about the incredible journey all of us make into recovery, it seems clear that our experience of forces beyond ourselves begins from the moment we reach out to help another suffering soul with our own vulnerability. The more efforts we make to reach out, the stronger and deeper is the bond we develop between ourselves and spiritual forces in the world. As bearers of these forces, we become a vital channel for them to function in our own lives as well as in the lives of others. In serving as a channel for this force, we receive the healing benefit ourselves. Through our efforts, we give ourselves a gift that none of our self-seeking could ever have given. It is a paradox that recovery is revealed to us not in some unusual or unique psychic experience but as we live it every day.

Life after Addiction

We did not set out on our journey to serve others; we came through the door because we wanted help and feared the consequences of not getting it. We did as others in recovery and those we selected to support us told us to do, not because we always understood the reasons but because we feared the alternatives if we rejected the help and continued doing more of what was not working. Often, with little faith or hope left in us, we began to work the Steps, not because we believed in them but because we wanted to believe they would work for us. Some of us feared death if we continued with our compulsive/dependent behavior; some of us feared life. It seems an appropriate question, now that we discover that we have a future after all, to ask ourselves: what are we now going to do with our lives?

It may take quite some time after being in recovery before you ask yourself this question. When you do, perhaps you will remember these words:

God has a unique purpose for your life. Find it! Do it!

A friend in San Francisco, who has been in recovery for over forty years, offered this counsel. He rarely, if ever, speaks about God, but this was his big exception. An implicit belief in our own uniqueness is capable of a startling realization when we connect this idea about ourselves with a Higher Power. The possibility of a Higher Power needing *me*—after recovery efforts have helped us to understand we are not as unique as we thought—constitutes a breakthrough into a totally different understanding of Step Eleven. In case this idea is difficult to hold on to, write it down and keep it in a special place for a while. Just allow it to be, without getting in the way:

I am not unique; I am unique!

At the heart of this paradox is the identical insight about aloneness that comes after working on Step Two in early recovery. At that time, it was not possible to be concerned with anything more than the devastating effects of compulsive/dependent behavior. In recovery, however, after working on the first ten Steps, we have prepared the foundation to see ourselves as *capable* of living fully and completely instead of waiting, like victims, for death to find us and take us out of our misery. With both a present *and* a future, like everyone else who lives in recovery, all of us have choices to make that will inevitably reflect our own individual nature—our uniqueness and our *un*-uniqueness.

Thinking back to what our lives were like at the beginning of our journey, back in Step Two, we will remember how we found ourselves caught between the two extremes: "I am alone; I am not alone." Instead of remaining stuck, we were encouraged to attend Twelve Step meetings or to find people in a counseling group who were just like ourselves—recoverers. Our initial efforts to interact with others created the way out of our past and began our journey into health. This happened only because we were willing to take this action. To break out of our isolation, we needed to use our energy to connect with others around us. This required conscious effort; and we had to choose to do this for ourselves, no matter how many reasons presented themselves to resist.

We have come much further in our journey into recovery, and we have learned a great deal more about ourselves and other people along the way. We have become far more conscious of our own actions, and theirs, than ever before in our lives. With this better-developed understanding of ourselves, we now allow Step Eleven to direct us to "*improve* our conscious contact" with a power greater than ourselves. The reason for this is basic. Just as using our energy to connect with the group introduced balance into lives that had been polarized and fragmented, so using our energy to connect with a Higher Power introduces the balance we need now and in the future to pursue our progress in recovery and create meaning out of our lives.

Through a conscious effort to improve this spiritual connection, we discover the way to set in balance those extremes that, no matter how far along we are in recovery, are always waiting for us. Our willingness to become available to this connection in our lives makes us a channel for resolving the conflict and confusion that can arise at any time. In this way, through the effects of prayer and meditation, we are able to create new patterns we can use no matter what the crisis or the victory. Relying on these new patterns, we will be able to introduce balance in our lives.

Back then, in the pain, in the despair and disappointment of compulsive/dependent behavior, we turned to someone or a group of someones for help. Some of us identified the group with a Higher Power; others of us did not. Now, from this vastly different place in ourselves, we know beyond a shadow of a doubt that we have not made this journey alone or without help.

Prayer and Meditation

Prayer is one of the ways we have of making conscious recognition of this understanding within ourselves. Just as honesty has provided us with a foundation for living in harmony with others, so prayer can create and extend in us a spiritual foundation for living in harmony with ourselves.

For many of us, "kill-for" petitions for things we wanted and ardent attempts to apologize for things we have done have figured heavily in the words we said when we tried to use the old patterns of praying given to us when we were children. In recovery, we need to be honest in our prayers about who we are now, instead of who we were, and about what we bring to the dialogue—our strengths along with our weaknesses. As gays, lesbians, and bisexuals, we need to use words that reveal who we are in recovery. For each of us, this can mean many things. Walt Whitman, a gay and great American poet, reminds us of something essential to this revelation of ourselves in these few lines of poetry:

> *Each of us inevitable,*
> *Each of us limitless—each of us with his or her right upon the earth,*
> *Each of us allow'd the eternal purports of the earth,*
> *Each of us here as divinely as any is here.*[1]

Unless we credit ourselves with these entitlements, we withhold ourselves from the healing experience of prayer that is waiting for us in recovery.

Through prayer and meditation we can find our voice. No matter how long it takes us to develop the courage to speak, we need to learn to do this. Only when we speak with our own voice can we stop pretending we are more OR less than ourselves. And, by accepting ourselves—and others—along with everything that is and everything that is not, we make ourselves available to support for living and changing. Only our own words, based on our own personal experience of honesty and gratitude for our lives, will open the way to a spiritual dialogue that begins the moment we are silent. After we have spoken and are ready to listen, the connection with a Higher Power can begin.

The story of our past was "self-will run riot." The account of our future is waiting for us to write as we live in the present. A day at a time, we are learning to live with the uncertainty of this new life. Egocentric behavior, whenever we find ourselves in the midst of it, is part of old patterns that the Steps help us to recognize. In recovery, we have the choice not to continue with this behavior and to act differently. With the new patterns of thinking and acting that we are developing, with the support of our dear ones, friends, sponsors, counselors, and the family who accept us, we create each new day out of the willingness to continue the journey. This creates a new past for ourselves.

Through prayer and meditation, we develop a spiritual bond with ourselves, with others, and with God/Higher Power which enriches our lives each day with greater self-esteem than any of our empty triumphs ever accomplished. The evidence of this will appear as we create a brand-new section of history for ourselves over the months and years ahead. We did not secure the benefits of recovery in one day or one week. The evidence of the benefits of spiritual bonding will only be revealed in time.

The effect of it on each of our lives is powerful. Prayer and meditation work. Those of us who develop a spiritual connection experience far deeper serenity in our lives than those who choose to omit Step Eleven from their efforts in recovery. Not only we, as individuals, are different without it, but so would the Twelve Steps be incomplete as well. Through the conscious efforts we make to be a channel for higher forces, of a God or a Higher Power, the narrow path of our journey through early recovery broadens into an open freeway on which each of us will experience the promises of recovery. (Perhaps not simultaneously, or continuously; nevertheless, we will know them in our recovery.)

The Big Book of Alcoholics Anonymous articulates these promises with great care and directness. They show us the way into the future:

> *If we are painstaking about this phase of our development, we will be amazed before we are half way through. We are going to know a new freedom and a new happiness. We will not regret the past nor wish to shut the door on it. We will comprehend the word serenity and we will know peace. No matter how far down the scale we have gone, we will see how our experience can benefit others. That feeling of uselessness and self-pity will disappear. We will lose interest in selfish things and gain interest in our fellows. Self-seeking will slip away. Our whole attitude and outlook upon life will change. Fear of people and of economic insecurity will leave us. We will intuitively know how to handle situations which used to baffle us. We will suddenly realize that God is doing for us what we could not do for ourselves.*
>
> *Are these extravagant promises? We think not. They are being fulfilled among us—sometimes quickly, sometimes slowly.*
>
> *They will always materialize if we work for them.[2]*

Step Eleven supports us each step along the way—if we work it!

※　　※　　※

✳ ✳ ✳

Relaxation and Stress Reduction Workbook[3] is an excellent sourcebook that provides clear directions to learn specific techniques for use in meditation. There are many different forms of meditation—structured or nonstructured. One example of a type of meditation is the following: read a passage in a meditation book before you go to sleep. The first thing after you wake up in the morning, spend a few moments reflecting on what you remember of the passage and what it means for your life! Try this and write about the experience in your journal.

✳ ✳ ✳

What advice would you give to another recovering individual who is struggling with the spiritual dimension of his or her life? Enter this in your journal.

✳ ✳ ✳

Reflect on the Serenity Prayer and what the words "serenity," "acceptance," "courage," and "wisdom" mean to you. Envision the prayer in a way that will be meaningful and personal for you, and write your thoughts about this in your journal.

✳ ✳ ✳

1. To be ready for change, we need to prepare ourselves physically, emotionally, and mentally. Growth depends on our readiness to grow. What evidence do you have of your readiness?

   _____

   _____

   _____

2. List some notable occasions you have used the Serenity Prayer.

   _____

   _____

   _____

3. If you have never spoken or thought of using the words of the Serenity Prayer, what words come to mind when you confront an obstacle that brings you up sharp or a situation that you think you might not be able to handle?

_____

_____

_____

4. What do *you* mean by the word "prayer"? Explain how you feel when others use this word.

_____

_____

_____

5. What does "meditation" mean to you?

_____

_____

_____

6. Is there a particular form of meditation that is comfortable for you?

_____

_____

_____

7. Who might help you explore different forms of meditation and find the type that best fits you at this time? Think of people familiar with meditation in their own lives.

_____

_____

_____

8. What obstacles stand in the way of your willingness to explore using these activities as tools for change?

_____

_____

_____

9. What do you think of the whole idea of praying and/or meditating on a daily basis?

_____

_____

_____

10. What link have you been able to understand between your own ability to live creatively and a spiritual dimension of life? Indicate below any new, creative efforts you have been making. *(You might make some journal entries on the new ideas you have about your own creativity.)*

_____

_____

_____

_____

_____

_____

_____

_____

11. What, if any, obstacles are in the way of your being creative?

_____

_____

_____

12. When you think of the idea of balance, what significance does spirituality have for you?

_____

_____

_____

13. Is there any area of your life in which you believe spirituality has no place? Why?

_____

_____

_____

14. Both with yourself and then with others, what have you become more conscious about in your recovery? Be as specific as possible.

    Myself:

    _____

    _____

    Other people:

    _____

    _____

15. Consider the list of promises from the AA Big Book that appear in this chapter (page 276). To this date, create an inventory of what you have experienced so far in your own life.

    _____

    _____

    _____

    _____

    _____

16. What are your personal expectations for these promises in the future?

    _____

    _____

    _____

17. What are your expectations about whether or not these promises will actually happen in your own life? How might your expectations influence what occurs?

    _____

    _____

    _____

18. If you have negative expectations, to whom can you go for help and support to alter your expectations?

    _____

    _____

    _____

19. Our efforts have been directed at forging a bond of love for ourselves and for others that homophobia, egocentricity, and mistrust could never have created. Consider the following in terms of how you acted before, and how you want to act now.

    • To share with others openly and directly (instead of using them or manipulating them indirectly out of fear of rejection if you were direct):

    _____

    _____

    • Intimacy and mutual self-disclosure (instead of relying on lies and secrecy):

    _____

    _____

    • Mutual appreciation (instead of only self-gratification):

    _____

    _____

20. How can your own availability to the spiritual in your life widen your road in recovery?

    _____

    _____

    _____

21. What further efforts do you need to make in order to widen the road you are journeying so that it becomes a freeway?

    _____

    _____

    _____

CHAPTER 24

Community and Service

Self-seeking

Some of us hung out a great deal in gay bars where there was laughter but not an abundance of joy. We tried desperately to fill the void inside ourselves. Our search focused more and more on selfish things; even these disappointed us. The more we got, the less satisfied we were. We lost hope of ever finding something good that lasted.

Communion with others—altruism

With acceptance of ourselves, with faith that we can find happiness, with acknowledgment of our own limitations and the availability of help from sources outside ourselves, with honesty and vulnerability and self-revelation, and with flexibility and humility, we enter into community.

Recovery is an environment for healing. We have been invited into this opportunity for wellness because we are exactly who we are—recovering gay men, lesbians, and bisexuals. We understand that in sharing with others our experience of taking action on the Twelve Steps, our own progress on the journey is accelerated.

Step 12

Having had a spiritual awakening as the result of these steps,
we tried to carry this message to alcoholics,
and to practice these principles in all our affairs.

Walking through the door of any consultation room, counseling group, or Twelve Step program with the intention of seeking help is the beginning of practicing Step Twelve. Even though we may not have understood its full significance, through sharing our experience of the journey with others, we begin carrying the message of recovery and participating in the process it initiates.

"Twelve Stepping"

Each time we talk with others about the efforts and actions we are taking to realize positive change in our lives, we "Twelve Step," or encourage them—as well as ourselves. As much as anyone else, we need to hear ourselves talk about the obstacles we are overcoming on a daily basis and how we feel about this. From sharing personal details about our lives in the past and the difference recovery makes to us in the present comes the support *we* need. We continue receiving the benefits of all the Twelve Steps as we take advantage of the opportunity to reveal and acknowledge to others our vulnerability and imperfection, along with our progress.

A large contingent of people in recovery take the first steps toward change and then jump headlong into telling their story to others without working any of the Steps between One and Twelve. They cheat themselves and those they want to help because they neglect all of their own potential for growing from Steps Two through Eleven. We cannot give away to others what we do not have. It is vitally important to our recovery that we stick with the real winners—people who have actually made significant personal changes, not just talked about making them (i.e., "walked the walk" instead of "talked the talk").

Perhaps some of us seriously believed, at the beginning of our journey, that we could sit through a few counseling sessions, attend a few self-help meetings, and be "fixed." By the time we get to Step Twelve, however, we understand that any idea of getting fixed was part of our past and has nothing to do with recovery. There are no "fixes" in recovery. Instead, we work each day at changing our lives, and as we do this, we share our experience of what it was like, what happened, and what it's like now. Then, instead of living in the past, we let it go, "turn it over." In the process of doing this, we find new support and hope inside ourselves, as well as from others, because we were willing to risk changing. We prove by our experience that we can change and live differently from the way we have lived in the past. That is the message we bring to others and to ourselves; sharing this is the work that is always waiting for us to do.

Because it is all too easy to forget this responsibility to ourselves until it becomes a way of life, we need others to remind us regularly of the two essential actions we must take to support our recovery: "Don't yield to the temptation to backslide! Move forward!" Our journey begins with Step One, but we must work through every one of the Steps—again and again—to discover for ourselves what the world of recovery is really like.

There are no shortcuts to Step Twelve. We are ready for it only *after* we have been through the process laid out in the first eleven Steps. Only through the results of the efforts we make can we begin to understand who we are and how we can grow beyond this place. No matter how many insightful ideas we may have about ourselves, we do not suddenly emerge into deeper self-understanding the moment we cease compulsive/dependent behavior. The damage we have suffered physically, emotionally, intellectually, and spiritually requires time in order to be healed. We deceive ourselves if we believe otherwise.

In the past, we lived in the isolation of our dreams and the extremes of our fantasies. Compulsive/dependent behavior excluded us from everything except the company of others behaving similarly; we were incapable of truly intimate and nurturing relationships. Had we not begun the recovery process, that is how we probably would have remained.

Alone, most likely, we would have succumbed. By finding our way into recovery where there were others working to change, we began our journey through the wilderness. The intensity of the isolation we experienced was diminished through our contact with others who shared the identical feelings we suffered. Many of us thought it miraculous to find people who were just as isolated and desperate as ourselves. We became part of a much larger group of gay men, lesbians, and bisexuals who did not want to go on suffering. This wish became a bond that linked us together no matter how isolated we continued to feel when we returned to our own rooms, apartments, or houses.

For most of us, there seems little doubt that recovery either *saved* our lives or gave us a life worth living. We needed to learn to use the tools to *transform* our lives. As we struggled with our past patterns of thinking, feeling, and behaving, we discovered we could rely on these tools to assist us through any ordeal we needed to face. This entire sequence of Steps, which we have used to create the foundation for understanding ourselves and others in a new way, is recapitulated in Step Twelve: "Having had a spiritual awakening *as the result of these steps . . . .*" Because it is an omnibus Step, one that depends on the effects of others, it is valuable for us to explore some of the linkages developed through the Steps preceding it.

Connecting the Steps

One of the most obvious connections is the relationship between Steps One, Two, and Three and Step Twelve. The journey into recovery could never have begun unless we accepted our desperate predicament and made ourselves available to help. This required acceptance, faith, and trust. The struggle to submit ourselves to these is the story of our wilderness days when our compulsive/dependent behavior seemed so alluring and powerful that we wondered if we would ever have strength enough to let it go. Unless we have worked, and continue to work these basic Steps, we do not get very far in our journey.

With the support of the group, many of us made it through the beginning Steps. The group helped us to overcome our denial, our sense of hopelessness, and our insistence on our own willfulness. The effect on us of these first three basic Steps made it possible for us to begin to change our lives. Until we had worked at them, we were not ready for Step Four that required intensive focus on ourselves. Only after the change process was begun were we prepared to develop a "fearless" and "thorough" moral inventory of ourselves. It was only then we experienced the beginning of a new kind of intervention that allowed us to know we no longer had to do anything alone, that there was help for us. This was the growing awareness that we relied on when we faced our secrets and identified the obstacles recorded in our inventories. Sharing this inventory with another human being, and a Higher Power (for those of us who have found one), we spoke in our own voices about the unspeakable. To our amazement, we survived! Step Five was not the end of the world for us, even though we feared that it would be.

In addition to the secrets we shared, this was a major move forward in relating in a totally different way with another human being. In the process of trusting someone else, we discovered that we were not abandoned or cast out because of the enormity of our shortcomings, nor were we alone in our vulnerability and imperfection. On this foundation of another person's acceptance, we began to build the bridge to *self-acceptance* that had never been there in our past lives as sexual minorities where compulsive/dependent behavior was the norm.

As we gradually link together the work we do in Steps Five, Nine, and Twelve, we begin to develop an ever-widening circle of acceptance. After the second inventory that we made in Step Eight, in Step Nine we reached out to make amends to all those we had harmed. These are the people from our past who have played a major role in our lives and account for much of the way we feel about ourselves. Through our efforts to mend our portion of our relationships with them, we accept responsibility for our previous actions, and begin creating the climate of honesty and trust needed for healthy and satisfying relationships with others. By willingly taking this responsibility on ourselves, we begin forging new links in the chain of *self-trust* and *self-caring*.

Through these amends, as well as those we continue to make, we are able to see that no one holds back the reins of our recovery except ourselves. Unless we are absolutely clear about this, we slip back into old habits of dependency in which new people we meet fill old needs that threaten our recovery.

In Step Twelve, the circle expands to include everyone in our lives—those in recovery, those not in recovery, those to whom we have made or still owe "amends," and those with whom we have a clean slate. By this time, we understand the role we have played in choosing everyone who has any significance in our lives. We become aware that from now on we must carefully and consistently consider our priorities in recovery. We need also to remember how vitally important these priorities are to our continued progress.

Haven't other people always been an enigma for us? In the past, we often looked for affirmation and for love from the very ones who were least able to give it. By taking responsibility for our choices, in Step Nine, we provide ourselves with the information we need to guide us as we meet new people in whom we can now develop trust and support. The honesty and trust in ourselves that is nurtured through Steps Five and Nine helps us interact with new patterns of thought and action with the people around us in our world. For us to consistently connect with others in the enlightened way that Step Twelve describes, we must have laid this foundation.

Perhaps of all the paradoxes in Twelve Step programs, the basic one is that we must share our recovery in order to keep it. Only through sharing with others what we have gotten along the way of working the Steps is it possible to hold onto the benefits. This sharing can take many forms within or outside the context of self-help groups. In our activities of sharing, we become the source of change and support for others who do not know there is an alternative to addiction. The willingness to do this becomes the cornerstone to our own further growth as we continue the journey.

That we have important work to do, that others depend on us to do it, that we need them as much as they need us are among the most amazing discoveries we make on our journey. What a paradox! By being a member of a group we can experience ourselves in a way that never seemed possible before. And what a revelation it is to begin now to understand that we are more *like* other people, gay or nongay, than we are *unlike* them! Participation as an equal with others is, for some of us, tantamount to a "spiritual awakening." Many gay men, lesbians, and bisexuals never thought such an experience possible! With it, we are able, day by day, to end the imprisoning isolation of our uniqueness and take part in life in the same way we see others participating.

This experience of ourselves as members of a group helps us to begin to examine old ideas that have always motivated our thoughts and actions and influenced our emotions. For the first time, we observe that everyone does not take the same things for granted or use the same rules we do. We see that many more choices are available than we ever believed. Through the Steps, we are able to put our old behavior into perspective and discover we are capable of change. While this is happening, the group around us provides us with the opportunity to unburden ourselves of the wreckage of the past and create the space in which to make new connections inside ourselves.

As we clear away old patterns of thought and behavior and replace them with the healthy new ones we develop through the Steps, our feelings about ourselves and others change and the space within us expands. This expanding space, this availability within each of us that opens in the process of recovery, is the focus of Steps Ten, Eleven, and Twelve.

Each of these Steps is about relationship and our own level of consciousness. The linkage between them is important for us to consider. Each Step is concerned with raising our consciousness about ourselves (Ten), our consciousness about our relationship with a Higher Power or spiritual dimension (Eleven), and our consciousness about our relationship with others in the world around us (Twelve). It is with new insights, which arise from honesty and trust instead of our old patterns, that we are now capable of creating and developing intimate, satisfying, and mutually rewarding relationships. These new relationships become the basis for living happy, healthy lives in recovery.

We are on the main road of the ongoing journey when we search for the answers to these questions:

- What efforts are we making to develop our relationship with ourselves, with a Higher Power, with others?

- Are we expanding our emotional, intellectual, and spiritual limits or maintaining them exactly as they are?

- What are the major challenges waiting for us in recovery?

The answers to any of these questions may change each time we work our way through the Steps. What remains constant is the awareness that these questions are there for us to work on with the tools we have acquired.

Practicing the Principles

Being capable of having a different relationship with ourselves and with the world around us does not mean that we will have one. We have to make a consistent and conscious effort in order to develop an expanding connection. The Tenth Step inventory and the need for prayer and meditation suggested by the Eleventh Step are examples of this exceptional kind of effort. The Twelfth Step suggests a *third* kind of effort we must make if we are going to create a new relationship with the world: "to carry this message" to others who are still suffering the effects of compulsive/dependent behavior and "to practice these principles in all our affairs."

This is strenuous work! The alternative to taking this action, unfortunately, is that we may find ourselves back again on the other side of the door. That door swings both ways, and for some who find themselves in and out of recovery every few months, it becomes a revolving door. Any of us can go through it as many times as we choose. Some of us, however, may not find this door again once we are outside because of feelings of shame and guilt, or accident and misfortune.

Is this effort we must make really such a burden? After our first Twelve Step meeting or recovery group session, we were invited to return in order to participate in the work of recovery. Given the state of collapse we were in, many of us could hardly believe the invitation. Nevertheless, we took our seats beside others with whom we gradually became more comfortable. We found relief from our pain and discovered that they did too. It is important to remember that it was not through silence, indifference, or "stuffing it," but through the effort to share our pain and suffering that relief came both for ourselves and for others. Healing began only as we exposed our wounds and our anguish.

In the process of sharing with others just like ourselves, we were able to change our perspective on everything. We became a witness to our agony; and, as we listened to others, we shared in their witness. There is a striking similarity between this and the recitation that Christians and Jews practice in reading from the Bible through the liturgical calendar. The prophets and the gospel writers were also witnesses to disaster, triumph, tragedy, sorrow, affliction, persecution, defeat, and the entire gamut of human experience. Men and women through the centuries have received hope, faith, strength, and joy for their own lives from the accounts that have been left behind. The recitations of these witnesses have consistently raised individual consciousness beyond any personal limit of suffering into an awareness of the human condition. In some vital way, the account of any witness changes the course of history.

We change our own individual history when we initiate the recovery process. Witnessing changes our lives. Through it, we come to realize that not only is each one a member of the group in which we share, but also a loving member of the human race instead of an outcast! This is 180 degrees from the way we lived. We are no longer victims; all of us have our experience, strength, and hope to share, and these are valuable to us and to others. Each story confirms this, for we learn from others how to make important connections that have been missing in our lives. Each story binds all of us together in a chain of recovery that works to support every one of us. We become participants in community and recognize that we are important to life. For many of us, until we have accepted ourselves as members with the responsibility of membership in the community in recovery, we remain outsiders looking at happiness like children in front of a candy store window. We see what is on the other side of the pane, but we cannot touch or taste it. This deprivation can, in itself, grow and become the source of bitter suffering.

Recovering from the effects of compulsive/dependent behavior with the help of the Steps is a major undertaking. Given the tremendous power of inertia or the ease with which we return to old habits, we find recovery is an ongoing effort. But the journey continues, with the help of the Steps, into recovering into life. For us, this means that we must continue to work on changing the rules we thought we needed in order to survive. No matter how committed we have been to any of them, we must be willing to grow beyond them. "If you change even one thing, you change everything." None of us understand how significant this truth about living is until we set out on the journey into recovery.

In recovery, we discover that we cannot share our lives with those around us without learning honesty, nor can we continue listening to others share their lives without learning acceptance. Next, we discover that the gaping abyss, the void, left open when we stopped self-medicating with mood-altering substances and compulsive/dependent behavior gets filled when we begin to work the Steps instead of pursuing our old ways of coping with pain or distress. With honesty, acceptance, and the tools of change, we finally discover the way to begin developing a connection between our heads and our hearts that had never been possible in the compartmentalized life most of us led as gay men, lesbians, and bisexuals in a heterosexual society.

The "Spiritual Awakening"

Because the Steps provide us with many tools we need to help us connect with ourselves, it becomes possible for us to connect with other people exactly the way they are instead of the way we may wish or want them to be. The desperate pursuit of perfection that motivated our lives is transformed in this process. When we search for something we consider beyond us, we will never find what we seek. By looking within ourselves, we learn the way to love what is—instead of what isn't.

Many of us truly believed we had taken a giant step beyond childhood when we first discovered what it was like to get "high." Instead of growing up, thousands of us found our way into addictive patterns of behavior and got stuck there. Consequently, we were never capable of developing a deep, personal connection with anyone around us. When we enter recovery, however, we begin learning to connect as individuals who are capable of evolving. We discover that we can find happiness, joy, and freedom in the world in which we knew only despair. *That* is the giant step waiting for us in recovery.

No one could have told us when we began this journey the place we would reach, how far we would travel or with whom. From where we stand now, we should be able to see that we could not have arrived at this moment unless we had come through all of the other moments along the way. Like many other answers that have found their way into our lives, this one reveals itself as we live-through the journey: *we can only get here from there!* We reach this place in our recovery because we have consciously made efforts to use our energy through each experience that led us to it.

Imagine the experience of visiting Yosemite National Park. (Many of Ansel Adams's photographs of Yosemite may assist you in this process.) Marvel at the effects of a prehistoric geological devastation that radically altered the mountains and valleys of that corner of California as you enter the park on the valley floor. Imagine looking down from Glacier Point into the valley 3,000 feet below; see the majesty of Half Dome rise across the way in the midst of its rocky wilderness! Seen from the perspective of time and distance, there is great beauty in nature's scars. Looking with wonder at those massive peaks and plunging chasms, and the space they are set in, we are able to understand that Yosemite would not be the miracle it is now without the disaster that overtook it all those millennia ago.

If we are willing to be taught, nature constantly provides us with valuable insights. For many of us, these insights are the basis of the "spiritual awakening" referred to in Step Twelve. The realization that each of us is remarkable *because* we have endured the devastation we have been through, and the daily struggle with recovery, comes only with time and distance in the journey itself. This understanding was not there when we started out. Our pain and our suffering were all that we knew. All of us are healed by our willingness to pass beyond our suffering, and we learn this again and again through Step Twelve.

Thousands of lesbians, gays, and bisexuals are out there in our world, but cut off from life because of the effects of addictive/compulsive behavior. None of them have any idea that help is even possible. For those of us who are learning to find our way, we have each other to help us. All of us need to remember that carrying this message to others is essential to our own journey into recovery and may be a life line to others.

"Will it save lives?" asked Bill W., cofounder of Alcoholics Anonymous, when asked for his approval for gay AA meetings in Boston in the early 1950s. As a member of this ever-expanding community in recovery, it is up to you to discover whether or not it saves your life—as well as the lives of others. There is help for us everywhere. The Twelve Steps of recovery are waiting for us to find them, and use them. The Steps won't work for you unless you use them and make them your own!

※   ※   ※

❋　　❋　　❋

Enter in your journal a few recollections about your last holiday (Thanksgiving, Christmas, New Year's, Passover, Independence Day, etc.) or last birthday before entering recovery. Write as much as you remember about your experience of your life at that time.

❋　　❋　　❋

Wait a few days, and then write in your journal some of the differences you observe in your life at this time in recovery. What does your own personal progress look like? What is the greatest change you observe? What has NOT changed?

❋　　❋　　❋

1. Most people in the world are not involved in a Twelve Step program or engaged in consistent, exerted efforts to alter compulsive/dependent behaviors. What are the implications of this for you? How does this impact your relationships with others?

_____

_____

_____

_____

_____

2. If you were to make a gratitude inventory of the good things that have happened to you since beginning recovery, what would it look like?

_____

_____

_____

3. What similarities do you share with others in your recovery or support group? List them.

_____

_____

_____

4. List some of the differences.

_____

_____

_____

5. What are your thoughts about the recovery community? If applicable, what does it feel like to be a member of the recovery community?

_____

_____

_____

_____

_____

6. It is important to see the inventories you have already completed as "results." List the inventories you have completed.

_____

_____

_____

7. Of the inventories that still need more work, identify what is left to be done on each one at this time.

_____

_____

_____

8. These inventories are "unfinished business in recovery." Record each one and give it a number; then set a date for completing it.

		Date
	Inventory	*for Completion*
_____		_____
_____		_____
_____		_____
_____		_____
_____		_____

9. If there are obstacles in the way of completing any of these inventories, identify the obstacles.

Inventory	Obstacle(s)
_____	_____
_____	_____
_____	_____
_____	_____
_____	_____

10. Taking positive action and getting positive results is a new experience for many of us. This is a change we need to acknowledge. How would you explain the benefits to you, personally, if you were talking with someone new to recovery who knew nothing about the Twelve Steps?

_____

_____

_____

11. How would you explain the benefits to someone who already has some time in recovery but who doesn't think the Steps have any use or value for him or her?

_____

_____

_____

12. After you have considered your answers to questions 10 and 11, try them out on appropriate people. Record the experience.

_____

_____

_____

13. How do you feel after sharing these ideas with others?

_____

_____

_____

14. What impact on the old pattern to isolate have Step Five and Step Nine had for you?

_____

_____

_____

15. Is it easier for you at this time to relate to others than to ideas about spirituality? Explore.

_____

_____

_____

16. What impact have Step Four, Step Eight, and Step Ten had for you with regard to honesty?

_____

_____

_____

17. In what areas of your life, or with whom, do you feel that you cannot be honest? Note your reason(s) in each case.

_____

_____

_____

_____

_____

_____

18. Detail your efforts at this time to continue developing your relationship with yourself, others, and the spiritual dimension of life.

_____

_____

_____

_____

_____

_____

19. What efforts are you making to expand your own emotional, intellectual, and spiritual boundaries?

_____

_____

_____

_____

_____

20. What do you see as the major challenges ahead for you:

a. in the next six months?

_____

_____

b. in the next year?

_____

_____

c. in the next two years?

_____

_____

21. What do you see as the major opportunities ahead for you:

a. in the next six months?

_____

_____

b. in the next year?

_____

_____

c. in the next two years?

_____

_____

22. Identify the individuals you will ask to support you in facing these challenges and opportunities.

Challenges/Opportunities	Individuals
_____	_____
_____	_____
_____	_____
_____	_____

23. Review your Action Plan and discover if there are gaps that now need to be filled.

CHAPTER 25

The Longer View

Steps Ten, Eleven, and Twelve

Connecting self-discipline and spiritual bonding and actively helping others find their way into recovery change our perspective of our own significance in the world we share with others. Developing self-esteem, caring about the well-being of others, and developing a spiritual connection result in a course correction in life that impacts all of our aspirations. This, in turn, calls for new efforts at acceptance and reevaluation of values. The process of forging new ideas is entirely open-ended. We find our way through finding our way.

No matter where we are in the Twelve Step cycle, recovery is an ongoing process in which each day is always the beginning. We need to continue being honest with ourselves about our relationship to mood-altering substances and compulsive/dependent behavior. We must remember that we are *recovering*, but not fixed just because we have abstained from substances and compulsive/dependent behavior.[1]

After getting high on whatever substance or behavior we tried, and then deciding that we liked it—or liked what it did for us—we did it again . . . and again. Having journeyed through the Twelve Steps, having had our first experience of affirming and supporting ourselves with love, validation, honesty, and companionship, we are responsible for continuing the same process, and working at it again . . . and again. We always have the choice, and, if we like what happens in our lives when we work at recovering, these Steps continue to provide us with an ever-unfolding road map to go on with the journey.

We often forget that no one except ourselves can always love us in precisely the way we want and need to be loved. Loving ourselves takes practice, and time. Perhaps you have heard other people in recovery say, from time to time, that those working the Twelve Steps will go on loving us until we can learn to love ourselves. The experience of this love can fill us with both pride and humility, for it means that we have become valuable members of the human family. As members, we embrace each other for exactly who we are, the way we are. This is tremendously freeing because it provides us with a place to stand and accept ourselves. It is the place from which our mountains are moved and our new lives begun.

Embracing Diversity in Community

There is vast energy in the power of love. Those who continue to work on all the Steps grow in understanding of this energy and its relationship with health. As we go on in recovery, what we are becomes the basis for continuing growth and development. We integrate our diversity more and more, and at the same time learn to appreciate each of the parts more deeply. The experience of wholeness and well-being within ourselves—and within society and the universe—extends our concept of who we are and what we mean to others. Recovery is the reentry into the heart of humanity.

We are the survivors of the devastating effects of addictive/compulsive behavior. We know many who are still suffering from its ravages, and we are right to feel ourselves lucky and grateful. Many of us joined recovery groups as isolated gay men, lesbians, and bisexuals; now we have become part of a much larger community. Through our participation in this community, we express our individuality. The paradox is that only by expressing our individuality do we actually become a member of the community.

In mobilizing against the AIDS crisis, the gay community has shown the way to a deep and humanitarian response to suffering and social ostracism. The hospices and home care projects are models for a humane, responsible, loving initiative that has made the lives of many who have fallen ill from this disease a little easier to bear. The gay community—in all its diversity—has reached out to embrace the exiles. Because of this action, gays, lesbians, and bisexuals have grown in love and understanding.

In recovery, the entire spectrum of individual diversity needs to be accepted. Embracing the diversity that exists within the gay and lesbian communities might, in the future, become the model of acceptance for *all* gay men, *all* lesbians, and *all* bisexuals whether or not they are chemically or behaviorally dependent. Just as the Steps have provided a new concept of fellowship and group participation throughout the world, so this same impulse for the acceptance of sexual diversity *by* the gay and lesbian communities seems a possibility waiting in the wings of the new century ahead of us.

We need first to accept our lesbian and bisexual sisters and gay and bisexual brothers ourselves before we expect the rest of the world to do this. Is it not possible that after our acceptance, the rest will follow? This is what has been happening with "alcoholics" and "addicts" over the past half-century of Twelve Step programs! First members welcomed each other into their own fellowship, and then a large portion of the rest of society began to follow their lead. Although stigma and discrimination continue to exist toward individuals who are chemically and/or behaviorally dependent, this prejudice has diminished. It is essential not to wait for others to change first or give us permission to change, before we allow ourselves the hope that change is possible and commit ourselves to make that change internally.[2]

If we want peace, we must live peacefully. If we want pride, let us live pridefully. If we want courage, let us live courageously.

The Longest Journey

We are all on an incredible journey. We have come many miles and years through space and time, through the mind and the heart, on the longest journey back into life. Back again in life, we encounter the reality of our sexuality, our virtue, and our merit as men and women who can be lovers—man to man, woman to woman. Is this important? Is it important to write a book about recovering into life as a gay man and as a lesbian and as a bisexual? Yes, because being who we are is important to us!

We have laughed and cried, alone and with others, at the wonderful insights and revelations that have come to us as we traveled. We have also known the miracle of being with those friends and strangers who love us because we shared our vulnerability with them. We have been made richer in understanding and experienced gratitude much deeper than we ever believed possible. Many of us have lived through the incredible paradox that the very disasters which befell us were the very experiences that helped us grow and discover the meaning of happiness.

As members of the community, we know we have the right to as much joy and freedom as anyone else. As recovering women and men, proud and responsible, we touch other people's lives with the richness of our diversity today and every day, and we continue our journey together. Wishing everyone the joy of the journey, may we meet along the way to celebrate our gifts and each other, the gift givers.

❋   ❋   ❋

❋　　❋　　❋

This exercise is another way of thinking about making your present and future different from your past. It is difficult to get to a new place without a map. In order to have a clearer idea of the old map you've used in your life, it will be helpful for you to understand what you need to redraw. Imagine this map to be a huge continent divided into many countries, islands, peninsulas, rivers, mountain ranges, and deserts. Identify your own "country" and then think about the names of people you selected in chapter 19 of the workbook. Imagine that the map helps you to see the distance these people are from you at the present time.

1.　What can you learn from this map?

_____

_____

_____

2.　What has the map been like in the past?

_____

_____

_____

3.　What do you want to change?

_____

_____

_____

4.　What distances between yourself and others do you want to work to alter?

_____

_____

_____

5.　What feelings do you have when you imagine this map?

_____

_____

_____

＊　＊　＊

*For such a long time, you had grown accustomed with living either
"high" or "low." Those feelings became natural. Learning to love
something in the middle, neither "high" nor "low," takes getting used
to. You can begin to value balance in your life by calling every day you
abstain from substances and compulsive behavior a "good" day. On a
regular basis, write these words in your journal: "I had a good day
today." Seeing this affirmation is the beginning of a pattern of
personal support that is important to continue throughout recovery.
Good days add up to better and better ones, if we let them. Begin
today's entry in your journal: "I am having a good day." Go on with
the rest of the entry.*

＊　＊　＊

*Sometimes, as we walk down the street, we catch a glimpse of
ourselves in a store window. Set aside five minutes each day, alone, in
which you can be with yourself in front of a mirror at home. Affirm
yourself with words that support your efforts in recovery. Write these
words in your journal and review them at the beginning of each day.*

＊　＊　＊

Looking back at our journey, from an eagle's eye view, we can observe the process.
After completing the basics—Steps One, Two, and Three—Step Four created an
inventory and forced our secrets out of hiding. Step Five shared them with another
human being (along with a Higher Power). Step Six encouraged our willingness to have
them removed; and Step Seven encouraged us to ask for help in dumping them.
Linking the four Steps together adds up to consistent action to change the conditions
of our past.

After Steps Eight and Nine in which we identified the people we had harmed in our
lives and began changing the way we related with them, we initiated a daily inventory
as daily maintenance for recovery. Steps Eleven and Twelve extended our boundaries
"beyond our wildest dreams."

Working on our own obstacles introduces a consistent approach to achieving equilibrium in our lives. Our old patterns of survival will always unbalance us—in thought and action. But by working on them consistently, we can make the changes that will permanently influence our lives. Embodied in the Twelve Steps is the wisdom that self-renewal depends on the unusual combination of individual effort *and* asking for help from others, the group or the source of Power beyond us. Personal effort, in these programs, does not mean recovering on one's own without outside assistance. Balance is difficult to achieve and even harder to maintain. For most people it requires, at times, outside help.

6. Ongoing recovery depends on asking for help. Asking for support from others, however, can put you in an uncomfortable place in yourself. How easy or difficult is it for you to ask for help now? Explore.

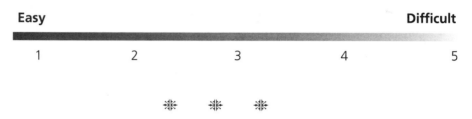

Easy				**Difficult**
1	2	3	4	5

In your journal over the next weeks and months, write further about your feelings and thoughts about asking for help. Reflecting on your willingness to ask for help can be another way to assess your progress.

7. What are some of the things you used to ask others for and the words you used to ask them?

_____

_____

_____

8. Who are the individuals from whom you would no longer ask for help? (Hint: those individuals in the past who couldn't or wouldn't give help when you asked.)

_____

_____

_____

9. How often did you manipulate others into giving you what you wanted? *(Circle your estimate.)*

Rarely   **All the Time**

1   2   3   4   5

10. What role does this play in asking for help now?

_____

_____

_____

11. Are there any differences when you ask others for help in your recovery? Identify the differences.

_____

_____

_____

12. Check off below the efforts/activities you use NOW to make progress in your recovery.

☐ a. not practicing addictive and/or compulsive behavior(s)

☐ b. attending Twelve Step meetings

☐ c. working regularly on the Steps

☐ d. reading literature to assist efforts to change and grow

☐ e. doing a regular service commitment

☐ f. staying in contact with a sponsor or friend committed to you in your recovery process

☐ g. sharing recovery with others

☐ h. using the telephone daily to be in touch with others

☐ i. maintaining a journal consistently

☐ j. spot-checking yourself; end-of-day inventorying

☐ k. meditating/praying/exploring your spiritual nature

☐ l. eating a balanced diet

☐ m. getting adequate rest

☐ n. checking out with a physician any troubling health issues

☐ o. doing physical exercise

☐ p. participating in individual therapy

☐ q. attending group therapy

☐ r. participating in couples therapy

13. Circle those activities you like to do best. Explain.

_____

_____

_____

14. Mark an "x" next to those activities you enjoy least (but think may be helpful to you as you continue to work on yourself). *Write in your journal* (1) what you dislike about doing these activities; (2) what kind of support you might need in order to do them; (3) under what circumstances you might want to incorporate these activities in your life in the future.

15. What are the likely areas in your life in which balance will be difficult to achieve and/or difficult to maintain?

_____

_____

_____

16. What tools will you use to help you maintain balance in these areas?

_____

_____

_____

17. How do you plan to fully integrate your life as a sexual minority into the larger community, while maintaining balance, integrity, dignity, and recovery?

_____

_____

_____

You may discover, after you have become well-grounded in one of the Twelve Step programs, that another Twelve Step group is working on issues appropriate to your recovery. Attend a few of these meetings with the intention of expanding your understanding of the issues and problems you experience and the way these groups may help your recovery.

❊ PART III ❊

For
Therapists

CHAPTER 26

Analysis of Alternative Models of Addiction

art I, chapter 1, an overview of four different treatment models and their impact on sexual minorities, provides an introduction to this chapter, which presents additional material that may be useful in working with clients.

Because of addiction's devastating effect on society, the cause and treatment of it have been, and will continue to be, the focus of attention of physicians, scientists, researchers, sociologists, psychologists, moral philosophers, and many others. As might be expected with this extensive array of professionals, there are many different approaches to explain the causes and treatment of addictive behaviors.

Each of the models deals with the causes and origins of addiction, and each differs most regarding whether or not addicted individuals are personally responsible for the development of their behavior, and whether or not they are responsible for changing their problem (Donovan & Chaney 1985).

The Moral Model

The *Moral Model* holds individuals responsible for both the development and resolution of their addiction. This model, the most damaging to self-esteem, is the one most prevalent in people's minds when they think about an "alcoholic"—"the skid-row bum." Even some individuals in recovery have the idea that chemical dependency is somehow related to having a moral deficiency. The Moral Model conjures up the sense that there is some "defectiveness" in the individual. In fact, these very words, "defect of character," are used in AA's Step Six. This model has serious implications for care providers working with gay, lesbian, and bisexual individuals who may already believe themselves such moral outcasts that recovery is not even a possibility.

The Medical Model

The second model, the Medical Model, widely endorsed in many treatment programs around the country, sees addiction as caused by an underlying disease from which individuals can recover with medical intervention. Addicted individuals are not responsible for the development of the disease, and they can be assisted in their recovery by putting themselves in the hands of trained professionals. This model relies on extensive education about the disease as a treatment intervention strategy.

Black, in *Double Duty,* records that the American Medical Association (AMA) first endorsed alcoholics' admission to general hospitals in 1956.[1] In November 1966, the AMA adopted a resolution formally recognizing alcoholism as a disease "that merits the serious concern of all members of health professions." The AMA's acknowledgment of alcoholism as a disease had significant impact on the delivery of care and firmly established the "disease concept"[2] in the mind of the general public.

Until 1980, homosexuality was also considered a disease. In that year, the American Psychiatric Association ceased to list it in the *Diagnostic and Statistical Manual of Mental Disorders.*[3] And, in 1981, the American Psychological Association also removed homosexuality from its list of disorders. However, some medical practitioners have failed to "update" their attitude and continue to act as if homosexuality were an infirmity or disorder. The result is that these practitioners perceive gays, lesbians, and bisexuals as *twice* as "sick" if they are diagnosed with "substance dependency" or "substance abuse."

The distinction between the diagnosis of "substance dependency" and "substance abuse" has important implications for treatment. Because it is difficult to make clear distinctions between the two conditions, individuals are often considered dependent for the sake of simplicity and safety. However, individuals who have been diagnosed with a condition that does not fit with their understanding or experience of their behavior are not likely to simply comply with the diagnosis either for simplicity or for safety's sake. With other conditions, disorders, or diseases, there are universal biological markers, blood tests, or other objective measures to clarify a diagnosis. None of these indicators are available, at this time, to confirm the diagnosis of either substance abuse or dependency.

In the absence of an objective test, the diagnosis is made on a variety of criteria. In some cases, it is based on criteria published in the *Diagnostic and Statistical Manual* published by the American Psychiatric Association (APA 1995). In other cases, the diagnosis will be based less strictly on such criteria and more heavily on an assessment of the individual's problems over his or her lifespan that may be connected in some fashion with substance use. For example, if the person uses alcohol and also admits to having occupational or social problems, this may be sufficient for some providers to assume that (1) there is a causal relationship between the two and (2) the use of alcohol is causing the occupational and social problems.

Another question often used to assist the assessment process is, "Have you ever sought assistance for this problem?" This method is quite circular: if you have problems and you drink alcohol in any fashion beyond what the provider deems to be "social drinking," you run the risk of being told that you have "alcoholism." Some treatment providers may define "alcoholism" as: "If you have problems as a *result* of your drinking, then you have a drinking problem. A drinking problem equals alcoholism." There is little room in the classification system for those who are "problem drinkers," but who are not "dependent." It may indeed be the case that individuals could determine they are drinking in an excessive fashion; but that does not make it true that these individuals, by definition, have "alcoholism."

In order to diagnose dependency, it is necessary to explore whether individuals have a complete inability to control their consumption of the substance, whether they have developed a significantly increased tolerance of the substance, and whether or not they experience withdrawal symptoms when the substance is removed.

There may be other reasons for problem drinking besides "alcoholism." Perhaps the individual is trying to self-medicate or manage an anxiety disorder with alcohol. Or perhaps he or she is a "problem drinker" in need of assistance to alter behavior.

In assessing research that suggests a higher incidence of alcoholism in the gay and lesbian population, it is important to know how "alcoholism" is defined in these studies. Research findings are sometimes misleading, and results sometimes over-generalized. Current results are inconclusive because the studies do not adequately distinguish between those who may have a diagnosis of "substance dependency" and those who simply are using substances in a problematic fashion, such as self-medication to cope with *other problems* that gays and lesbians are experiencing.

The Spiritual/Enlightenment Model

Alcoholics Anonymous and all of the other Twelve Step programs are based on the Spiritual Model, which assumes that addicted individuals are powerless over the development of their addiction—and powerless over their recovery as well. Reliance on a power greater than the individual self—God or a Higher Power—and use of the Twelve Steps on an ongoing basis brings about recovery. Some people modify this and allow that association with the group is an adequate higher power to bring about recovery.

Some implications of this model for gays and lesbians are related to patriarchal concerns about religion, an external "fixing" power, and feeling "less-than," which have been discussed in earlier chapters. Another concern with the Enlightenment Model is the emphasis on the idea of a "group force." Some people who attend a Twelve Step meeting to discover whether or not they are "alcoholics" or "addicts" may feel pressured to identify themselves in this fashion, just to receive help. It is possible that some gays and lesbians who find themselves in AA, or another Twelve Step group, are in such pain that they are willing to identify themselves *in any fashion* necessary in order to get help and support. Once the pain subsides and they have developed a network of friends, they may fear the loss of these friends if they reconsider their identification and reexamine their behavior in a new light. They may suffer lost authenticity and lower self-esteem if the identification doesn't seem to fit but is nevertheless retained for fear of losing friends and network in order to correct the error.

The Social Learning Model

The sense of responsibility in the Social Learning Model is different from that of the Moral Model. There is no implication of a moral or an intellectual deficiency. Instead, individuals who have developed addictive behaviors have learned these behaviors as strategies to cope with problems. The learning is the problem, not the individual. Individuals learn many things, and the issue of responsibility raises two important questions. First, to what extent are individuals responsible for what they have learned? Second, if no pejorative label is attached, and no stigma, what harm is there in admitting that they have learned nonadaptive strategies?

The Social Learning Model is particularly interested in assisting individuals to focus on altering the addictive behavior, instead of on discovering why the behavior developed. Individuals are considered to have the power and the capability to learn alternative coping strategies and then change the addictive behavior. Learning new behaviors may be a slow and systematic process, with successes as well as setbacks. This approach, termed "relapse-prevention therapy" (Marlatt & George 1984), is built on social learning theory.

Relapse-prevention therapy uses a variety of techniques, such as helping individuals to identify situations that may have a high risk for relapse. The treatment focuses on developing strategies and coping skills to prevent such relapses. Education about a "lapse" is included; the model focuses on how to regain abstinence immediately before a full relapse develops. Interventions, for those who have relapsed, involve helping individuals cope with the relapse and make new attempts to change instead of giving up completely.

The Social Learning Model does not assume that someone has an illness or that someone is characterologically deficient. Instead, it suggests that all individuals learn to make the most with what they have at hand. With billions of dollars of drugs sold over-the-counter each year, the use of substances to relieve physical pain is both common and acceptable. Individuals with addictive/compulsive behavior have adapted the practice of using substances to ease emotional pain. In one sense, there is the expectation that people are responsible for the development of the maladaptive strategy, but there is no stigma *per se* about having learned this. Most people learn to use some type of strategy to cope with problems in our culture. Some strategies are effective and others are not. This model suggests that the individual *can learn* to cope differently by learning alternative strategies (Monti et al. 1989).

The Power of Expectations

One way of coping differently is abstinence from compulsive/dependent behaviors. Another is the moderation of such behavior. An interesting feature of the Social Learning Model is the "abstinence-volition effect" (Marlatt & Gordon 1985). If people are taught that they are powerless, and they relapse, they tend to think they have absolutely no control and must ride the elevator to the bottom of the abyss. For example, if they take a sip from the wrong glass, or do something they hadn't intended, they have internal permission to go the limit. There is no expectation they should do anything different because they've been programmed to say, "I'm powerless."

A different understanding of relapse is possible within the context of the Social Learning Model. People can be helped to understand that they will be in high-risk situations and will need to learn alternative methods of coping when these arise. They learn, as well, that relapse is part of what happens on the way to change. (This is frequently talked about in smoking-cessation literature: the more frequently individuals try to quit, the more likely they are to be successful because of what they learn from their efforts to quit along the way. Taking one cigarette does not mean you have to throw it all in and return to smoking like a fiend. Recovery doesn't have to work that way either.)

There is great power in expectations. For example, telling people in a vulnerable state that it is totally unacceptable for them to consume any alcohol, and that if they do they will die, is a setup. By hearing horror story after horror story about others' experiences on going back to using alcohol, they may come to believe that what has happened to others will, by definition, happen to them. Then, if they consume any alcohol, they are far more likely to believe that they have no control over their lives and are therefore doomed.

This has direct implications for sexual minorities who may already have diminished expectations of themselves, low self-esteem, and feelings of unworthiness because of their sexual orientation. Programming for disaster may hamper sexual minorities' attempts to alter addictive/compulsive behavior.

Treatment Approaches

There is a close relationship between individuals' perceptions of their ability to effect change (self-efficacy) and their actions (Marlatt & Gordon 1985; Marlatt 1978). Marlatt and Gordon propose that self-efficacy based on expectations of the ability to cope in a particular situation is a factor in the decision to abstain from or consume alcohol. In turn, success in coping with high-risk situations increases the perception of self-efficacy. When disbelief in self-efficacy in such a situation exists, lapse, and possibly relapse, will occur. Treatment, therefore, can focus on learning to abstain and to use alternative coping skills in high-risk situations (Curry & Marlatt 1986; DiClemente 1986). It may be beneficial to direct treatment efforts at altering the addicted individual's self-image in the direction of greater self-efficacy and greater personal control.

The close relationship between how individuals perceive their effectiveness and the actions they engage in (Bandura 1982a, 1982b) takes on enormous relevance in the treatment of addiction in gays, lesbians, and bisexuals. In general, sexual minorities do not enjoy the same kind of success stories heterosexuals may experience. While there are exceptions, especially in the arts, even when fame or fortune occurs, many gays and lesbians suffer deeply from destructive self-doubt and lack of confidence because of their sexual orientation. Their perception of success is often filtered through daily dishonesty and self-deprecation. Because success in any area is constantly mitigated by a distorted self-image, addicted individuals can easily fall prey to the belief that nothing they ever do to begin recovery will work. This self-fulfilling prophesy keeps many individuals stuck in addiction.

A fair number of interventions that are not entirely consistent with the "disease concept" of addiction have been incorporated into Medical Model treatment programs. Coping-skills training and other strategies are extremely valuable for some people.[4] In general, chemical dependency treatment providers seem to lack information about alternative explanations for addictive disorders beyond the disease concept. As indicated earlier, ideas and interventions from other models have been modified and incorporated into Medical Model treatment programs without understanding that these interventions stem from an approach that does not require abstinence or powerlessness as the underlying construct of the treatment philosophy.

Inpatient, Outpatient

There is considerable controversy about what types of treatment are best suited for whom and at what time. In the absence of definitive research to settle the controversy, it may be best to start with the least restrictive treatment environment and monitor progress. If the client is having difficulty making progress with the initial level of treatment selected, the intensity of the intervention can be increased.[5]

Another treatment intervention is medical detoxification. The assessment of the need for medical detoxification should consider such factors as the quantity and frequency of substance(s) consumed, the duration of this pattern, the length of time the individual has been able to remain abstinent without intervention, the presence or absence of withdrawal symptoms, the co-occurrence of other disorders (e.g., functional, organic), and the risk of harm to self and/or others. It is obviously not possible to reduce this to a recipe or a formula. Consequently, in the absence of experience in making this assessment, it is wise for clinicians to defer to providers experienced in this area.

For the most part, research in the addiction treatment area focuses on outcomes that compare outpatient with inpatient programs. The results are inconclusive because in many clinical settings individuals with alcohol dependencies and those with other drug dependencies are treated together, along with individuals with different histories of substance abuse and substance dependence. While there have been explorations into modified drinking, predominantly in the United States, chemical dependency treatment programs stress complete abstinence from all forms of alcohol and all self-prescribed medications, regardless of the diagnosis of substance abuse or substance dependence.

Although the predominant treatment orientation is toward complete abstinence as the goal, some people choose reduced consumption instead. Guided Self-Change (Sobell & Sobell 1993b) is a motivational intervention, premised on the idea that individuals "with alcohol problems can solve their problems on their own if they are sufficiently motivated and are provided with some guidance and support" (Sobell & Sobell 1993b, xi). This intervention strategy is particularly important for providers to become aware of.

Another alternative for individuals who feel that they have a drinking problem is Moderation Management™, a nine-step program aimed to help people reduce their alcohol consumption. This approach is detailed in Kishline's *Moderate Drinking: The Moderation Management ™ Guide for People Who Want to Reduce Their Drinking* (1994). The approach is intended for individuals who have encountered mild-to-moderate degrees of alcohol-related problems. It is connected with the Moderation Management Network, a support group network intended to help people reduce their drinking.[6]

As pointed out in earlier chapters, the majority of individuals with drinking problems do not seek formal treatment (Imber et al. 1976; Narrow et al. 1993; Sobell et al. 1992), and many individuals who never receive professional treatment become stably abstinent or moderate drinkers (Humphreys et al. 1995).

Vast amounts of money have been spent on the implementation of some of these models in treatment programs across the country; nevertheless, research has failed to reveal that any one model is better than another. What has frequently occurred is the integration of aspects of one model into another, creating a multimodal treatment approach.

"Alcoholism"—A Disease?

Whether alcoholism should be classified as a disease or as the result of mal-adaptive learning is a complex debate conducted with great vehemence in the literature. The definition of alcoholism has changed over time and as the result of both cultural consensus and medical foundation (Lewis 19; Miller & Chappel 1991). The conceptualization of alcoholism as a disease dates back to the work of Rush (1814, 1834) and was eventually followed by the American Medical Association's (WHO 1967) formal classification in 1956. A recent definition by the American Society of Addiction Medicine (ASAM) represents current thought:[7]

> *Alcoholism is a primary, chronic disease with genetic, psychosocial, and environmental factors influencing its development and manifestations. The disease is often progressive and fatal. It is characterized by continuous or periodic impaired control over drinking, preoccupation with the drug alcohol, use of alcohol despite adverse consequences, and distortions in thinking, most notably denial.*[8]

Many consider loss of control to be a defining and enduring characteristic of alcoholism (Jellinek 1960; Keller 1976; Vaillant 1983). This refers to the "alcoholic's" lack of certainty regarding the consequences of the decision to initiate the consumption of alcohol. Jellinek (1960) arrays the identifiable set of symptoms that support the characterization of alcoholism as a disease in *The Disease Concept of Alcoholism*. This work includes a typology of "alcoholics," a differentiation between physiological and psychological dependency, and the importance of tolerance for the diagnosis of physiological dependency. Vaillant (1983) notes that extensive longitudinal studies support the conclusion that alcoholism is a primary disorder with loss of control as the distinguishing feature. However, such studies are generally done with chronic, severely alcohol-dependent individuals.

Further evidence for the disease definition comes from family studies, as well as from research with twin and adoption samples. Relatives of "alcoholics" are much more likely to develop alcoholism than the general population (Cotton 1979). Twin and adoption studies (Cloninger 1987; Goodwin 1985) support the idea that an inherited predisposition to alcoholism exists; Schuckit's (1986) related work supports the contention that alcoholism is a primary disorder independent of other personality or psychiatric disorders. Dinwiddie and Cloninger (1991) state that alcoholism is "at the end of a lengthy causal chain beginning with the expression of genes and gene products, which subsequently interact in a highly complex way with a variety of environmental influences."[9] However, many questions remain about the nature and strength of this genetic predisposition to alcoholism.

Research is being conducted on the biochemical and neurological differences between "alcoholics" and nonalcoholics. Metabolization of alcohol has been shown to be different between these two groups (Schuckit & Rayses 1979), as has brainwave activity (Begleiter et al. 1984; Noble1991). Although findings are far from conclusive, there is some empirical support for the contention that some genetic and/or physiological differences exist with "alcoholics" and their offspring.

The majority of clinicians in U.S. chemical dependency treatment centers probably subscribe to the Medical Model. However, those professionals who are not part of the chemical dependency treatment field strongly oppose this definition. Nathan (1985) argues forcefully against viewing alcoholism as a disease. Instead, he asserts that the behavior of those individuals addicted to alcohol results from their belief

> that craving and loss of control are inevitable components of alcoholism rather than simply [from] the pharmacologic impact of alcohol . . . the realization grows that what we think and what we believe in and what we are convinced of is much more important in determining our behavior than [is] a narrow physiologic response.[10]

These beliefs are created by the definition of addiction as a disease. Fingarette (1988) proposes that alcohol-related problems are best understood as behavioral disorders that are established and maintained by a range of physical, personal, and social factors that together predispose a person to drink to excess.

Studies designed to examine the relationship between level of alcohol dependence and controlled drinking versus abstinence outcomes have failed to confirm the assertion that alcoholism is progressive in a linear fashion. Instead, there is evidence that the participants' "persuasion" that one type of outcome was more achievable was a more significant factor (Orford & Keddie 1986). Vaillant (1983) notes that the subjects' ethnic group's understanding of alcoholism (disease concept versus concern with moderate drinking and drunkenness) was a factor that contributed to differences in outcome between controlled drinking versus abstinence conditions.

The disease concept is not the cornerstone of addiction treatment in other countries. Peele (1984) cites a British survey that found 93 percent of treatment facilities accepted the principle that controlled-drinking therapy has merit. In the United States, however, the consensus against controlled drinking for more serious alcoholism problems began to form in the 1970s, and currently such an option is anathema for clinicians. Peele (1984) explains that this shift is based on evidence that the more severe the drinking problem, the greater the likelihood of a successful outcome using an abstinence as opposed to a modified-drinking model. Peele asserts that "what makes this resolution less than decisive is the consistent finding that drinking problems occur along a continuum, one that is not well ordered. There is no distinct point at which genuine alcoholism or addiction to alcohol can be said to exist" (1984, 1342). This logically leads to the question whether individuals can benefit from behavior therapy techniques aimed at moderating drinking.

It is difficult to identify subjects for whom modified drinking (as opposed to abstinence) is likely to produce positive outcomes. Therefore, one treatment strategy is to allow individuals to choose their treatment goals themselves, along with input from informed, objective professionals who can assist in the risk-benefit assessment of each treatment goal (abstinence or modified consumption). In addition, professionals can assist individuals to more clearly assess the severity of the substance abuse or dependency. Individuals with severely dependent alcohol problems more often become abstinent when they recover (Vaillant 1983). "Problem drinkers," those who are mildly dependent on alcohol, are more likely to become moderate drinkers (Rosenberg 1993).[11]

An ethical issue exists with the presentation to subjects that abstinence is the only strategy. Provider-selected objectives of abstinence are controversial because there is evidence that when subjects choose their outcome goal, modified drinking or abstinence, successful achievement is predicted during follow-up periods (Booth et al. 1984).

Research on Controlled Drinking

In a review of the literature, Miller (1983) notes that major criticism of controlled drinking consists of the following points: (1) total and permanent abstinence works; (2) countless alcoholics have tried controlled drinking on their own and have failed; (3) there is little research in favor of controlled drinking and its results are mixed; (4) individuals who become controlled drinkers have a higher risk of relapse and show less improvement on other life problems; and (5) it is not possible to unerringly differentiate appropriate candidates for controlled drinking as opposed to abstinence treatments.

However, Miller contends that longer-term (one to three years) follow-up data show that controlled-drinking treatment interventions produce comparable success rates with abstinence approaches. For subjects who have been trained in abstinence models, 5 to 20 percent establish a pattern of nonproblem drinking over the years following treatment. On the average, at one-year follow-up, controlled-drinking training produced successful outcomes for about 65 percent of the subjects.[12] Findings support the hypothesis (Polich et al. 1980) that positive outcomes with controlled-drinking interventions are generally found in subjects with less severe drinking problems. Marlatt (1985a and 1985b) makes a case for the importance of clear diagnosis, at least between abuse and dependency, since studies report that those with the most severe dependencies do better with abstinence versus controlled-drinking interventions.

More research is needed to explore individual differences that yield alternative outcomes with these interventions. There is great need for increased clarity, in terms of theoretical premises of treatment interventions and additional methodological components, to more adequately assess which types of treatment interventions are suited to which types of clients.

✳   ✳   ✳

CHAPTER 27

Assessing Homophobia

Research on homophobia indicates that mental health professionals generally hold more positive attitudes about sexual minorities than does the general public (DeCrescenzo 1984). This does not, however, prevent gay, lesbian, or bisexual clients from encountering a psychotherapist with homophobic and heterosexist attitudes (Garfinkel & Morin 1978). Research conducted in the mid-1980s showed that mental health professionals were often uninformed about sexual minorities' lifestyles and issues (Graham et al. 1983) and hold many of the same stereotypes about sexual minorities as the general public (Casas et al. 1983; DeCrescenzo 1984).

This situation fosters distorted assessments of sexual minorities' issues and concerns. Little research has been done on psychotherapists' heterosexism and homophobia, and training programs pay little attention to these concerns (Buhrke & Douce 1991). Research further indicates that there is greater posttherapy psychological distress for gay and lesbian clients of psychotherapists who have been perceived to hold negative attitudes about homosexuality (Paulsen 1991). External and internalized homophobia, for both clients and psychotherapists, is often an unexplored factor that complicates and interferes with therapeutic work because of complicated transference and countertransference issues (Cabaj 1988).

Framework and Definitions

In discussing homophobia, we begin by setting out some definitions on which to build.[1]

Gender identity. The male or female designation based on genitality.

Gender role. The socially constructed concepts of masculinity and femininity.

Sexual orientation. The same-sex or opposite-sex object choice. It is a complex combination of behaviors, emotions, attitudes, and personal identification, including sexual and lifestyle choices regarding one's selection of intimates.[2]

Sexual attraction. One dimension of sexual orientation, with affectional/emotional and political dimensions.[3]

Homophobia. The irrational fear of gayness or same-sex loving; Brown and Zimmer (1986) define this operationally as the fear and hatred of same-sex intimacy, love, sexuality, and relationships, and of those individuals and institutions that participate in, affirm, and support same-sex relating. Homophobia also manifests itself in hatred, revulsion, disgust, and culturally sanctioned prejudice and violence (homosexual-panic defense).

Internalized homophobia. The unconscious or conscious incorporation and acceptance of negative and derogatory societal beliefs about homosexuality.

Biphobia. The fear of intimacy and closeness to people who don't identify with either the hetero- or homosexual orientation; manifested as homophobia in the heterosexual community and heterophobia in the homosexual community.

Bisexual. People who have erotic, affectionate, romantic feelings for, fantasies of, and experiences with women and men, and/or who self-identify as bisexual.

Heterosexism. The assumption that heterosexuality is superior to homosexuality.

Heterosexual privilege. The benefit of basic civil rights and familial recognition heterosexuals accord themselves as the "norm" (e.g., marriage, job security, tax breaks, parental rights, foster parenting, visitation, and inheritance rights). For women, such privilege often also means the material and physical security of being with a man who has more access to earning power (financial security) and who can protect her from other men. For men, it can mean protection from homophobic "faggot" attacks by other men and benefit from women's free labor in patriarchy—for example, in the forms of housework, cooking, child rearing, and emotional nurturing. This varies depending on race, class, culture, age, and physical abilities.

Closeted. Being secretive (in varying degrees) about sexual orientation.

Out. Being open (in varying degrees) about sexual orientation.

Passing. Appearing to others to be heterosexual based on looks, speech, or attire.

Separatism. The choice to maintain distance from the other gender and from those who relate to the other gender.

Homophobia: External and Internal

Homophobia operates on many levels. One of the levels is punitive. For example, many states make a felony of the sexual activities most common in same-sex relationships. This punitive attitude is also evidenced in denial of custody and visitation rights, loss of employment, discrimination in military service, and barriers to certain government jobs that require security clearances.

A second level is invisibility. There is no socially sanctioned acknowledgment of same-sex relationships. Individuals in these relationships are usually treated as single. For example, their employers often transfer them to other parts of the country without compensation for the costs of moving their families. Some of the most frequently encountered obstacles that result from being denied the rights and privileges of married status include the following:

- the right to file joint income tax returns, and other tax deductions;
- the opportunity to recover damages based on injury to the significant other;
- the right to receive survivor's benefits;
- the opportunity to enter places restricted to "immediate family" such as hospitals and jails;
- the ability to receive family health and dental insurance policies, bereavement leave, and other employment benefits;
- the right to collect unemployment benefits if one partner leaves a job to follow the other to a new location because of a job change;
- getting residency status for a noncitizen spouse;
- the opportunity to make medical decisions in the event that the significant other is injured or incapacitated;
- the right to inherit the property of the significant other in the absence of a will.

Additional obstacles that sexual minorities must overcome involve the lack of social supports for couples, and the lack of sanctioned rituals such as marital showers and weddings.

Many sexual minorities have developed creative ways of coping with these obstacles. For example, although same-sex partners are not included in each other's legal family (and thus can be barred from visiting in intensive care units if the biological family insists), preexisting legal agreements between the partners can allow such visitation. Many sexual minorities have adapted existing rituals or created new ones; many have used commitment ceremonies as a way to validate themselves and their relationships.

There are two clear types of homophobia, external and internal. Hate crimes, such as "queer bashing," are an obvious manifestation of external homophobia. Assaults and murders motivated by external homophobia are reported on from time to time in the newspapers. In addition, recent studies reveal that 92 percent of gays and lesbians report being targets of verbal abuse or threats, and more than one-third are survivors of violence related to their sexual orientation. As much as 90 percent of antigay violence goes unreported. The impact of this vulnerability must not be overlooked.

Another clear type of homophobia is internal. Internal homophobia includes the explicit and the implicit—conscious and unconscious—attitudes, beliefs, and values in individuals socialized in homophobic cultures. For example, beliefs about the inability of gay/lesbian relationships to endure, or of gay men to be monogamous, may be held implicitly or explicitly. The same is true for negative feelings that gays, lesbians, or bisexuals may have about themselves, their sexual behavior, or other sexual minorities.

Sensitivity to Homophobia

Gays and lesbians are hypersensitive to homophobia in others, whether it be total disconnection or polite avoidance. Stereotypes of gays and lesbians result from homophobia, as well as ignorance. Some stereotypes of lesbians and gays that come to mind are sinners, misfits, child molesters, diesel dykes, swishy hairdressers, and drag queens. It is important to examine these stereotypes.

Many gays and lesbians develop dual identities because of the stigma of homosexuality. Lesbians and gays also develop finely tuned radar to detect homophobia in others. Some choose to remain invisible or attempt to "pass as straight." But this invisibility or "passing" has negative consequences on self-esteem, self-concept, and the ability to develop and maintain honest, genuine, and fulfilling relationships. Hiding or passing results in a loss of authenticity and integrity; individuals who adopt this behavior tend to become alienated and isolated.

But let us acknowledge the difficulties and risks of the alternatives. Coming out—identifying oneself as gay, lesbian, or bisexual—risks rejection or worse. Being out risks security because of reprisals from employers or landlords, rejection from family and friends, expulsion from religious groups, and possible loss of child custody and visitation rights. It also risks physical abuse and attack. For some, just buying a gay- or lesbian-related book is a source of anxiety or terror. It is essential that every psychotherapist be aware of the risks clients run in disclosing their sexual orientation in therapy.

(Psychotherapists need to be aware that language used by sexual minorities to describe themselves may not be acceptable when used by "mainstream" psychotherapists. For example, a lesbian may refer to herself as a "dyke" in conversation with her friends, but may not be open to that term when used by a nongay psychotherapist. It is essential to discuss this issue directly with the client.)

Sexual Attraction

In the 1950s, Kinsey and his colleagues discovered that people experience sexuality along a continuum (Kinsey et al. 1953). This scale is an equal-interval scale with continuous gradations between heterosexuality and homosexuality. An individual rating is based on relative amounts of heterosexual and homosexual response. Kinsey used the scale to rate individuals on overt experiences and psychological reactions. The ratings are as follows:

(0) Exclusively heterosexual

(1) Predominantly heterosexual, only incidentally homosexual

(2) Predominantly heterosexual, but more than incidentally homosexual

(3) Equally heterosexual and homosexual

(4) Predominantly homosexual, but more than incidentally heterosexual

(5) Predominantly homosexual, only incidentally heterosexual

(6) Exclusively homosexual[4]

At one end of the continuum are those who feel sexual attraction only for those of the opposite gender; at the other end are those who feel sexual attraction only for those of the same gender. Kinsey concluded that most people fall somewhere in between the two extremes. Kinsey et al. proposed the idea that people choose their sexual identities for a variety of reasons—social, religious, cultural, and political—in addition to physical attraction.

The Klein Sexual Orientation Grid (Klein et al. 1985) was developed to measure a person's sexual orientation as a dynamic multivariable process. It was designed to extend the scope for the Kinsey scale by including attraction, behavior, fantasy, social and emotional preference, self-identification, and lifestyle. These characteristics are also measured in the past, in the present, and as an ideal. The Klein grid provides a framework for understanding sexual orientation on a theoretical level. On a practical level it enables the researcher to separate groups more precisely, and to focus on the individual while noting some of the common configurations.[5]

A preponderance of individuals identify experiences of sexual attraction somewhere between the two extremes on the sexual continuum. This is particularly important for psychotherapists to acknowledge and understand. Those psychotherapists who have not confronted their own hidden or forbidden homoerotic feelings are likely to find themselves very uncomfortable when faced with a client's homosexuality.

Homosexual Orientation

Some psychotherapists may believe that adolescents are too young to know about their orientation. The Kinsey Institute study of sexual development (Bell et al. 1981) found, however, that most homosexual males could identify themselves as homosexual on the basis of their erotic feelings by the time of puberty (around age thirteen), and most homosexual females by age fifteen or sixteen. Approximately nine out of ten recognized their erotic orientation through romantic infatuations, dreams, or masturbation fantasies, or they simply knew they were sexually "different" some years before they became (homo)sexually active. When they did become active, the behaviors merely reflected their already-present feelings.

The Kinsey Institute research indicates that homosexuality will be the enduring adult orientation of adolescents who are confused because of feeling both homosexual and heterosexual attractions (perhaps one year having a crush on a boy, and the next year having a crush on a girl, or feeling capable of both types of sexual experience). The heterosexual control group almost never reported this sort of confusion or variability in erotic attractions.

This same research had additional findings:

1. Parents and family environment have little to do with the determination of sexual orientation.

2. Homosexuality does not result from recruitment.

3. Homosexuality does not develop through social learning or sexual conditioning (early pleasurable experiences with members of one's own sex, traumatic experiences with members of the opposite sex, or a same-sex environment).

4. Sexual orientation is not a matter of choice.

5. Sexual orientation is related to some degree to gender differentiation.

Bisexuals, those in the middle of the Kinsey scale, face many of the same issues as gays and lesbians in terms of homophobia, gender socialization, same-sex relationships, and discrimination. However, bisexuals confront unique problems stemming from their marginality in both the gay and nongay communities.[6] *BI Any Other Name* (Hutchins & Kaahumanu 1991) is a useful resource for more in-depth understanding of specific issues.

Heterosexism

Heterosexism, or heterosexual bias, is insidious. It is inculcated into individuals from birth via direct and indirect messages. Most people are not even aware that they are raised with the general assumption that heterosexuality is superior to homosexuality. They frequently express shock and surprise when their heterosexual bias is identified and challenged.

Heterosexism also means assuming that everyone is heterosexual. We have frequently heard psychotherapists question why it is so important for clients to come out and tell others of their orientation. One reason is that coming out helps to combat stereotypes and heterosexism. Individuals who fit certain physical and behavioral stereotypes are thought to be homosexual, whereas anyone else is assumed to be heterosexual (Eldridge 1987). This results in the reinforcing of stereotypes.

Psychotherapists' attitudes about homosexuality are related to their level of homophobia. Homophobia gives rise to anxiety and discomfort; therefore, psychotherapists may experience great anxiety when confronted with gay, lesbian, or bisexual clients and may respond to this anxiety in a number of different ways. Psychotherapists may avoid, deny, or minimize the issues of gay, lesbian, and bisexual clients. Or they may respond with token acceptance or overtolerance. Psychotherapists who have successfully overcome their homophobia are able to respond with real tolerance, honest acceptance, affirmation, support, and advocacy.

It is difficult for psychotherapists to make honest self-assessments about their degree of homophobia because ethical codes require tolerance. They often have idealized beliefs about what they should think and feel. They know they are not supposed to be racist, sexist, ageist, or homophobic. However, this *expectation* of tolerance and acceptance may not match internal reality because of socialization and life experiences. This is understandable, even though it may not be ethically acceptable to remain that way. These discrepancies between what psychotherapists are supposed to think and believe and what they actually believe create fear and distance in forming a therapeutic relationship. This incongruence can also lead to inconsistency in treatment and interventions, and may result in premature termination by either the psychotherapist or the client.

Unresolved Homophobia

There are several indications of the presence of unresolved homophobia. One is negative attitudes regarding physical affection between gays or lesbians, in or outside of counseling sessions. Another is discomfort with addressing a client's comfort with sex practices, or sexual identity. Still another is difficulty understanding the problems and complications of gay and lesbian lifestyles (e.g., insensitivity to issues related to oppression and marginalization): "Why do they keep having to make such an issue of it? I don't mention to people that I'm heterosexual. Why do they have to tell people that they're gay or lesbian?"

Homophobic attitudes are not limited to heterosexuals. All of us grow up in a culture that inculcates heterosexist attitudes and beliefs. Gays, lesbians, and bisexuals may be *most* homophobic at the beginning of their recovery process because of lifelong sensitivity to cultural homophobic comments and messages. Young people who are questioning their sexuality or wondering about their orientation or attraction are more likely to have heard homophobic comments—and to have taken in and reflected on the comments more deeply—than someone not concerned about whether the comments apply to them.

All psychotherapists need to work through issues related to homophobia. If the psychotherapist is homosexual and out, concern over self-revelation for fear of distracting clients from their issues, crossing boundaries, and giving unclear messages about the nature of the relationship needs to be resolved.

Looking at Biases

It is also important to examine biases that psychotherapists may have about sexual minorities. Here are some of the most common biases: gay men are not capable of fidelity; all gay men are promiscuous; lesbians are not happy if they're not in a relationship; lesbians have boundary problems and create fused connections. Each of these may be an issue for the individual client, or it may not. Psychotherapists need to look at the meaning and function of such issues for the individual client.

There are many common stereotypes regarding gays, lesbians, and bisexuals: all same-sex couples have a butch/femme polarization; gay men are effeminate and lesbians are not; bisexuals are "just sitting on the fence." Such stereotypes hinder understanding of the particular experiences and reality of the individual or couple that comes to a psychotherapist for assistance. These stereotypes are maintained by fear and lack of information; they can be changed by contact and open minded interaction with a diversity of individuals who identify themselves as lesbian, gay, or bisexual.

It is also important for psychotherapists to be aware of the existence of violence in some homosexual relationships, and to have a clear understanding of specific sexual practices such as sadism and masochism ("S and M"). A discussion of "S and M" is beyond the scope of this book. However, a psychotherapist may need to assist clients in exploring the differences between alternative sexual practices and exploitive and abusive behaviors.

Relevance of Racial/Ethnic Issues

There are both similarities and differences in the experiences of sexual minorities and racial and ethnic minorities. It may be helpful for psychotherapists to modify the developmental schema in the literature on racial identity development to include the dimension of sexual identity development.

Psychotherapists need to work through their own racial or ethnic identity development process[7] in order to more effectively work with others of similar and different racial and ethnic groups. It is also imperative that psychotherapists, regardless of sexual orientation, work through a similar process with regard to their sexual identity. This is Cross's (1971) model for black racial identity:

Stage 1. Pre-encounter—Identifies with White culture, rejects and or denies membership in Black culture.

Stage 2. Encounter—Rejects previous identification with White culture, seeks identification with Black culture.

Stage 3. Immersion-Emmersion—Completely identifies with Black culture and denigrates White culture.

Stage 4. Internalization—Internalizes Black culture, transcends racism.

Stage 5. Internalization-Commitment—Internalizes Black culture, fights general cultural oppression.[8]

This model can be modified to track the development of sexual orientation identity. Psychotherapists, regardless of orientation, may be in any of these stages: either blind to issues related to sexual orientation or overwhelmingly identified with this orientation; rejecting the "culture" of their own orientation and over-valuing that of the other orientation; transcending both positions to have an integrated, transcultural understanding of sexual orientation and the relevant issues and implications. Applying this model to sexual orientation, psychotherapists need to explore their own development process.

In cross-cultural counseling, along with certain similarities, there are differences between racial/ethnic minorities and sexual minorities. For many African Americans, the immediate and extended family is a haven from discrimination and racism. It is a place where the individual can receive guidance for coping with societal and institutional racism and discrimination. The family can model a positive self-identity and can provide acceptance and affirmation even though the outside environment is racist or hostile.

For many sexual minorities, however, the family is not a safe haven. Coming out risks loss of ties to individuals or to the entire family depending on the level of family members' homophobia. Even if the loss is less than complete, it is likely that relationships will be profoundly altered for some time. Some sexual minorities live a dual life with the possible attendant reduction in self-esteem and integrity.

Sexual minorities can "pass" more easily than racial minorities. Passing may help diminish the overt results of discrimination and oppression, but it is costly to self-esteem and integrity. For example, a police officer may successfully hide his sexual orientation behind his charade of the "flight-attendant" girlfriend who is always conveniently out of town for the annual picnic or holiday party. However, if he does have a partner, there will be costs to his relationship because of the charade. Another cost of "passing" is hearing all the homophobic comments of others who might have curbed their remarks if they'd known the truth. Unable to challenge these remarks, the police officer may feel angry, frustrated, and isolated, and suffer significant dis-ease.

Another difference arises over the substantial controversy about whether homosexuality or bisexuality is an orientation or a preference.[9] (No one asks whether being of African or Asian descent is a choice!) Racial and ethnic minorities are not given the message that they could choose not to be a member of their race or ethnicity. However, gays, lesbians, and bisexuals are often asked not to value or affirm or promote that identity. Psychotherapists who already work with racial and ethnic minorities, and who are seeking to become more effective with sexual minorities, can easily build on their existing expertise. (This can work the other way as well. Psychotherapists can utilize the insights and awareness gained working with sexual minorities to enhance their work with other individuals who identify themselves as having minority affiliation.)

Dual Relationships

Gay and lesbian psychotherapists need to acknowledge and address the issue of dual relationships—being "out" to some people while at the same time remaining in the closet with others. This is particularly essential in a small or rural community. Even in a metropolitan community, because of past and present interconnections, the psychotherapist is likely to confront many challenges with regard to an intricately related community. Brown (1989) explores in depth many issues that psychotherapists may wish to consider.

For gay and lesbian psychotherapists in small communities, being out has important consequences: for example, the possibility of developing a reputation for specializing in gay and lesbian issues and thus limiting one's referral options; or developing a practice of gay, lesbian, and bisexual clients and having limited social options because of the probability of encountering one's current and former clients. If psychotherapists are not out, they may fear exposure to coworkers or supervisors and the impact this will have on case assignments and advancement. However, a psychotherapist not willing to be out loses an important opportunity for modeling a healthy, positive identity for clients. Choosing to remain closeted with the supervisor can put the psychotherapist in jeopardy because it places certain issues off-limits for discussion. For example, issues of transference and countertransference are not likely to be addressed and resolved as effectively.

Consider the following hypothetical situation. You are working in a residential treatment program for chemical dependency. You identify yourself as homosexual and have come out to a couple of your coworkers. However, you are not out with your clinical supervisor. One of your clients is a young man or woman who believes that he or she may be homosexual. The client has limited information about sexual orientation and many misconceptions. In addition, the client believes that being homosexual will doom him or her to an awful existence. The client has no gay or lesbian contacts or role models.

The client relates negative beliefs about himself or herself, as well as a possible connection between these beliefs and the individual's abuse of substances. You weigh the relative benefits and costs of coming out to the client. You think it to be in the client's best interest for you to self-disclose in a limited fashion, and to give the client as much information about the coming-out process, positive identity development, and community resources as possible. However, since you are not out to your supervisor, you do not discuss this decision in supervision prior to coming out to the client.

As the treatment progresses, you begin to suspect that this client is developing romantic feelings toward you. Under the circumstances, this may be quite anxiety provoking. What do you do? Having come out to this client places you in a vulnerable position because your sexual orientation is a "secret" in supervision. This is not advisable.

After much consideration of this question, it appears wise only to be out with clients if one is willing to be out in public. It is essential to be out in supervision in order to use supervision effectively to address the client's feelings and issues as well as the clinician's. This hypothetical situation highlights one of the risks for lesbian and gay psychotherapists when working with sexual minorities. If gay and lesbian psychotherapists are not open and comfortable with their own sexual orientation, they are likely to face many more risks in clinical situations.

Regardless of personal sexual orientation, it is essential for psychotherapists who work or are planning to work with sexual minorities to be conscious of their own homophobia and heterosexism, and to be as fully aware as possible of the impact of externalized homophobia on sexual minorities. It is also imperative for psychotherapists to closely monitor their personal reactions toward each gay, lesbian, and bisexual client and couple. It is essential for psychotherapists to acknowledge their limitations related to knowledge, tolerance, or awareness. Psychotherapists need to obtain supervision or consultation when encounters with clients press on the limits of their knowledge or awareness (Buhrke 1989). They should also be willing to refer clients to other therapists when their own levels of tolerance or understanding are breached without possibility of resolution.[10]

❊   ❊   ❊

CHAPTER 28

Working with Gay, Lesbian, and Bisexual Clients

Therapists should not expect their clients to train them about issues relevant to sexual minorities or to work through homophobic attitudes generated by their clients' sexual orientation. On-the-job training is particularly ill-advised with sexual minorities, who are extremely sensitive to criticism, rejection, and oppression.

Studies estimate that 10 to 15 percent of the population is gay or lesbian in the United States—about 22 million; yet, only about 1.5 million are considered to constitute the "out" population of gays and lesbians (Rudolph 1989). Men and women who choose to come out confront negative societal attitudes as well as their own internalized homophobia, and they must repeat the process over and over in each new situation in which their gayness is not known. The process occurs in the context of few, if any, role models; inadequate support systems; lack of legal protection; and—for gays and lesbians of some racial/ethnic groups—added isolation and potential loss of primary racial/ethnic identification and community.

Brown (1989) has asserted that coming out also entails addressing the following three elements thought to be common to all sexual minorities: first, biculturalism resulting from simultaneous participation in two cultural realities; second, marginality and the experience of being an outsider from the cultural majority; third, "normative creativity," i.e., the need to invent intrapsychic and interpersonal boundaries and rules that are often developed without existing models or guidelines, or may be adapted from other situations that may not be entirely applicable. This normative creativity encourages numerous alternatives—and often inspired solutions—to demanding interpersonal challenges.

Identity Development

Whether identity development is seen as a series of stages (Cass 1979; Lewis 1984; Woodman & Lenna 1980) or as a more fluid process (Golden 1987; Gramick 1984; Ponse 1978), it is not a fixed and sequential series of developments. Rather, identity development is individualized and varying, and may even be cycling over time based on environmental or developmental forces.

Cass sees development as follows:

1. *Identity Confusion*—characterized by feelings of turmoil, in which one questions previously held ideas about one's sexual orientation.

2. *Identity Comparison*—characterized by feelings of alienation, in which one accepts the possibility of being gay and becomes isolated from nongay others.

3. *Identity Tolerance*—characterized by feelings of ambivalence, in which one seeks out other gays, but maintains separate public and private images.

4. *Identity Acceptance*—characterized by selective disclosure, in which one begins the legitimization (publicly as well as privately) of one's sexual orientation.

5. *Identity Pride*—characterized by anger, pride, and activism, in which one becomes immersed in the gay subculture and rejects nongay people, institutions, and values.

6. *Identity Synthesis*—characterized by clarity and acceptance, in which one moves beyond a dichotomized worldview to an incorporation of one's sexual orientation as one aspect of a more integrated identity.[1]

This model may be clinically useful but it has limitations. In addition to its linear approach, the model is not sensitive to diversity in race/ethnicity, age, class, locale, or occupation. It also assumes that political activism is a necessary part of identity development, and it gives little attention to the significance of homoerotic intimacy. Finally, it does not address the parallel and reciprocal processes involved in identity development for sexual minorities noted by McCarn and Fassinger (1990): first, self-identification; second, group-membership identification and awareness of marginalization and oppression. Stage models also do not adequately capture the differences in identity development for men and women based on gender differences stemming from sex-role socialization (McCarn & Fassinger 1990). In working with any client, the therapist needs to adapt any model of identity development to the unique experience of that client.

Specific Issues for Counseling

Research indicates that homosexuals are two to four times more likely than heterosexuals to seek out treatment, and a significantly larger proportion of homosexuals is dissatisfied with that counseling. Rudolph (1989) suggests that this dissatisfaction is caused by psychotherapists' being either ignorant of or prejudiced toward homosexuality.

Many sexual minorities will not reveal their identities unless they feel comfortable in the setting. Nondisclosure produces censorship and distance; disclosure risks rejection and isolation (Zigrang 1982).

With appropriate support and affirmation, it is possible for lesbians and gays to accept their homosexuality and to develop a positive gay or lesbian identity. A positive identity is essential for self-esteem and leads to enhanced psychological adjustment of sexual minorities. Literature consistently shows that homosexuals do not differ significantly from heterosexuals in their psychological adjustment (Hooker 1957). However, research has also shown a correlation between psychological health and the degree of "being out" (Bell & Weinberg 1978; Gartrell 1984). Moreover, cross-cultural studies suggest that any maladjustment stems from societal homophobia rather than from inherent pathology (Atkinson & Hackett 1988).

There are differences between the gay and lesbian cultures, and it is not appropriate to apply the conclusions of research on gay men to lesbians without empirical verification. Some differences between lesbians and gay men are readily apparent with regard to love and sexuality. For example, lesbians appear to place the highest value on an intimate, love relationship, with all other things being significantly less important (Gilligan 1982). Many gay men do not make their relationships their highest priority.

There are also differences in the meaning of sex and love for gays and lesbians. Some people quip that gay men have sex first and later they may fall in love, and vice versa for lesbians (Falco 1991). There are also differences in the frequency of sexual activity between lesbians and gay men. Lesbians often have less frequent genital sensuality than gay men. However, lesbians have a higher rate of affection, touching, caressing, and nongenital sensuality (Loulan 1984).

Some studies (Colgon & Riebel 1981; Isay 1989; Johnson 1985) show that ideal identity development results from an ongoing interaction between the individual's personal sense of self-worth and the response of significant individuals (particularly parents) in the individual's life. Consistently negative responses harm the capacity for self-valuing and halt or disturb identity development. An identity disorder will have a profound effect on the individual, particularly in the development of self-esteem and fulfilling interpersonal relationships. If the responses from others are generally positive, however, individuals will develop a positive sense of self-worth. Optimally, as individuals grow and mature, they will come to depend on an internal sense of self-worth and become less sensitive to the reactions of others when making decisions or self-perceptions (Shannon & Woods 1991).

Shannon and Woods suggest exploring the following areas in order to assess individuals' level of identity development:

a) early relationships with parents, siblings, and other significant caretakers; b) ways in which affection was or was not expressed in the family; c) how conflict was handled within the family; d) at what age the individuals knew they were "different" from other boys or girls, and their understanding of this difference; e) their first awareness of sexual/affectual feelings for others of their gender; f) a careful description of their process of "coming out"; g) a history of significant romantic relationships (i.e., dating, boy and girl friends, and lover relationships); h) a thorough sexual history, including a frank discussion of sexual fantasies and sexual preferences; i) gender role conformity and nonconformity, and its impact on the individual's process of "coming out."[2]

It is not possible to overemphasize the importance of developing a positive identity. Positive identity and intimacy interact and reinforce each other (Colgon 1987). Individuals who lack a positive identity will have great difficulty establishing and maintaining healthy relationships of any sort.

Because gays and lesbians have often experienced rejection, disapproval, and unrealistic expectations from parents and other authority figures, it is essential to develop a trusting relationship. Developing trust and coping with the client's pain, anger, and confusion can be particularly challenging, especially for psychotherapists who are coping with their own confused feelings about the client and the client's sexual orientation.

Working with Couples

Same-sex couples have very different sets of dynamics than heterosexual couples for two reasons—gender-role socialization and homophobia.

Gender-role socialization shows up in such areas as expressing and sharing power, expressing anger and hostility, initiation of sexual activity, and tolerance of conflict and differences. Because they were likely socialized in a similar way, both partners in a same-sex relationship play the same gender roles. This has both benefits and drawbacks. To work with same-sex couples, therapists must have a clear comprehension of the strengths and deficits of each gender role.

For same-sex partners, there is no equivalent of "Ozzie and Harriet." The metamessage for each partner is that the couple doesn't or shouldn't exist. This leads to internalized negative attitudes about the couple's viability and worth. Many couples structure their relationships for the inevitable breakup: financial resources are often kept separate; individual partners often have their own set of friends and interests; and career planning is rarely coordinated. Berzon's book *Permanent Partners* (1988) is a helpful resource for both psychotherapists and couples alike.

Also, there may be significant differences in each partner's sexual identity development. Although they may be about the same age, they may be in very different stages of their development, with correspondingly different feelings about their sexual orientation.

For lesbian couples, there may be boundary problems, such as intolerance for distance and difference. The mother-infant daughter relationship—including such features as perfect empathy, mutuality of needs, and poorly defined boundaries—becomes the paradigm for close and loving relationships between women. Often, the therapist needs to help women in couples counseling define appropriate boundaries. Sometimes fusion results in problems with sexual activity, and some lesbian couples attempt to gain sufficient distance by avoiding sexual contact. This avoidance may also stem from internalized homophobia or other unresolved conflicts in the relationship.

Gay male couples may have boundary problems too, of course. Because gays (and men in general) are not socialized to nurture and build relationships, they often need help in the work of maintaining those relationships. Often gays have very rigid ideas about masculinity that interfere with their ability to be intimate. Therapy often involves helping men become more expressive of their needs and feelings. Because gay couples have fewer models of effective relationships than lesbians have, it may be necessary to help dysfunctional gay couples connect with functional couples.

Therapists may need to help gay men define relationship boundaries and levels of monogamy. (Simultaneous emotional monogamy and sexual nonmonogamy is quite common.) It is important to assist individuals and couples to define explicitly their needs and expectations for their relationship.

Also, it is important to address competitiveness in the areas of power and status in gay relationships because competitiveness can become destructive to the relationship. Money and status differences can become major sources of conflict. Status differences can lead to the devaluation of the partner with the lesser status, but both men may need help in understanding the dynamics of the situation.

Gay and lesbian couples may also have problems accessing a community of other well-functioning couples. The biggest gathering place for gays and lesbians is in bars. Couples often do not frequent the bars.

Nonexclusivity is the most common pattern for long-term gay male relationships (Harry 1983). Of lesbian couples, 75 to 85 percent are sexually exclusive, while less than half of gay couples are sexually exclusive. Agreement on the open or closed nature of the relationship is the critical factor.

Many psychotherapists measure the health of a same-sex couple by the couple's similarity to ideal heterosexual unions. Some therapists ask their gay or lesbian couple clients, "Who plays the 'male' and who plays the 'female' role?" This kind of question is based on heterosexist stereotypes and oversimplifies relationship dynamics. (It is also likely to raise doubt in the couple's mind about the therapist's level of competence.)

Married (heterosexual) couples automatically have a "legitimate relationship"; societal and legal procedures help clarify each partner's rights and responsibilities. The couple automatically becomes a family, with or without the presence of children. This social and legal legitimacy provides a supportive environment for the relationship that is often lacking in same-sex relationships.

Through different rituals, some sexual minorities are inventing different forms of marriage and creating experiences of greater social acknowledgment, such as commitment ceremonies. They often attempt to create legal relationships through partnership agreements, powers of attorney, and living wills. However, because legal marriage is not possible, often gays and lesbians do not have the legal or social support of "divorce" rituals either.

Therapists need to be especially careful not to imply that nonheterosexual relationships are less meaningful or are less painful to dissolve. Therapists must be careful not to be judgmental of the couple's negotiated rules about such things as monogamy and finances. Individuals are likely to be extremely sensitive to messages that devalue or diminish the legitimacy of their pain. On top of the expected emotions that divorce produces—guilt, hurt, anger, fear—sexual minorities have additional pressure because of discrimination, stigmatization, and the insensitivity of society.

During divorce, internalized homophobia may be particularly destructive and may surface as stereotypes that gays and lesbians can't have successful relationships or that such relationships are wrong. It's also easy to romanticize heterosexual relationships at this time and to envy the social approval and comfort of heterosexual marriage (and divorce).[3]

Working with At-Risk Adolescents

Psychotherapists face numerous challenges in working with adolescent sexual minorities. The biggest challenge may be refraining from the assumption that all adolescents are heterosexual (Paroski 1987). Therapists should always use language sensitive to sexual minorities to help safeguard against the assumption of heterosexuality and make it safe for adolescents to self-disclose. A gay, lesbian, or bisexual adolescent who chooses to disclose to a therapist is overcoming substantial familial and peer pressures to remain hidden.

Prior to any intervention, the therapist should make a careful exploration of the adolescent's history and developmental level. This assessment should include an investigation into the adolescent's values and social mores.

The therapist needs to maintain a nonjudgmental attitude in this process, particularly with regard to the adolescent's possible sexual experiences with peers or adults. Sexual experience (heterosexual or homosexual) or lack thereof may not accurately reflect interest or orientation. Assessing possible reasons for lack of experience—such as negative attitudes about sexual minorities, possible feelings of guilt and fear, religious beliefs, or parental injunctions—is important. It is also important to assess carefully when teens have had experiences with adults because such contacts may not have been consensual. Determining the adolescent's understanding of intimacy as well as the cultural and social dimensions of sexual orientation is part of this assessment.

Once therapists have clarified the adolescent's perceptions about sexual orientation, they can construct an appropriate intervention. Adolescents' sexual identity confusion can be significantly diminished if therapists effectively assist them to explore personal attitudes toward homosexuality or bisexuality, foster understanding and self-acceptance, and facilitate safe and appropriate experimentation.

Therapists need to facilitate and support such experimentation for homosexual and bisexual adolescents as they would for heterosexual adolescents. This is difficult for some therapists to do (Coleman & Remafedi 1989). Some therapists may minimize an adolescent's homosexual interests (Gonsiorek 1988), which is likely to be quite harmful. Other therapists, not accepting that sexual orientation appears to be established relatively early in childhood, may fear that discussion of homosexuality or bisexuality may foster or promote both. It is important for therapists not to encourage a premature foreclosure on the issue of sexual orientation and identity. Understanding and acceptance of any sexual orientation is a process that unfolds and develops over time; it cannot be rushed or mapped out on a time line.

Instead, therapists should work to assist adolescents to develop effective coping skills, fulfilling interpersonal relationships, and age appropriate sexual exploration. Teens have great difficulty accessing information about sexual minorities or getting feedback and validation about their behavior or feelings (Wakelee-Lynch 1989). Therapists can offer much needed information about human sexuality and provide affirming messages about adolescents' intrinsic worth independent of their sexual orientation. Therapists also need to provide messages to counteract social and cultural homophobic and heterosexist messages.

Most importantly, therapists must not give adolescents the message that "it's just a stage" or that they are too young to know whether or not they are homosexual or bisexual. This is clearly not the message given to heterosexual teens. It is perfectly appropriate for bisexual and homosexual adolescents to question their homoerotic feelings. This questioning is not a sign of latent heterosexuality. It is very important for therapists to value and affirm adolescents' internal experiences and thus help to develop reality-based self-concepts (Slater 1988). This will go a long way to help prevent adolescents from developing serious and life-threatening behaviors that result when they are not able to positively resolve sexual identity confusion or obtain adequate social and familial support.

For lesbian and gay teens, finding a supportive environment, much less a peer group, is particularly problematic. In a society that pretends that gays and lesbians shouldn't exist, it isn't surprising that sexual orientation confusion has been identified as a possible major factor in teenage suicide, which is the third leading cause of death in adolescents age fifteen to twenty-four (and the eighth-leading cause of death in the United States across the population).[4]

There are many dangerous outlets for adolescents who are struggling to cope with sexual orientation conflicts: drug and alcohol abuse, homelessness, prostitution, HIV, and suicide. Teens experience a great deal of conflict over society's view that it is wrong to be gay, lesbian, or bisexual. Those who accept society's view that their orientation is wrong experience tremendous psychological turmoil. This, in turn, exposes them to tremendous risk for suicide, possibly related to inner psychological conflict.[5]

Coleman and Remafedi (1989) report that as many as 7 percent of gay men and 12 percent of lesbians have attempted suicide, with the majority of suicide attempts for gay men occurring before the age of twenty-one. (However, this must not be assumed to mean that those who attempt suicide are necessarily the same as those who complete suicide.)

Psychotherapists need to assist teens in resolving their conflict between the negative societal messages about homosexuality and bisexuality and their need to develop a positive sense of self-worth. Psychotherapists can foster this resolution by helping adolescents to develop internalized positive identity. They can also help adolescents to cease defining themselves based on external pressures to conform or to deny their own identity, and to resist the temptation to drop out of school or drop out of life.

Therapy can assist adolescents to put their sexual identity into perspective as one dimension of who they are by discussing the advantages and disadvantages of coming out to parents, teachers, and friends. Such a discussion can help the adolescent weigh the costs and benefits of coming out and plan for all possible reactions. The therapist should encourage caution and careful planning if disclosure is chosen. Therapists can also work to help parents process reactions. Parents can be expected to go through a process of acceptance, and it is necessary to be realistic about the time dimension of that process.

Schneider and Tremble's (1986) experience may be a useful reference for developing curricula for group interventions:

- Homosexuality is not an obstacle in and of itself to developing into happy, productive adults.

- Gay and lesbian adolescents need to be helped to view sexual orientation in a positive fashion and not as an excuse to avoid the challenges and responsibilities of maturation and development.

- The issues and concerns of adolescent sexual minorities are frequently the same as heterosexual adolescents although the context or specifics may be different. (Schneider and Tremble give as an example a gay adolescent making advances to other male students. A psychotherapist should intervene in the same fashion as with a heterosexual male making unwanted advances toward female students.)

- There are no easy answers or boilerplate approaches for working with adolescent sexual minorities. The therapist should use good counseling practices and techniques and acknowledge limitations.

In working with adolescents, therapists need to confront negative stereotypes in the media and the shortage of positive role models, as well as difficulties developing a peer group of other gays, lesbians, and bisexuals in many locales. It is wise to address other realities such as the increased risk of physical assault, peer pressure to deny homosexual or bisexual orientation, and possible rejection by family, friends, and religious groups.

One interesting training program for student leaders to diminish prejudicial attitudes has been developed by Iasenza and Troutt (1990). The program's goal is to sensitize student leaders on issues relevant to racism, sexism, homophobia, and anti-Semitism. Through a word-association prejudice exercise and a small-group prejudice-problem-solving exercise, students express their hurt, fears, and anger about prejudice by discussing the development of stereotypes and the implications for all groups. Iasenza and Troutt report significant positive effects of being able to confront and discuss these beliefs and attitudes in a safe environment that helps to develop a more open and tolerant atmosphere.[6]

Some Practical Suggestions

Psychotherapists must be conscious of their own homophobia, heterosexism, and personal reactions toward the client. They need to acknowledge their limitations related to knowledge, tolerance, or awareness. All therapists need to obtain supervision or consultation when encounters with clients press on their limits of knowledge or awareness. Psychotherapists should also be willing to refer clients to others when their own levels of tolerance or understanding are breached without possibility of resolution.

Psychotherapists should be familiar with sexual minorities' language and jargon, and for this purpose should have firsthand knowledge and familiarity with sexual minorities. Graham et al. (1984) discovered that most therapists in their survey had positive attitudes about homosexuality. For example: 81 percent agreed that homosexuality is not a mental disorder (in accordance with American Psychological and American Psychiatric associations positions); 77 percent thought homosexuals could be as well-adjusted as heterosexuals; and 94 percent agreed homosexuals should be in teaching, parental, religious, and human service roles.

Although their attitudes were generally positive, therapists in the study had little basic information about sexual minorities—information that was available in the scientific literature. For example: only one-half of the respondents were aware that most homosexuals have had sexual experiences with members of the other gender; about one-quarter thought it irrelevant to help clients make others aware of their sexual orientation, despite evidence of the connection between openness about sexual orientation and psychological health; and two-thirds agreed that it is possible for counseling to alter an individual's sexual orientation, although no empirical evidence supports this statement.

Issues of attraction and sexual energy in the process of therapy may be especially challenging. Therapists may need supervision to work through other countertransference issues. If the client is in the coming-out process, the therapist should encourage the client to develop new friendships and explore community supports. This will broaden the client's support network and reduce dependence on the psychotherapist.

Many gay and lesbian clients may prefer lesbian and gay psychotherapists. There is a clear difference between the statements "I know what you feel" and "I know how you must feel." Clients may ask psychotherapists direct questions about their sexuality, training, and values. These questions represent a legitimate trust-building activity, and psychotherapists can learn to respond to clients' concerns without necessarily divulging personal information they regard as private. Gay and lesbian psychotherapists may not wish to divulge their sexual identity. This is an issue to process in supervision as well.

It is important for nongay psychotherapists to learn to interpret requests for a lesbian or gay psychotherapist as a positive identity issue for the client rather than as a personal rejection. The psychotherapist can refer accordingly if this seems to be in the client's best interest.

The provider's sexual orientation is less salient when the therapeutic issue is not sexual. The psychotherapist must determine to what degree homosexuality is a part of the issues bringing the individual to therapy. However, even when the issues are not specifically related to sexual orientation, sexual orientation is never irrelevant because it is an essential component of the client's life.

Further Considerations and Recommendations

Until clients specify the sex of their partners, therapists should use gender-neutral language with all clients. For example, when the client says, "This person I met at a party," the psychotherapist should respond with a gender neutral comment such as, "Tell me more about this person." This also helps counter heterosexual clients' heterosexism by subtly raising their consciousness. It gives sexual minorities a message that the psychotherapist doesn't automatically assume heterosexuality, and may encourage individuals to come out if they haven't already.

Psychotherapists will need to examine their feelings and thoughts, both rational and irrational, about HIV/AIDS, as well as their ability to deal with death and dying issues. It is also important to explore the issue of suicide with all HIV-positive clients and allow them to process this openly. Grief and loss are widespread issues in the gay and lesbian communities. Some gay men are going to more than one friend's funeral service per week and have been for some time. In some areas, AIDS has brought the lesbian and gay communities somewhat closer together because of shared losses.

There are other relevant issues to consider as well. Theory courses either ignore homosexuality or have a bias against it. For example, Sigmund Freud considered homosexuality a stage prior to the development of heterosexuality; others thereafter framed homosexuality as arrested development and pathologized it or ignored the issue in their theory construction altogether.

Psychotherapists have an ethical responsibility to remedy limitations of knowledge about all diversity issues, including sexual orientations. This has significant implications for all therapeutic encounters, not just those with sexual minorities.

Breaches of confidentiality may be even more serious for sexual minorities—with consequences related to eligibility for health insurance coverage, future military service, and employment with some government agencies.

Value conflicts and identity confusion of the coming-out process can produce symptoms that mimic psychopathology. It is necessary to tease out real psychopathology from developmental identity crises, cultural differences, and assessment biases.

It is important to address the issue of multiple levels of oppression: sexual orientation, gender, racial, ethnic, religious, socioeconomic. These factors will also have a significant impact and will need to be examined for their relevance for particular clients.

Some questions on questionnaires and assessment instruments are irrelevant for gays and lesbians because they ask about intimate relationships with the opposite gender. There also is a lack of norm groups for gays and lesbians. Because it is performed with clinical samples only, the little research that is available on gay/lesbian issues does not take the nonpatient ("normal") population into account.

There are substantial effects of misdiagnosis, such as attributing clients' problems to their sexual orientation without fully exploring their symptoms and the sources of their current distress, and treating intimate relationships and family dynamics totally in terms of sexuality issues and heterosexual sexual development models.

Psychotherapists must be prepared to work with sexual minorities with a wide range of problems. Just to name a few: a substance-abuse problem or other compulsive/dependent behaviors; the individual's HIV/AIDS status and that of friends and significant others; sexual orientation confusion; and developmental issues seemingly unrelated to sexual orientation that may be influenced by either external or internal homophobia. Knowing what sexual minorities are looking for in a therapist is also valuable. As mentioned in chapter 7, Picucci's 1993 study of 130 clients and workshop participants in recovery found specific attributes that recovering people look for in therapists. Individuals in recovery wanted therapists:

- to encourage growth outside the therapy setting.
- to show lack of fear in revealing the therapist's own weaknesses.
- to allow themselves to make mistakes and show their humanity.
- to be familiar with and respectful of varied addictions' self-help groups.
- to engender a safe, nonjudgmental atmosphere so that shame can surface.
- to encourage the client to take healthy risks.
- to give feedback, without which therapy would be frustrating.
- to provide a role model of what a fuller recovery might look and feel like.
- to be interactive and help illuminate dynamics that are debilitating.
- to compassionately include, and have understanding of, one's "shadow-self."
- to understand that therapy is ineffective if a client is suffering a substance addiction.
- to recognize that a new approach/strategy is required if the process becomes stagnant.[7]

Awareness of these attributes will greatly facilitate interaction with gay, lesbian, and bisexual clients who are struggling to find their way out of addictive/compulsive behavior.

❋　　❋　　❋

CHAPTER 29

Approaches to Specific Issues

Creating a Safe Environment

Setting the stage for people to feel comfortable to disclose their orientation is an important first step. Using gender-neutral language and interacting without making assumptions about the client's sexual orientation facilitate the sharing of this information.

Setting the stage is useful in interacting with ethnic and racial groups as well. Discussing how it feels to the client, as a *"purple"* person, to be working with an obviously not-*"purple"* person is frequently an important point to address. To encourage clients to talk about certain kinds of behavior, therapists need to encourage talk about everything relevant and to provide the message of openness and tolerance.

Many therapists may think they have really good "gay-dar." (The ability to know who is gay/lesbian and who isn't.) But "gay-dar" is often simply stereotyping. For this reason, therapists need to be aware of their own stereotypical attitudes. No matter how much clients may fit the stereotype, they may prove to be heterosexual (or clients who seem heterosexual may turn out to be gay/lesbian/bisexual).

Therapists who use gender-neutral language at all times encourage those who are gay and lesbian to self-identify. And for those people who are not sexual minorities, it will help them to become more tolerant and more understanding about the need to recognize differences in orientation.

The more therapists know, the more effective they will be with their clients, who will feel more open to discuss the challenging issues, problems, and circumstances that have brought them to seek help. Working in a group therapy setting with clients who are not able, ready, and willing to come out is quite a challenge for therapists who know of their clients' orientation. It is essential to make the environment a safe place for all the members of the group without breaching anyone's right to privacy. If someone in the group has made homophobic comments or has been joking about gays or racial or ethnic minorities (whether or not a gay, lesbian, or bisexual client is in the group), it is appropriate to address these behaviors at the moment they occur. For example, one might ask, "If such a person were here, and you knew they were gay or lesbian, would you still be saying that?" Or, "Let me stop you for a moment. Try to imagine if you were gay, what it would be like for you to hear something like that said. What would that mean for you whether this was a safe place or not?"

Recognizing the impact of discrimination and cruelty helps people become more empathetic. Helping them imagine what such cruelty would feel like and would mean to them expands awareness and increases tolerance.

People Pleasing

It is common for many clients to want to please their therapists. This is not unique to therapy. Many want to be good patients . . . good students . . . good learners . . . good children . . . good coworkers, etc. Therapists can anticipate that clients will want to please them, or want to displease them, for much the same reasons. Clients care about what therapists think, and they may be fearful that therapists are not going to approve of them. Often, the therapist's opinion matters to them. Many clients are looking for validation, approval, and support for what they are doing and for the choices they are making.

It is important, therefore, to look at the dependency that may develop as a result of therapy. Clients who are externally focused (i.e., looking for support, validation, and approval from others in order to feel worthy or acceptable to themselves) are particularly vulnerable to becoming excessively dependent on a therapist. It is essential for the therapist to be aware of this and to assist the client in developing autonomy and the ability to self-validate, with or without others' approval.

People come to the therapist seeking answers. Asking the therapist "What would *you* do?" is flattering. Therapists need to resist succumbing to this kind of invitation. Empathy is one thing. Too much sympathy may allow clients to avoid taking responsibility for their choices.

Gay and lesbian clients are particularly astute because of many years of trying to figure out who is safe and who is not. They are quite likely to be sensitive about the client-therapist relationship, in varying degrees. Therapists need to explore and inquire about the client's perceptions of the therapist and of the relationship, modeling that it is okay to talk about this, and that the therapist is open to discussing this as well. Clients benefit from experiencing a therapist responding honestly and genuinely: "Yes, that is something difficult for me." Or, "I am feeling uncomfortable." Therapists should not hide behind a mask of professionalism in order to cover up feelings of discomfort or lack of information. Being honest about these things is much better and may even foster a better therapeutic relationship than the alternatives.

Therapists need to evaluate whether any discomfort they may feel is a matter of internalized homophobia or lack of experience. One of the ways to determine "Is it me, or is it the issue?" is to ask: "Would I be reacting this way if a heterosexual were saying this? Would I be reacting with this couple in this way if it were a man and a woman, instead of two men, or two women? Would I have the same response to a client telling me he was experiencing discrimination on the job if this were not a gay man?"

Therapists need to be careful with clients about where they are with what they are doing, and why they are doing it. Are they doing it to get the therapist's approval? Is their locus of control completely external, or is their locus of control completely internal? Can therapists help clients to become more balanced about what they do or do not have control over? Frequently, when people who are compulsive about anything come into recovery, they look at the external environment to discover what is going to help them or hurt them. Part of the change process is learning to become more internally controlled, to manage for themselves, and to take responsibility for their actions with substances or compulsive behavior.

There are plenty of people who say, "Oh yes, I'm an alcoholic" or "I'm an addict." And to them this label makes their behavior acceptable. "If I weren't an addict, I wouldn't be doing these things." Part of the recovery process is helping these people to understand what it is about *them* that may even be creating these behaviors. Or what is it within them that interacts with these behaviors? Or what forces or temptations pull them into that kind of behavior? Developing conscious awareness that they have control and responsibility helps to achieve balance.

What's the Difference?

Many therapists express surprise about the need for a book on gays, lesbians, and bisexuals in recovery. "You mean to say that gays and lesbians have different issues from others in recovery? What are they?" The fact that therapists are not aware of the existence of so many issues affecting gays and lesbians in recovery is an issue for therapists.

Not nearly enough research has been done to demonstrate all the ways that gays' and lesbians' issues are different from those of heterosexuals. It is also not possible to say that being gay or lesbian is going to mean the presence of this or that issue. Some issues—such as the problem of being honest and open about sexual orientation in a homophobic environment; spiritual abuse; and victimization— have already been identified in earlier chapters. Here are several more issues.

The commitment of gay and lesbian couples to maintain their relationships is not formal as it is with married heterosexuals. The ties that hold two people together are often not as tight, partially because society refuses to sanction gay/lesbian relationships, and partially because gays and lesbians don't sanction them either. Berzon in her book *Permanent Partners* says:

> *We need a concept of permanent partnership for our relationships, a concept that sends the same message that heterosexual marriage does: these two people are bound together in love and in life, functioning as a family unit, mutually committed and invested in one another's future. The integration of such concepts into our thinking about our relationships is the precondition necessary to turn the tradition of failure that we have lived with for so long [impermanent partners] into a tradition of success.*[1]

This is a call to action for gays and lesbians to become self-empowering, in spite of the obstacles, to create relationships and families that are fulfilling and nurturing.

Another issue for most gays and lesbians is that there is usually no built-in, solid family support system for coping with intolerance in an external, harmful environment, because most gay and lesbian individuals were born to nongay individuals. People of color may learn from their families about how to deal with society's attitudes and prejudice; however, gays and lesbians do not have the benefit of hearing from their parents how they (the parents) managed to survive discrimination. Nor do they have the security that no matter what happens to them out in the world, it is possible to come home to the family for support. This is a major difference. Gays and lesbians can be coached through difficult experiences to cope with bigotry and discrimination in different circumstances. Familial, extended-family subculture support can be developed over time. But it still is not the same and this reality must be faced.

There is so much diversity in the gay and lesbian community that it may be much more difficult to identify role models that might provide support for the client. Appropriate models may even be invisible. (And some of these models may, over time, discount their gay and lesbian experience as merely being just a phase.) Taking pride in gay and lesbian accomplishments as a next step in supporting identity may not be easy for some individuals struggling with the broad diversity and/or invisibility of sexual minorities.

Another issue also relates to society: the sense of being "sinners outside the pale." Being a "sinner" in recovery programs that maintain a spiritual center at the heart of the recovery process is of particular significance.[2] Sexual minorities also find the chauvinism, the dogmatism, and the tremendous amount of heterosexism in recovery literature to be problematic (e.g., "Boy meets girl on AA campus"[3] and "This is the Step that separates the men from the boys"[4]).

One significant issue is the terror that HIV disease creates for gay men. A terrible sense of vulnerability and frustration that results in extreme pessimism and despair can immobilize a client: "I can't do anything; I'm in a straight jacket." Safe sex is an important practice for *everyone*. It is even more crucial in the gay and lesbian community because of the incidence of HIV disease.

Not Dealing with Sexual Issues

Some health care providers believe that sexual issues should only be dealt with *after* the client is sober. Conflicts over sexuality are often so fundamental, however, that it is impossible to make any progress with compulsive/dependent behavior unless sexuality is dealt with from the very start of treatment.

Because sexual orientation is an issue of great complexity, it makes the recovery treatment plan far more complex. But *anything* that is an add-on makes the treatment more difficult. Would therapists say to a client with cancer, "Oh, we won't deal with your cancer until after you're sober"? The chemically dependent Holocaust survivor or Vietnam veteran is another example. "Let's not think about your core issues until you are free of chemicals! Let's talk only about why you shouldn't use heroin anymore." How inconvenient for the provider to have to deal with the fact that the addicted individual is plagued with guilt and despair over what happened in Vietnam!

Therapists need to understand what it means to ask that sexual issues be dealt with only after the individual is sober. Getting sober means ending denial. Yet, therapists are asking the client not to be in denial about the use and effect of substances, but to remain in denial about sexual orientation *because it is harder to deal with*.

It is entirely possible that the provider really does not know enough about homosexuality and doesn't want to do the homework. There may be discomfort from homophobia or other unresolved sexual issues. It is one thing to say, "I'm really okay with gays and lesbians and bisexuals," without knowing any. But in the flesh, it is quite different.

Consider a related example of working with gay couples. Therapists may believe they have no problem with the homosexual client who has a lover. But to have the lover in the same room and to observe a display of physical affection may be quite another matter. Being presented with the actual display of emotion may result in the discovery that the therapist is not so comfortable after all! That is understandable. Therapists need to gain knowledge about homosexuality on their own and not work through the entire learning curve with their clients!

It is extremely important to understand the issues and complications that may need to be addressed. For example, what is considered acceptable for gays, lesbians, and bisexuals, and who is making these decisions? Who is deciding what is acceptable? Is it the client or others? How is it that the client is empowering others to make these decisions? Whose authority makes certain behavior correct? Part of the challenge for therapists is to help clients address these questions.

Clients need to be helped to see that their family of origin, their partners, or their churches are not right merely by virtue of the positions they hold. Therapists need to help disabuse clients of their unrealistic expectations of others and of themselves, whether it is overvaluing, or undervaluing. Even with their skills, therapists need to acknowledge their own limitations as well in this regard.

Personal Values

Therapy does not take place in a value-free setting. Therapists need to be clear about their personal values and to be able to articulate them when clients raise issues that have an impact on them. Values are not a question of "this is my opinion versus this is your opinion." For example, learning that an HIV-positive client is practicing unsafe sex without informing partners means confronting the client. Not to do this would violate ethical principles. The client is not simply the client, but is also a member of a society to which the therapist has a responsibility. However, breaching the client's confidentiality and telling the partner may also be unethical.[5] Certainly, the first priority is to the client, and the therapist must avoid harming the client and should aim to avoid harming the therapeutic relationship. However, therapists need to be clear about their own ethical principles so that they can consciously choose how to intervene in such situations. Therapists must be clear about their own values and principles in order to guide therapy. These principles should help to guide how explicitly and directly the therapist decides to work with the client to change life-threatening behavior and what strategies the therapist chooses to use with regard to disclosure of the client's HIV status to the partner.[6]

Working with any individual calls into play the therapist's values and beliefs. The more in opposition therapists are with the client, the greater the need for expert supervision to make sure they are being effective rather than damaging.

In addition to the ethical principles of the American Psychological Association or the American Counseling Association, the following ethical principles are invaluable in guiding professional practice: "*Nonmalfeasance:* do no harm; *beneficence:* doing good; *autonomy:* right to be autonomous and the responsibility to treat others as autonomous; *justice:* be fair; and *fidelity:* be loyal."[7]

Ethical Principles to Guide Professional Practice

1. Autonomy: Freedom of action and freedom of choice; right to be autonomous and the responsibility to treat others as autonomous. 2. Nonmalfeasance (Do no harm): Cause no harm through intention nor through risking others. 3. Beneficence (Doing good): Contribute positively to another's welfare. 4. Justice (Be fair): Treat persons equally without regard to gender, race, or socioeconomic background. 5. Fidelity (Be loyal): Keep promises and be loyal.[8]

Ethically, therapists should not be working with clients for whom they are not adequately prepared. People need to have the preparation of interacting with gays and lesbians who are not patients so that they can know what nonclinical or "normal" looks like. Being comfortable with gays and lesbians as people is essential before beginning to work with them as clients.

Serving Clients' Needs

The therapist needs a great deal of education about homosexuality, not only from books and reading materials but also from going to training sessions, interacting with nonpatients, and being exposed to cultural opportunities that demonstrate gay and lesbian life. And they need to be able to work through whatever reactions they may have to what they experience in order to become more comfortable and serve their clients effectively.

Therapists also need to ask themselves why they are going to the effort to know about gays and lesbians. And, if they are *not* willing to do this, why not? It's okay if they choose not to. Therapists don't have to be therapists for everyone! They can decide this is not the group of people with whom they want to work. However, they need to consciously know the reasons why not.

Therapists conscious of their strengths and limitations act responsibly either to remedy the limitation or to not have other people suffer their limitations. They can make appropriate and responsible referrals to other providers. Sometimes, however, a network of competent providers is unavailable. Other therapists may be entirely well-meaning, kind, empathetic, and sympathetic, but they simply do not have the information, at present, to help someone who is gay or lesbian deal with compulsive/dependency issues.

A clinician working in a rural community mental health center in Wyoming does not have the same referral options as a therapist in San Francisco, who can refer a client to a care giver who advertises professional services in a gay or lesbian publication. Clinicians in Wyoming may not have the option of saying, "I don't need to become educated about this!" They *do* need to learn in the event they serve the gay or lesbian client in a city or town without competent referral options. In this case the clinician is ethically compelled to learn to work with gay, lesbian, or bisexual clients effectively.

Many therapists may not be comfortable initially, but they will *want* to become comfortable. The people who do not choose to do this need to acknowledge that the issue is so large for them that they are not going to be able to work with sexual minorities. Acknowledging it as a limitation of their own—and not because there is some intrinsic problem with gays, lesbians, and bisexuals—is essential as well as ethical and responsible.

❈   ❈   ❈

CHAPTER 30

Using This Book with Clients

After examining parts I, II, and III, you may find the following suggestions helpful in using this book. Much of the material in part I can be used as an adjunct to therapy. The issues explored in this section will, for many clients, provide a broader perspective for them to consider.

In part II, the material in the workbook sections can help identify what are problems for the client and what are not. These exercises are a way to help clients become clearer about issues they might want to work on in therapy. After completing the exercise(s), the client might indicate, "In all these things, this is the ONE INCIDENT that is so important. It is really, really, really irking me." You can then assist clients to explore how this incident might replicate some other matters that come up repeatedly in their lives.

Part III provides psychotherapists with a more extensive examination of the issues; how these issues relate to the problems of gays, lesbians, and bisexuals; and the optimal therapeutic environment for assisting the recovery process. Exploring and analyzing these areas should improve the quality of care for sexual minorities.

Appendices A and B provide two checklists for use with individuals who are unclear about how their use of substances or their compulsive behavior—or the addictive/compulsive behavior on the part of individuals around them—impacts their lives. The resources section offers access to networks that individuals may find useful in their quest for increased understanding. The references/bibliography section provides additional resources for study and reading in these areas.

Anyone can use this book, alone or with a psychotherapist. For people in therapy for issues other than substance dependency, the exercises can be a resource to explore some relevant areas of their lives. "Read this book; see whether you see yourself."

Psychotherapists can use the book in many different ways. For example, in a brief therapy context, therapists can select material to help clients investigate on their own whether they do, in fact, have a substance abuse problem, and how to deal with it. In this approach, staggered sessions can be arranged. "Work on some of these exercises; then come back and we will talk about what you have discovered." Or, the material can be incorporated in regular sessions; it can become another objective the client decides on.

Part II can be used with people who have never gone to a Twelve Step program, as well as with people who have gone but have been dissatisfied with the experience. The Twelve Steps can be used by anyone to find assistance in recovery; no one need be put off by the words. The Steps were written with the *intention* to assist people to change.

Many who are familiar with the Steps have only heard them read at meetings or looked at them on the wall of a Twelve Step meeting room. They have no idea of the possibilities of working them to explore a wide range of personal issues. Those who wish to do so may find these exercises useful.

Therapists should carefully review the material in the book in order to select and tailor exercises to work on specific objectives with clients. This can best be accomplished after you are completely familiar with what is covered.

This book is NOT for people who are looking for a way out of being responsible, and who don't want to change. Individuals in recovery need to understand that while this book can be useful for setting goals, it isn't useful for justifying remaining stuck in compulsive/dependent behavior. *Accepting Ourselves and Others* helps them to understand what they need to know about their patterns of behavior, and what it might take to change these patterns. It does not take the place of individuals' assuming responsibility for setting their own goals.

This book will not break through anyone's deep denial. The book is very gentle; it offers a strategy for people who wish to enter and remain in recovery. The exercises have proven useful in assisting gays, lesbians, and bisexuals, as well as non-gays, to get help for their recovery. The book is based on the authors' experience working with clients and reflects a commitment to assist sexual minorities to enjoy the benefits of recovery from addictive/compulsive behavior.

The authors have not intended to answer every question related to addiction or recovery or to gay, lesbian, or bisexual issues. The book is intended to be there for people who lack other resources for finding out this information. It may be an introduction to getting additional, specific information and help for applicable issues. The authors hope it is useful in your work and look forward to receiving any information you would like to share from your experience with it.

❉   ❉   ❉

Signs of Alcoholism/Addictive Behavior*

1. Do you occasionally drink or use substances after a disappointment or a quarrel, or when the boss gives you a hard time? ☐ Yes ☐ No

2. When you have trouble or feel under pressure, do you always drink or use more heavily than usual? ☐ Yes ☐ No

3. Have you noticed that you are able to handle more liquor/mood-altering substances than you did when you first began? ☐ Yes ☐ No

4. Did you ever wake up on the "morning after" and discover that you could not remember part of the evening before, even though your friends tell you that you did not pass out? ☐ Yes ☐ No

5. When drinking or using with other people, do you try to get in a few extra ones when others will not know it? ☐ Yes ☐ No

6. Are there certain occasions when you feel uncomfortable if alcohol or mood-altering substances are not available? ☐ Yes ☐ No

7. Have you recently noticed that when you begin drinking or using you are more in a hurry to get the first one than you used to be? ☐ Yes ☐ No

8. Do you sometimes feel a little guilty about your drinking or using? ☐ Yes ☐ No

9. Are you secretly irritated when your family or friends discuss your drinking or using? ☐ Yes ☐ No

10. Have you often found that you wish to continue drinking or using after your friends say they have had enough? ☐ Yes ☐ No

11. Do you usually have a reason for the occasions when you drink or use heavily? ☐ Yes ☐ No

---

* Checklist adapted from the National Council on Alcoholism: "What Are the Signs?"

12. Have you recently noticed an increase in the frequency of your memory blackouts? ☐ Yes ☐ No

13. When you are sober, do you often regret things you have done or said while drinking or using? ☐ Yes ☐ No

14. Have you tried switching brands or substances or following different plans for controlling your drinking or using? ☐ Yes ☐ No

15. Have you often failed to keep the promises you made to yourself about controlling or cutting down on your drinking or using? ☐ Yes ☐ No

16. Have you ever tried to control your drinking or using by making a change in jobs or moving to a new location? ☐ Yes ☐ No

17. Do you try to avoid family or close friends while you are drinking or using? ☐ Yes ☐ No

18. Are you having an increasing number of financial and work problems? ☐ Yes ☐ No

19. Do more people seem to be treating you unfairly without good reasons? ☐ Yes ☐ No

20. Do you eat very little or irregularly when you are drinking? ☐ Yes ☐ No

21. Do you sometimes have the "shakes" in the morning and find that it helps to have a little "pick-me-up"? ☐ Yes ☐ No

22. Have you recently noticed that you cannot drink or use as much as you once did? ☐ Yes ☐ No

23. Do you sometimes stay under the influence of alcohol or other substances for several days at a time? ☐ Yes ☐ No

24. Do you sometimes feel very depressed and wonder whether life is worth living? ☐ Yes ☐ No

25. Sometimes after periods of drinking or using, do you see or hear things that aren't there? ☐ Yes ☐ No

26. Do you get terribly frightened after you have been drinking or using heavily? ☐ Yes ☐ No

If you answered yes to any of the questions, you have some of the symptoms that may indicate alcoholism or addiction to substances. Yes answers to several of the questions indicate the following stages of alcoholism/addiction: questions 1 through 8, early stage; questions 9 through 21, middle stage; questions 22 through 26, the beginning of the final stage.

Indications of Codependency*

Have you ever:

1. Been embarrassed at the behavior of someone you know after he or she drinks or uses mood-altering substances? ☐ Yes ☐ No

2. Disposed of alcohol or substances to keep someone from using them? ☐ Yes ☐ No

3. Felt your behavior was making someone else drink or use? ☐ Yes ☐ No

4. Threatened to leave someone because of too much drinking or using? ☐ Yes ☐ No

5. Called work to give an excuse for someone who could not work that day because of excessive alcohol or substance use the day/night before? ☐ Yes ☐ No

6. Felt angry that the basic necessities of life were not being taken care of because so much money was being spent on alcohol or substances? ☐ Yes ☐ No

7. Felt fearful at what would happen to you and/or others dependent on you if drinking or using continues in your relationship/family? ☐ Yes ☐ No

8. Left home to look for someone who you think might be out drinking or using? ☐ Yes ☐ No

9. Called bars, neighbors, friends, looking for someone you believe is either drinking or using? ☐ Yes ☐ No

10. Increased your own consumption of alcohol or substances in order to keep up with someone who is a heavy drinker/user? ☐ Yes ☐ No

11. Wished that alcohol/mood-altering substances could be outlawed? ☐ Yes ☐ No

---

* Adapted from a checklist developed by the National Council on Alcoholism - Bay Area.

12. Wanted to move and start over as a solution to the drinking and/or using problem going on around you? ☐ Yes ☐ No

13. Been revolted by others' drinking/using behavior? ☐ Yes ☐ No

14. Been unable to sleep because someone has stayed out late drinking/using or not come home at all? ☐ Yes ☐ No

15. Resented the fact that there is heavy drinking/using going on in the life of someone close to you? ☐ Yes ☐ No

16. Felt hopeless about a drinking/using situation? ☐ Yes ☐ No

17. Felt that it was a disgrace or that it was simply not possible to talk about a drinking/using problem? ☐ Yes ☐ No

18. Cut down on activities outside your own home in order to keep an eye on someone who is drinking or using? ☐ Yes ☐ No

19. Complained, nagged, or quarreled with someone who drinks/uses? ☐ Yes ☐ No

20. Felt that if the substance abuser would just stop drinking/using, everything would be okay? ☐ Yes ☐ No

Part I: Understanding and Navigating the Issues

Chapter 1: Alternative Models of Addiction

1. The Moral Model has not been incorporated into any chemical dependency treatment program, as far as the authors know.

2. The American Psychiatric Association stopped listing homosexuality as a disease in 1980; the American Psychological Association followed suit in 1981. Some medical professionals still have not revised their thinking.

3. Steven L. Berg reviews this and other issues related to spirituality in his doctoral dissertation, "A.A., Spiritual Issues, and the Treatment of Lesbian and Gay Alcoholics," Michigan State University, 1989.

4. For discussion of useful assessment instruments, see N. Heather, "Brief Intervention Strategies," *Handbook of Alcoholism Treatment Approaches: Effective Alternatives,* ed. R. K. Hester and W. R. Miller (New York: Pergamon Press, 1989). For further information about the disease concept, refer to N. Heather and I. Robertson, "Introduction: Disease Conceptions of Alcoholism," *Controlled Drinking* (London/New York: Methuen, 1981, 1983), 1–20.

5. This approach is detailed in *Moderate Drinking: The Moderation Management™ Guide for People Who Want to Reduce Their Drinking* by Audrey Kishline.

6. Moderation Management Network is a nonprofit charitable organization founded by Audrey Kishline. For more information, write to P.O. Box 6005, Ann Arbor, MI 48106.

7. Pride Institute, founded 10 years and 4,000 graduates ago, is the nation's only inpatient treatment facility exclusively for sexual minorities. Pride Institute also has inpatient psychiatric, dual, and halfway house programs nationally. For more information about these gay, lesbian, and bisexual specific programs call 1-800-54-PRIDE.

This is the only inpatient treatment program specifically for sexual minorities of which the authors are aware. We would appreciate learning of any other programs.

Chapter 2: The Recovery Process in Perspective

1. This list appears in R. L. Atkinson, R. C. Atkinson, and E. R. Hilgard, *Introduction to Psychology,* 8th ed. (New York: Harcourt Brace Jovanovich, 1983), 486.

2. See N. Heather, "Brief Intervention Strategies," *Handbook of Alcoholism Treatment Approaches: Effective Alternatives,* ed. R. K. Hester and W. R. Miller (New York: Pergamon Press, 1989).

3. Stephanie Brown, *Treating the Alcoholic* (New York: John Wiley and Sons, 1985), 30–54.

4. Ibid., 54.

Chapter 3: A New Look at the No-Nos

1. Sonja Johnson, "Twelve Steps into the Fog," *Wildfire: Igniting the She/volution* (Albuquerque: Wildfire Books, 1989).

2. Jean Kirkpatrick, *Turnabout: Help for a New Life* (New York: Doubleday, 1978), 64.

Chapter 4: Recovery Issues for Gays, Lesbians, and Bisexuals

1. John Fortunato, *Embracing the Exile: Healing Journeys of Gay Christians* (San Francisco: Harper and Row, 1982), 35.

2. One of the authors (SBK) of this book was not renewed on his yearly contract as dean at City College in Chicago, in 1982, after the president learned of a paper he had delivered on homophobia sponsored by the Gay Academic Union.

3. We need a better word, but until we have one, choose your own.

4. See H. Curry and D. Clifford, *A Legal Guide for Lesbian and Gay Couples* (Berkeley, Calif.: Nolo Press, 1992).

Chapter 5: Dealing with Internalized Homophobia

1. The categories for defining addiction may themselves be misleading because they suffer from definitional confusion. For example, those individuals with a mild drinking problem (the majority) may be included with those with a moderate or severe problem (the minority).

2. Scholarship reveals that in biblical times there were no words for homosexuality; neither are there statements or references of any kind in the New Testament attributed to Jesus about homosexuality. Dr. Virginia R. Mallenkott points out that late-nineteenth-century English translators of the Bible introduced the word "homosexuals" in place of "masturbators." In 1 Tim. 1:5–10, the Greek word "arsenokoitai" referred to what we, today, call "homosexual acts"—but committed by heterosexuals! For an in-depth review of biblical texts, see chapter 4, in John Boswell, *Christianity, Social Tolerance and Homosexuality* (Chicago: University of Chicago Press, 1980).

Chapter 6: Choosing a Therapist

1. To secure a list of providers, you might peruse local or regional periodicals targeting sexual minorities. Providers sometimes advertise psychotherapy services in these publications. You could also contact the local mental health association, community mental health center, or state branches of national professional organizations such as the American Psychological Association or the American Counseling Association. Specifically request a list of providers who identify themselves as having expertise working with sexual minorities. See the list of resources beginning on page 373 for further information.

2. For an in-depth analysis of different psychotherapeutic orientations, see Gerald Corey, *Theory and Practice of Counseling and Psychotherapy* (Monterey, Calif.: Brooks, Cole, Faber, 1995).

3. The following definitions are from the glossary section of *Abnormal Psychology and Modern Life,* 7th ed., by J. C. Coleman, J. N. Butcher, and R. C. Carson (Glenview, Ill.: Scott, Foresman, 1984). "Psychosis: severe psychological disorder involving loss of contact with

reality and gross personality distortion. Hospitalization is ordinarily required," page xiv. "Neurosis: nonpsychotic emotional disturbance characterized by exaggerated use of avoidance behavior and defense mechanisms against anxiety," page xii.

4. In my professional duties (KDK), a supervisor once took issue with my use of the word "oppression" to describe the experience of sexual minorities. The term "discrimination" was acceptable, but "oppression" was too strong. This comment helped me to realize that I was not going to feel very safe working with this supervisor.

Chapter 7: Assessing Progress with a Therapist

1. Michael Picucci, *Complete Recovery* (New York: Mombaccus Publications, 1996), 178–79.

Part II: Exercising the Twelve Steps in Your Life

Chapter 11: The Wilderness of Isolation

1. Another choice may include Rational Recovery Therapy, or another orientation.

2. This is an excerpt from a letter from Jung to Wilson, dated January 23, 1961. It was first published in the *Grapevine,* January 1963.

Chapter 12: Taking Positive Action

1. Claudia Black, *It Will Never Happen to Me!* (Denver: MAC Publishing, 1982), 31–49.

Chapter 14: Looking into the Mirror

1. Refer to the resource section of this book for a list of gay, lesbian, and bisexual groups who can put you in touch with groups in your area.

2. See, for example, *Alcoholics Anonymous* (New York: Alcoholics Anonymous World Services, 1976), 64–71; and *The Twelve Steps of Alcoholics Anonymous, interpreted by the Hazelden Foundation* (San Francisco: Harper and Row, 1987), 28–58.

Chapter 23: Antidote to Egotism

1. Walt Whitman, "Salut Au Monde!" *Leaves of Grass and Selected Prose* (New York: Rinehart, 1951), 122.

2. *Alcoholics Anonymous* (New York: Alcoholics Anonymous World Services, 1976), 83–84.

3. Martha Davis, Elizabeth Robbins, and Matthew McKay, *Relaxation and Stress Reduction Workbook* , 4th ed. (Oakland, Calif.: New Harbinger Publications, 1995).

Chapter 25: The Longer View

1. The issue of "recovered" versus "recovering" relates to whether or not it is deemed appropriate or advisable to return to using these substances and/or behaviors and is the source of continuing debate.

2. Sonja Johnson, *Wildfire: Igniting the She/volution* (Albuquerque: Wildfire Books, 1989).

Part III: For Therapists

Chapter 26: Analysis of Alternative Models of Addiction

1. Claudia Black, *Double Duty: Dual Identity* (New York: Ballantine, 1990), 9.

2. We note the use of the term "disease concept" instead of "disease" by professionals is an indication of equivocation. Apparently, "alcoholism" is like a disease—but not exactly.

3. See the *Diagnostic and Statistical Manual of Mental Disorders III (DSM-III),* Washington, D.C. Currently, in *DSM-IV,* there is a minor reference to sexual orientation under the category "302.9 Sexual Disorder Not Otherwise Specified." It lists "persistent and marked distress about sexual orientation."

4. It is beyond the scope of this book to address the divide between the mainstream approach to chemical dependency treatment in the United States, the larger social and political forces that operate, and the results of empirical research on addictive disorders and relapse prevention.

5. For a discussion of useful assessment instruments, see N. Heather, "Brief Intervention Strategies," *Handbook of Alcoholism Treatment Approaches: Effective Alternatives*, ed. R. K. Hester and W. R. Miller (New York: Pergamon Press, 1989); and NIAAA, *Assessing Alcohol Problems: A Guide for Clinicians and Researchers* (Washington, D.C.: National Institute of Health, 1995).

6. Moderation Management Network is a nonprofit charitable organization founded by Audrey Kishline. For more information, write to P.O. Box 6005, Ann Arbor, MI 48106.

7. For more information see D. K. Flavin and R. M. Morse, "What Is Alcoholism? Current Definitions and Diagnostic Criteria and Their Implications for Treatment," *Alcohol Health and Research World* 15 (1991): 266–71.

8. D. K. Flavin and R. M. Morse, "What Is Alcoholism? Current Definitions and Diagnostic Criteria and Their Implications for Treatment," *Alcohol Health and Research World* 15 (1991): 266–71.

9. S. H. Dinwiddie and C. R. Cloninger, "Family Adoption Studies in Alcohol and Drug Addiction," *Psychiatric Annals* 21 (1991): 213.

10. P. Nathan, "Alcoholism: A Cognitive Social Learning Approach," *Journal of Substance Abuse Treatment* 2 (1985): 171–72.

11. For further discussion see N. Heather, op. cit.

12. As an example of a controlled-drinking intervention, see D. W. Foy et al., "Broad-Spectrum Behavioral Treatment for Chronic Alcoholics: Effects of Training Controlled Drinking Skills," *Journal of Consulting and Clinical Psychology* 52 (1984).

Chapter 27: Assessing Homophobia

1. When not otherwise indicated, the definition appears in the glossary of *BI Any Other Name,* ed. Loraine Hutchins and Lani Kaahumanu (Boston: Alyson Publications, 1991), 369-71.

2. Fritz Klein et al., "Sexual Orientation: A Multi-variable Dynamic Process," *Two Lives to Lead: Bisexuality in Men and Women* (New York: Harrington Park, 1985), 35–50.

3. L. Faderman, *Odd Girls and Twilight Lovers: A History of Lesbian Life in Twentieth-century America* (New York: Columbia University Press, 1984).

4. Fritz Klein et al., "Sexual Orientation: A Multi-variable Dynamic Process," *Bisexualities: Theory and Research,* No. 11 of the book series Research on Homosexuality, ed. Fritz Klein and Timothy J. Wolf (Binghampton: N. Y.: Haworth Press, 1985), 37.

5. Ibid.

6. See *Journal of Homosexuality,* vol. 11, Spring 1985.

7. See J. E. Helms, "An Overview of Black Racial Identity Theory," *Black and White Racial Identity: Theory, Research, and Practice*, ed. J. E. Helms (Westport, Conn.: Greenwood Press, 1990), 9–32.

8. Ibid., 12, 13.

9. For a detailed discussion, see Eric Marcus, *Is It a Choice?* (San Francisco: Harper/Collins, 1993).

10. For a historical discussion of psychology's approach to gay people, see Ruth Fassinger, "The Hidden Minority: Issues and Challenges in Working with Lesbian Women and Gay Men," *The Counseling Psychologist* 19 (1991): 157–76.

Chapter 28: Working with Gay, Lesbian, and Bisexual Clients

1. This summary of Cass's (1979) model of identity development is from Ruth Fassinger, "The Hidden Minority: Issues and Challenges in Working with Lesbian Women and Gay Men," *The Counseling Psychologist* 19 (1991): 157–76.

2. J. W. Shannon and W. J. Woods, "Affirmative Psychotherapy for Gay Men," *The Counseling Psychologist* 19 (1991): 198.

3. L. M. Markowitz presents some examples of therapists' approaches for working with same-sex couples who are in the process of divorcing. See "When Same-Sex Couples Divorce," *The Family Therapy Networker* May/June (1994): 31–33.

4. Comments made in a presentation by Nancy Bacher, president of the American Suicide Foundation, South Florida Division, at "Suicide: Prevention, Intervention, Postvention" conference in Ft. Lauderdale, Florida, January 26, 1996.

5. Based on comments by Karen Dunne-Maxim, University of Medicine and Dentistry of New Jersey at Piscataway, co-coordinator, UMDNJ Suicide Prevention Project, at "Suicide: Prevention, Intervention, Postvention" conference held in Ft. Lauderdale, Florida, January 26, 1996. There are some complications about investigating the possible connection between sexual orientation and teenage suicide. Research studies often investigate completed suicides and make inferences postmortem about possible motivations for the suicide. Often parents and peers of the teen are unaware of whether or not the adolescent was experiencing any issues related to sexual orientation. Another, perhaps greater problem is that often this question is not asked.

6. For more information see James B. Teague, "Issues Relating to the Treatment of Adolescent Lesbians and Homosexuals," *Journal of Mental Health Counseling* 14 (1992): 422–9.

7. Michael Picucci, *Complete Recovery* (New York: Mombaccus Publications, 1996), 178–79.

Chapter 29: Approaches to Specific Issues

1. Betty Berzon, *Permanent Partners* (New York: E. P. Dutton, 1988), 8.

2. Since 1989, following the publication of *Accepting Ourselves*, the author (SBK) received many letters from readers about the problem god-centered belief creates for gays and lesbians who feel this focus does not reflect in any way their understanding of their lives.

3. *Twelve Steps and Twelve Traditions* (New York: Alcoholics Anonymous World Services, 1953), 119.

4. Ibid., 63.

5. In some states, such as California, courts have ruled that therapists have a duty to warn nonclients when a client reveals information that would lead a therapist to believe that the client is a danger to the nonclient. See *Tarasoff v. Regents of the University of California* (1976)—Cal.3d. Also, in California, and perhaps some other states, any communication that would lead a therapist to believe that another person is in danger from a client may not be protected by the psychotherapist-patient privilege.

6. For further discussion of these issues see R. Standard and R. Hazler, "Legal and Ethical Implications of HIV and Duty to Warn for Counselors: Does *Tarasoff* Apply?" [Italics in original.] *Journal of Counseling and Development* 73 (1995): 397–400.

7. From a handout from a presentation by Karen Kitchener, Ph.D., University of Denver Counseling Center, Fall 1994.

8. Derived from T. L. Beauchamp and J. F. Childress, *Principles of Biomedical Ethics* (Oxford: Oxford University Press, 1979); P. Ramsey, *The Patient as Person* (New Haven: Yale University Press, 1970), as delineated by K. S. Kitchener, "Intuition, Critical Evaluation, and Ethical Principles: The Foundation of Ethical Decisions in Counseling Psychology," *The Counseling Psychologist* 12 (1984): 43-55 and "Ethical Principles and Ethical Decisions in Student Affairs," *Applied Ethics in Student Services,* ed. H. Canon and R. Brown (San Francisco: Jossey-Bass, 1985).

Alcoholics Anonymous. 1976. New York: Alcoholics Anonymous World Services.

Altman, D. 1982. *The Homosexualization of America.* New York: St. Martin's Press.

American Psychiatric Association. 1980. *Diagnostic and Statistical Manual of Mental Disorders.* 3d ed. Washington, D.C.: American Psychiatric Association.

American Psychiatric Association. 1994. *Diagnostic and Statistical Manual of Mental Disorders.* 4th ed. Washington, D.C.: American Psychiatric Association.

American Society of Addiction Medicine. 1990. Addiction Review.

Annis, H. M. 1990. Relapse to substance abuse: Empirical findings within a cognitive-social learning approach. *Journal of Psychoactive Drugs.* 22:117–24.

Atkinson, D. R., and Hackett, C. 1988. *Counseling Non-Ethnic American Minorities.* Springfield, Ill.: Charles C. Thomas.

Atkinson, R. L.; Atkinson, R. C.; and Hilgard, E. R. 1983. *Introduction to Psychology.* 8th ed. New York: Harcourt Brace Jovanovich.

Baer, J. S.; Holt, C. S.; and Lichtenstein, E. 1986. Self-efficacy and smoking reexamined: Construct validity and clinical utility. *Journal of Consulting and Clinical Psychology.* 54:846–52.

Bandura, A. 1982a. The assessment and predictive generality of self-percepts of efficacy. *Journal of Behavior Therapy and Experimental Psychiatry.* 13:185–89.

———. 1982b. Self-efficacy mechanism in human agency. *American Psychologist.* 37:122–47.

Bass, E., and Davis, L. 1988. *The Courage to Heal: A Guide for Women Survivors of Child Sexual Abuse.* New York: Harper and Row.

Beattie, M. 1987. *Codependent No More.* New York: Harper/Hazelden.

———. 1989. *Beyond Codependency.* San Francisco: Harper/Hazelden.

Beauchamp, T. L., and Childress, J. F. 1979. *Principles of Biomedical Ethics.* Oxford: Oxford University Press.

Begleiter, H.; Porjesz, B.; Bihari; and Kissin, B. 1984. Event-related potentials in boys at risk for alcoholism. *Science.* 225:1493–96.

Bell, A. P., and Weinberg, M. S. 1978. *Homosexualities: A Study of Diversity Among Men and Women.* New York: Touchstone.

Berzon, B. 1988. *Permanent Partners.* New York: E. P. Dutton.

Berzon, B., and Leighton, R. 1979. *Positively Gay.* Millbrae, Calif.: Celestial Arts.

Bill B. 1981. *Compulsive Overeater.* Minneapolis: CompCare.

Black, C. 1982. *It Will Never Happen to Me*. Denver: MAC Publishing.

———. 1990. *Double Duty: Dual Identity*. Denver: MAC Publishing.

Booth, P. G.; Dale, B.; and Ansari, J. Problem drinkers' goal choice and treatment outcome: A preliminary study. *Addictive Behaviors*. 9:357–64.

Boswell, J. 1980. *Christianity, Social Tolerance, and Homosexuality*. Chicago: University of Chicago Press.

Brown, L. S. 1989. Beyond thou shalt not: Thinking about ethics in the lesbian therapy community. *Women and Therapy*. 8:13–25.

Brown, L. S., and Zimmer, D. 1986. "An Introduction to Therapy Issues of Lesbian and Gay Male Couples." In *The Clinical Handbook of Marital Therapy*, edited by N. S. Jacobsen and A. S. Gurman. New York: Guilford Press.

Brown, S. 1985. *Treating the Alcoholic*. New York: John Wiley and Sons.

Bruckner-Gordon, F.; Kuerer Gangi, B.; and Urbach Wallman, G. 1988. *Making Therapy Work*. New York, Harper and Row.

Buber, M. 1958. *I and Thou*. New York: Charles Scribner's Sons.

Buhrke, R. A. 1989. Lesbian-related issues in counseling supervision. *Women and Therapy*. 8:195–206.

Buhrke, R. A., and Douce, L. A. 1991. Training issues for counseling psychologists in working with lesbian women and gay men. *The Counseling Psychologist*. 19:216–34.

Bullough, V. L. 1979. *Homosexuality: A History*. New York: New American Library.

Burns, D. D. 1980. *Feeling Good: The New Mood Therapy*. New York: Avon Books.

Cabaj, R. P. 1988. Homosexuality and neurosis: Considerations for psychotherapy. *Journal of Homosexuality*. 15:13–23.

Carnes, P. 1983a. *Out of the Shadows*. Minneapolis: CompCare.

———. 1983b. *The Sexual Addiction*. New York: CompCare.

Casas, J. M.; Brady, S.; and Ponterotto, J. G. 1983. Sexual preference biases in counseling: An information processing approach. *Journal of Counseling Psychology*. 30:139–45.

Cass, V. C. 1979. Homosexual identity formation: A theoretical model. *Journal of Homosexuality*. 4:219–35.

Cavanagh, M. E. 1982. *The Counseling Experience: A Theoretical and Practical Approach*. Monterey, Calif.: Brooks/Cole.

Clark, D. 1977. *Loving Someone Gay*. New York: Signet.

Cloninger, R. C. 1987. Neurogenetic adaptive mechanisms in alcoholism. *Science*. 236:410–16.

Coleman, E., and Remafedi, G. 1989. Gay, lesbian, and bisexual adolescents: A critical challenge to counselors. *Journal of Counseling and Development*. 68:36–40.

Coleman, J. C.; Butcher, J. N.; and Carson, R. C. 1984. *Abnormal Psychology and Modern Life*. 7th ed. Glenview, Ill.: Scott, Foresman.

Colgon, P. 1987. Treatment of identity and intimacy issues in gay males. *Journal of Homosexuality*. 14:101–23.

Colgon, P., and Riebel, J. 1981. *Sexuality Education for Foster Parents*. Minneapolis: University of Minnesota.

Condiotte, M. M., and Lichtenstein, E. 1981. "Self-efficacy and relapse in smoking cessation programs." *Journal of Consulting and Clinical Psychology*. 49:648–58.

Corey, G. 1995. *Theory and Practice of Counseling and Psychotherapy*. Monterey, Calif.: Brooks, Cole, Faber.

Cotton, N. S. 1979. The familial incidence of alcoholism: A review. *Journal of Studies on Alcoholism*. 40:89–116.

Crawford, D. 1990. *Easing the Ache*. New York: Dutton.

Cross, W. E., Jr. 1971. The Negro-to-Black conversion experience: Toward a psychology of Black liberation. *Black World*. 20 (9):13–27.

Curry, H., and Clifford, D. 1991. *A Legal Guide for Lesbian and Gay Couples*. Berkeley, Calif.: Nolo Press.

Curry, S. G., and Marlatt, G. A. 1986. "Building Self-Confidence, Self-Efficacy and Self-Control." In *Treatment and Prevention of Alcohol Problems*, edited by W. M. Cox. Orlando: Academic Press.

Davis, M.; Robbins, E.; and McKay, M. 1995. *Relaxation and Stress Reduction Workbook*. 4th ed. Oakland, Calif.: New Harbinger Publications.

DeCrescenzo, T. A. 1984. Homophobia: A study of the attitudes of mental health professionals toward homosexuality. *Journal of Social Work and Human Sexuality*. 2:115–36.

Delaney, M., and Goldblum, P. 1987. *Strategies for Survival*. New York: St. Martin's Press.

DiClemente, C. C. 1981. Self-efficacy and smoking-cessation maintenance: A preliminary report. *Cognitive Therapy and Research*. 5:175–87.

———. 1986. Self-efficacy and the addictive behaviors; Special Issue: Self-efficacy theory in contemporary psychology. *Journal of Social and Clinical Psychology*. 4:302–15.

Dinwiddie, S. H., and Cloninger, C. R. 1991. Family and adoption studies in alcoholism and drug addiction. *Psychiatric Annals*. 21:206–14.

Donovan, D. M., and Chaney, E. F. 1985. "Alcohol Relapse Prevention and Intervention: Models and Methods." In *Relapse Prevention: Maintenance Strategies in the Treatment of Addictive Behaviors*, edited by G. A. Marlatt and J. R. Gordon. New York: Guilford Press.

Eldridge, N. S. 1987. Gender issues in counseling same-sex couples. *Professional Psychology: Research and Practice*. 18:552–57.

Faderman, L. 1984. The "new gay" lesbians. *Journal of Homosexuality*. 10:85–95.

———. 1991. *Odd Girls and Twilight Lovers: A History of Lesbian Life in Twentieth-century America*. New York: Columbia University Press.

Falco, K. L. 1991. *Psychotherapy with Lesbian Clients: Theory into Practice*. New York: Brunner/Mazel.

Fassinger, R. E. 1991. The hidden minority: Issues and challenges in working with lesbian women and gay men. *The Counseling Psychologist*. 19:157–76.

Fingarette, H. 1988. *Heavy Drinking: The Myth of Alcoholism as a Disease*. Berkeley, Calif.: University of California Press.

Finnegan, D. G., and McNally, E. B. 1987. *Dual Identities*. Center City, Minn.: Hazelden.

Flavin, D. K., and Morse, R. M. 1991. What is alcoholism? Current definitions and diagnostic criteria and their implications for treatment. *Alcohol Health and Research World*. 15:266–71.

Fortunato, J. 1982. *Embracing the Exile: Healing Journeys of Gay Christians*. San Francisco: Harper and Row.

———. 1987. *AIDS: The Spiritual Dilemma*. San Francisco: Harper and Row.

Fossum, M. 1989. *Catching Fire*. San Francisco: Harper/Hazelden.

Foy, D. W.; Nunn, L. B.; and Rychtarik, R. G. 1984. Broad-spectrum behavioral treatment for chronic alcoholics: Effects of training controlled drinking skills. *Journal of Consulting and Clinical Psychology*. 52:218–30.

Fricke, A. 1981. *Reflections of a Rock Lobster*. Boston: Alyson Publications.

Fricke, A. and Fricke, W. 1991. *Suddenly Strangers*. New York: St. Martin's Press.

Garber, M. 1995. *Vice Versa*. New York: Simon and Schuster.

Garfinkel, E. M., and Morin, S. F. 1978. Psychologists' attitudes toward homosexual psychotherapy clients. *Journal of Social Issues*. 34:101–12.

Gartrell, N. 1984. Combating homophobia in the psychotherapy of lesbians. *Women and Therapy*. 3:13–29.

Gilligan, C. 1982. *In a Different Voice*. Cambridge, Mass.: Harvard University Press.

Glaus, K. O. 1989. Alcoholism, chemical dependency and the lesbian client. *Women and Therapy*. 8:131–44.

Golden, C. 1987. "Diversity and Variability in Women's Sexual Identities." In *Lesbian Psychologies*, edited by Boston Lesbian Psychologies Collective. Urbana: University of Illinois.

Gonsiorek, J. C. 1988. Mental health issues of gay and lesbian adolescents. *Journal of Adolescent Health Care*. 9:114–22.

Goodwin, D. W. 1985. Alcoholism and genetics: The sons of our fathers. *Archives of General Psychiatry*. 42:171–74.

Gorski, T. T. 1989. *Passages Through Recovery*. San Francisco: Harper/Hazelden.

Graham, D. L. R.; Rawlings, E.; Halpern, H. S.; and Hermes, J. 1984. Therapists' needs for training in counseling lesbians and gay men. *Professional Psychology: Research and Practice*. 15:492–96.

Gramick, J. 1984. "Developing a Lesbian Identity." In *Women-Identified Women*, edited by T. Darty and S. Potter. Palo Alto, Calif.: Mayfield.

Halpern, H. M. 1982. *How to Break Your Addiction to a Person*. New York: McGraw-Hill.

Harford, T. C., Haack, M. R., and Spiegler, D. L. 1987/1988. Positive family history for alcoholism. *Alcohol Health and Research World*. 12:138–43.

Harry, J. 1983. "Gay Male and Lesbian Family Relationships." In *Contemporary Families and Alternative Lifestyles: Handbook on Research and Theory*, edited by E. D. Macklin and R. H. Rubin. Beverly Hills, Calif.: Sage.

Hart, S. 1988. *Rehab: A Comprehensive Guide*. New York: Harper and Row.

Heather, N. 1989. "Brief Intervention Strategies." In *Handbook of Alcoholism Treatment Approaches: Effective Alternatives*, edited by R. K. Hester and W. R. Miller. New York: Pergamon Press.

Heather, N., and Robertson, I. 1983. *Controlled Drinking*. Cambridge, England: University Press.

Helms, J. E. 1990. "An Overview of Black Racial Identity Theory." In *Black and White Racial Identity: Theory, Research, and Practice*, edited by J. E. Helms. Westport, Conn.: Greenwood Press.

Herek, G. M. 1989. Hate crimes against lesbians and gay men: Issues for research and policy. *American Psychologist*. 44:948–55.

Hooker, E. 1957. The adjustment of the male overt homosexual. *Journal of Projective Techniques*. 21:18–31.

Humphreys, K.; Moos, R. H.; and Finney, J. W. 1995. Two pathways out of drinking problems without professional treatment. *Addictive Behaviors*. 20:427–41.

Hutchins, L., and Kaahumanu, L., eds. 1991. Overview, in *BI Any Other Name*. Boston: Alyson Publications.

Iasenza, S., and Troutt, B. V. 1990. A training program to diminish prejudicial attitudes in student leaders. *Journal of College Student Development*. 31:83–84.

Imber, S.; Schultz, E.; Funderburk, F.; Allen, R.; and Flamer, R. 1976. The fate of the untreated alcoholic: Toward a natural history of the disorder. *Journal of Nervous and Mental Disease*. 162:238–47.

Isay, R. A. 1989. *Being Homosexual: Gay Men and Their Development*. New York: Giroux.

Jaffe, J. H. 1980. "Drug Addiction and Drug Abuse." In *The Pharmacological Basis of Therapeutics*, 6th ed., edited by A. G. Gilman, L. S. Goodman, and A. Gilman. New York: Macmillan.

Jellinek, E. M. 1952. Phases of alcohol addiction. *Quarterly Journal of Studies on Alcohol*. 13:673–38.

———. 1960. *The Disease Concept of Alcoholism*. New Haven, Conn.: College and University Press.

———. 1971. "Phases of Alcohol Addiction." In *Studies in Abnormal Behavior*, edited by G. D. Shean, 86–98. Chicago: Rand McNally.

Johnson, S. 1985. *Characterological Transformation: The Hard Work Miracle*. New York: Norton.

Johnson, S. 1989. *Wildfire: Igniting the She/Volution*. Albuquerque: Wildfire Books.

Katz, J. 1978. *Gay American History*. New York: Discus.

Keller, M. 1976. The disease concept of alcoholism revisited. *Journal of Studies on Alcoholism*. 37:1694–1717.

Kinsey, A. C.; Pomeroy, W. B.; Martin, C. E.; and Gebbhard, P. H. 1953. *Sexual Behavior in the Human Female*. Philadelphia: W. B. Saunders.

Kirkpatrick, J. 1978. *Turnabout: Help for a New Life*. New York: Doubleday.

Kishline, A. 1994. *Moderate Drinking: The Moderation Management™ Guide for People Who Want to Reduce Their Drinking*. New York: Crown Trade Paperbacks.

Kitchener, K. S. 1984. Intuition, critical evaluation, and ethical principles: The foundation of ethical decisions in counseling psychology. *The Counseling Psychologist*. 12:43–55.

———. 1985. "Ethical Principles and Ethical Decisions in Student Affairs." In *Applied Ethics in Student Services*, edited by H. Canon and R. Brown. San Francisco: Jossey-Bass.

Klein, F. 1978. *The Bisexual Option*. New York: Arbor House.

Klein, F.; Sepekoff, B.; and Wolf, T. 1985. "Sexual Orientation: A Multi-variable Dynamic Process. In *Two Lives to Lead: Bisexuality in Men and Women*, edited by F. Klein and T. Wolf, 35–50. New York: Harrington Park.

Kominars, S. B. 1995. Homophobia: The Heart of the Darkness. *Journal of Gay and Lesbian Social Services*. 2(1):29–39.

Kopp, S. 1976. *If You Meet The Buddha On the Road, Kill Him!* New York: Bantam.

———. 1978. *An End to Innocence*. New York: Bantam.

Kurtz, E. 1988. *A.A.: The Story*. San Francisco: Harper/Hazelden.

Larsen, E. 1985. *Stage II Recovery: Life Beyond Addiction*. San Francisco: Harper and Row.

———. 1987. *Stage II Recovery: Relationships*. San Francisco: Harper and Row.

Lewis, D. C. 1991. Comparison of alcoholism and other medical diseases: An internist's view. *Psychiatric Annals*. 21:256–65.

Lewis, L. A. 1984. The coming out process for lesbians: Integrating a stable identity. *Social Work*. Sept.–Oct.:464–69.

Lindbergh, A. M. 1955. *Gift from the Sea*. New York: Random House.

Living Sober. 1975. New York: Alcoholics Anonymous World Services.

Loulan, J. 1984. *Lesbian Sex*. San Francisco: Spinsters Ink.

Marcia, J. E. 1966. Development and validation of ego identity statuses. *Journal of Personality and Social Psychology*. 3:557–58.

———. 1980. "Identity in Adolescence." In *Handbook of Adolescent Psychology*, edited by J. Adelson. New York: John Wiley and Sons.

Marconi, J. T. 1959. The concept of alcoholism. *Quarterly Journal of Studies on Alcohol*. 20:216–35.

Marcus, E. 1993. *Is It a Choice?* San Francisco: Harper/Collins.

Markowitz, L. M. 1994. When same-sex couples divorce. *The Family Therapy Networker*. May/June:31–33.

Marlatt, G. A. 1978. "Craving for Alcohol, Loss of Control, and Relapse: A Cognitive-behavioral Analysis." In *Alcoholism: New Directions in Behavioral Research and Treatment*, edited by P. E. Nathan, G. A. Marlatt, and T. Loberg. New York: Plenum.

———. 1985a. "Cognitive Assessment and Intervention Procedures for Relapse Prevention." In *Relapse Prevention*, edited by G. A. Marlatt and J. R. Gordon. New York: Guilford Press.

————. 1985b. "Relapse Prevention: Theoretical Rationale and Overview of the Model." In *Relapse Prevention: Maintenance Strategies in the Treatment of Addictive Behaviors*, edited by G. A. Marlatt and J. R. Gordon. New York: Guilford Press.

————. 1990. Cue exposure and relapse prevention in the treatment of addictive behaviors. *Addictive Behaviors*. 15:395–99.

Marlatt, G. A., and George, W. H. 1984. Relapse prevention: Introduction and overview of the model. *British Journal of Addictions*. 79:261–73.

Marlatt, G. A., and Gordon, J. R. 1980. "Determinants of Relapse: Implications for the Maintenance of Behavior Change." In *Behavioral Medicine: Changing Health Lifestyles*, edited by P. O. Davidson and S. M. Davidson. New York: Brunner/Mazel.

————. 1985. *Relapse Prevention*. New York: Guilford Press.

Marotta, T. 1982. *Sons of Harvard*. New York: William Morrow.

McCarn, S. R., and Fassinger, R. E. 1990. Development of a model of sexual minority identity development. Unpublished manuscript, University of Maryland. Cited in R. E. Fassinger's (1991) article.

McLellan, A. T.; Luborsky, L.; and O'Brien, C. P. 1980. An improved evaluation instrument for substance abuse patients: The Addiction Severity Index. *Journal of Nervous and Mental Disorders*. 168:26–33.

McKay, M.; Rogers, P. D.; and McKay, J. 1989. *When Anger Hurts*. Oakland, Calif.: New Harbinger Publications.

McNaught, B. 1981. *A Disturbed Peace*. Washington, D.C.: Dignity.

McWhirter, D. P., and Mattison, A. M. 1984. *The Male Couple*. Englewood Cliffs, N.J.: Prentice-Hall.

Mellody, P., and Miller, A. W. 1989. *Breaking Free: A Recovery Workbook for Facing CoDependence*. San Francisco: Harper and Row.

Mendola, M. 1980. *The Mendola Report*. New York: Crown Publishers.

Miller, N. 1989. *In Search of Gay America*. New York: Atlantic Monthly Press.

Miller, N. S., and Chappel, J. N. 1991. History of the disease concept. *Psychiatric Annals*. 21:196–205.

Miller, W. R. 1983. Controlled drinking: A history and critical review. *Journal of Studies on Alcohol*. 44:68–82.

Monti, P. M.; Abrams, D. B.; Kadden, R. M.; and Cooney, N. L. 1989. *Treating Alcohol Dependence: A Coping Skills Training Guide*. New York: Guilford Press.

Moore, T. 1992. *Care of the Soul*. New York: HarperCollins.

Mueller, L. A., and Ketcham, K. 1987. *Recovering: How to Get and Stay Sober*. New York: Bantam Books.

Narcotics Anonymous, It Works: How and Why. 1987. Van Nuys, Calif.: World Service Conference Literature Committee.

Narrow, W. E.; Regier, D. A.; Rae, D. S.; Manderscheid, R. W.; and Locke, B. Z. 1993. Use of services by persons with mental and addictive disorders. *Archives of General Psychiatry*. 50:95–107.

Nathan, P. 1985. Alcoholism: A cognitive social learning approach. *Journal of Substance Abuse Treatment*. 2:169–73.

National Institute on Alcohol Abuse and Alcoholism (NIAAA). 1995. *Assessing Alcohol Problems: A Guide for Clinicians and Researchers*. Publication No. 95–3745. Washington, D. C.: National Institute of Health.

Noble, E. P. 1991. Genetic studies in alcoholism: CNS functioning and molecular biology. *Psychiatric Annals*. 21:215–29.

Orford, J., and Keddie, A. 1986. Abstinence or controlled drinking. *British Journal of Addiction*. 81:495–504.

Padesky, C. 1989. Attaining and maintaining positive lesbian self-identity: A cognitive therapy approach. *Women and Therapy*. 8:145–56.

Paroski, P.A. 1987. Health care delivery and the concerns of gay and lesbian adolescents. *Journal of Adolescent Health Care*. 8:188–92.

Paulsen, J. 1983. Homophobia in American psychiatrists. Paper presented to the Group for the Advancement of Psychiatry, Philadelphia, cited in R. E. Fassinger's (1991) article.

Peele, S. 1984. The cultural context of psychological approaches to alcoholism. *American Psychologist*. 39:1337–51.

Pharr, S. 1988. *Homophobia: A Weapon of Sexism*. Little Rock, Ark.: Chardon Press.

Picucci, M. 1996. *Complete Recovery*. New York: Mombaccus Publications.

Polich, J. M.; Armor, D. J.; and Braiker, H. B. 1980. *The Course of Alcoholism: Four Years after Treatment*. Santa Monica, Calif.: Rand Corporation.

Ponse, B. 1978. *Identities in the Lesbian World*. Westport, Conn.: Greenwood.

Prochaska, J. O.; DiClemente, C. C.; and Norcross, J. C. 1992. In search of how people change: Applications to addictive behaviors. *American Psychologist*. 47:1101–14.

Ramsey, P. 1970. *The Patient as Person*. New Haven, Conn.: Yale University Press.

Rist, F., and Watzl, H. 1983. Self-assessment of relapse risk and assertiveness in relation to treatment outcome of female alcoholics. *Addictive Behaviors*. 8:121–27.

Robertson, N. 1988. *Getting Better: Inside Alcoholics Anonymous*. New York: William Morrow.

Robson, E., and Edwards, G. 1980. *Getting Help: A Woman's Guide to Therapy*. New York: Dutton.

Rosenberg, H. 1993. Prediction of controlled drinking by alcoholics and problem drinkers. *Psychological Bulletin*. 113:129–39.

Ross, S. M.; Miller, P. J.; Emmerson, R. Y.; and Todt, E. H. 1990. Self-efficacy, standards, and abstinence violation: A comparison between newly sober and long-term sober alcoholics. *Journal of Substance Abuse*. 1:221–29.

Rudolph, J. 1989. The impact of contemporary ideology and AIDS on the counseling of gay clients. *Counseling and Values*. 33:96–108.

Rush, B. 1814. *An Inquiry in the Effects of Ardent Spirits upon the Human Body and Mind*. South Waterford, Maine: Merriam and Co.

————. 1834. *Medical Inquiries and Observations upon the Diseases of the Mind*. New York: Doubleday.

Russell, P. 1995. *The Gay 100*. New York: Citadel Press.

Schaef, A. W. 1987. *When Society Becomes an Addict*. San Francisco: Harper and Row.

Schneider, M. S., and Tremble, B. 1986. Training service providers to work with gay or lesbian adolescents: A workshop. *Journal of Counseling and Development*. 65:98–99.

Schuckit, M. A. 1986. Genetic and clinical implications of alcoholism and affective disorders. *American Journal of Psychiatry*. 143:140–7.

Schuckit, M. A., and Rayses, V. 1979. Ethanol ingestion: Differences in blood acetaldehyde concentrations in relatives of alcoholics and controls. *Science*. 203:54–55.

Searles, J. S. 1988. The role of genetics in the pathogenesis of alcoholism. *Journal of Abnormal Psychology*. 97:153–67.

Shannon, J. W., and Woods, W. J. 1991. Affirmative psychotherapy for gay men. *The Counseling Psychologist*. 19:197–215.

Shilts, R. 1987. *And the Band Played On*. New York: St. Martin's Press.

————. 1993. *Conduct Unbecoming*. New York: St. Martin's Press.

Silverstein, C. 1982. *Man to Man*. New York: Quill.

Slater, B. R. 1988. Essential issues in working with lesbian and gay male youths. *Professional Psychology: Research and Practice*. 19:226–35.

Small, J. 1981. *Becoming Naturally Therapeutic*. Austin, Tex.: Eupsychian Press.

Sobell, M. B., and Sobell, L. C. 1993a. "Treatment for Problem Drinkers: A Public Health Priority." In *Addictive Behaviors Across the Life Span: Prevention, Treatment and Policy Issues*, edited by J. S. Baer, G. A. Marlatt, and R. J. McMahan. Newbury Park, Calif.: Sage.

————. 1993b. *Problem Drinkers: Guided Self-Change Treatment*. New York: Guilford Press.

Sobell, L. C.; Sobell, M. B.; and Toneatto, T. 1992. "Recovery from Alcohol Problems without Treatment." In *Self-control and Addictive Behaviors*, edited by N. Heather, W. R. Miller, and J. Greely, 198–242. New York: Macmillan.

Solomon, K. E., and Annis, H. M. 1990. Outcome and efficacy expectancy in the prediction of post-treatment drinking behavior. *British Journal of Addiction*. 85:659–65.

Sontag, S. 1988. *AIDS and Its Metaphors*. New York: Farrar, Straus and Giroux.

Standard, R., and Hazler, R. 1995. Legal and ethical implications of HIV and duty to warn for counselors: Does *Tarasoff* apply? *Journal of Counseling and Development*. 73:397–400.

Swallow, J., ed. 1983. *Out from Under: Sober Dykes and Our Friends*. San Francisco: Spinsters Ink.

Teague, J. B. 1992. Issues relating to the treatment of adolescent lesbians and homosexuals. *Journal of Mental Health Counseling*. 14:422–29.

Tessina, T. 1991. *The Real Thirteenth Step*. New York: Tarcher/Perigee.

Twelve Steps and Twelve Traditions. 1952, 1953, 1981. New York: Alcoholics Anonymous World Services.

Vaillant, G. E. 1983. *The Natural History of Alcoholism: Causes, Patterns, and Paths to Recovery.* Cambridge, Mass.: Harvard University Press.

Wadsworth, R.; Spampneto, A. M.; and Halbrook, B. M. 1995. The role of sexual trauma in the treatment of chemically dependent women: Addressing the relapse issue. *Journal of Counseling and Development.* 73:401–6.

Wakelee-Lynch, J. 1989. Gay and lesbian youths face danger and isolation. *Guidepost.* 32:1, 4, 7.

Wegscheider-Cruse, S. 1985. *Choicemaking.* Pompano Beach, Fla.: Health Communications.

Weinberg, M. S.; Williams, C. J.; Pryor, D. W. 1994. *Dual Attraction.* Oxford and New York: Oxford University Press.

Willerman, L., and Cohen, D. B. 1990. *Psychopathology.* New York: McGraw-Hill.

Woititz, J. G. 1983. *Adult Children of Alcoholics.* Pompano Beach, Fla.: Health Communications.

———. 1989. *Healing Your Sexual Self.* Deerfield Beach, Fla.: Health Communications.

Wolf, J. G., ed. 1989. *Gay Priests.* San Francisco: Harper and Row.

Wolfe, S. J., and Stanley, J. P., eds. 1980. *The Coming Out Stories.* Watertown, Mass.: Persephone Press.

Woodman, N. J., and Lenna, H. R. 1980. *Counseling with Gay Men and Women.* San Francisco: Jossey-Bass.

World Health Organization. 1967. *Manual of the International Statistical Classification of Diseases, Injuries, and Causes of Death.* Albany, N.Y.: Q Corp.

Yates, A. J., and Thain, J. 1985. Self-efficacy as a predictor of relapse following voluntary cessation of smoking. *Addictive Behaviors.* 10:291–98.

Ziebold, T. O. 1978. *Alcoholism and the Gay Community.* Washington, D. C.: Blade Communications.

Zigrang, T. A. 1982. Who should be doing what about the gay alcoholic? *Alcoholism and Homosexuality.* 35:27–35.

At the time of this publication, access to sources of information for gays, lesbians, and bisexuals is developing at such an incredible rate that many of these suggestions may already be out-of-date. The national sites listed will refer you to specific resources in your area of the country. We encourage anyone seeking professional counseling or other assistance regarding recovery from addictive/compulsive behavior or information on gay/lesbian/bisexual issues, as well as opportunities to interact with others interested in these areas, to explore additional references.

Access to these sources is through written requests, telephone, fax, and Internet communication. Hazelden, our publisher, has a Web page address on the World Wide Web that will provide on-line access to all of its publications, including *Accepting Ourselves and Others*.

The Hazelden address is: **http://www.hazelden.org**

Accepting Ourselves and Others also has a Web page of its own for interactive reader response at: **http://sibyllineofbooks.com/acceptingourselves.html**

Accessing Local Resources for Your Needs

The obvious place to begin your search for resources is with the Yellow Pages of the local telephone directory. "Gay and Lesbian Organization" may be listed in your area and you might explore this first. In addition, the Yellow Pages in your city may list Mental Health Services; Psychologists; Physicians: Psychiatry; Social Service Organizations; Alcoholism Information and Treatment Centers; Drug Abuse and Addiction Information and Treatment Centers; Crisis Intervention Services; Women's Organizations and Services.

The *GAYELLOW PAGES*, published by Renaissance House, Box 533, Village Station, New York, NY 10014-0533 has extensive listings in all categories for the United States and Canada. It is available in bookstores. Many cities also publish local gay/lesbian/bisexual weekly or monthly newspapers that list service providers, care facilities, Twelve Step meetings, and social opportunities. Local or regional consumer directories are an additional source for information.

(*The Canadian Women's Directory*, 3585 St. Urbain, Montreal, QC H2X 2N6; (514) 844-1761; this directory lists over 2,000 women's groups. *The Bisexual Resource Guide*, P.O. Box 391611, Cambridge, MA 01239; e-mail: Ochs@world.std.com.)

National Referral Resources

[IAC] The International Advisory Council for Homosexual Men and Women in Alcoholics Anonymous, Inc., P.O. Box 18212, Washington, D.C. 20036-8212, provides lists of Twelve Step meetings for gays and lesbians in the United States and abroad.

[NALGAP] The National Association of Lesbian and Gay Alcoholism Professionals, 1208 East State Boulevard, Fort Wayne, IN 46805; (219) 483-8280, provides counseling referrals. Their clearinghouse address is NALGAP, 204 West 20th Street, New York, NY 10011; (212) 807-0634. This association is actively involved in the gay and lesbian recovery field.

Gay and Lesbian National Organizations Providing Health and Legal Information

Lambda Legal Defense and Education Fund . . . . (212) 995-8585

National Gay and Lesbian Task Force . . . . (202) 332-6483

National Lesbian and Gay Health Foundation . . . . (202) 797-3708

Other National Information Health and Recovery Resources

Adult Children of Alcoholics World Service Org. . . . . (310) 534-1815

Al-Anon Family Groups *(general information)* . . . . (800) 356-9996

Alcoholics Anonymous World Services, Inc. . . . . (212) 870-3400

BiNet USA. . . . . (202) 986-7186
P.O. Box 7327
Langely Park, MD 20787-7327
e-mail: Virago@slip.net

Bisexual Resource Center *(international listings)*
P.O. Box 639
Cambridge, MA 02140
e-mail: BRC@panix.com

Canadian AIDS society . . . . (613) 230-3580

National AIDS Clearinghouse. . . . . (800) 458-5231

National AIDS Hotline. . . . . (800) 342-AIDS
(Spanish) (800) 344-7432
(Hearing Impaired) (800) 243-7889

National Center for Sexually Transmitted Diseases. . . . . (800) 227-8922

National Clearinghouse for Alcohol and Drug Information . . . . (800) 729-6686

P-Flag (Parents and Friends of Lesbians and Gays). . . . . (202) 638-4200

Gay and Lesbian Inpatient Facility for Recovery from Addictive/Compulsive Behavior

Pride Institute . . . . (800) 547-7433
14400 Martin Drive
Eden Prairie, MN 55344

Outpatient Facilities

Call your local community center. For a listing of lesbian and gay community centers by state, contact "The NY City Lesbian and Gay Center" on the World Wide Web: **http://www.panix.com/~dhuppert/gay/center/**

National Associations Providing Counseling Referral

American Association for Marriage and Family Therapy
133 15th Street NW Suite 300
Washington, D.C. 20005-2710
(Send stamped/self-addressed envelope to receive referral.)

American Counseling Association . . . . (703) 823-9800, ext. 222
    5999 Stevenson Avenue
    Alexandria, VA 22304-3300
        (A new affiliate has just formed: Association for Gays, Lesbians and Bisexuals in Counseling. Request listing.)
American Psychological Association . . . . (202) 336-5500
    750 First Street NE   *(Gay and lesbian issues)* (202) 336-6037
    Washington, D.C. 20002-4242

World Wide Web Addresses for Recovery from Addiction

Access to the Recovery Home Page for information about any of the Twelve Step recovery programs is through: **http://www.shore.net/~tcfraser/recover.html**

Web sites include these Twelve Step programs and chat groups

Adult Children of Alcoholics	Emotions Anonymous
Al-Anon	Food Addicts Anonymous
Alateen	Gamblers Anonymous
Alcoholics Anonymous	Incest Survivors Anonymous
A.R.T.S. Anonymous	Narcotics Anonymous
Cocaine Anonymous	Nicotine Anonymous
Codependents Anonymous	Overeaters Anonymous
Codependents of Sex Addicts	Sex and Love Addicts Anonymous
Co-Sex and Love Addicts Anonymous	Workaholics Anonymous.
Debtors Anonymous	

Through the Recovery Home Page, it is also possible to access specialized groups—such as Christians, Jews, and Dignity/USA—as well as professional groups (pharmacists, psychologists, clergy, anesthetists, dentists, lawyers, doctors, nurses, realtors, athletes, academics), bisexual, gay, and lesbian youth; children of lesbians and gays; gay and lesbian parents; and Rainbow Alliance of the Deaf.

We suggest you use this information as a starting place to explore the specific kind of assistance you desire. At the same time we encourage you to explore these suggestions, we also believe it is equally important to check out carefully each one to determine how well it meets your needs.

Dignity, 110
diversity, 59, 298-99, 341, 346
divorce, 336
Doctor Bob, 200
dual relationships, 329

F
family, 22, 34-36, 41, 78, 91, 113, 146, 185,
    201, 223, 233, 239, 316, 328
Fortunato, John, 33

G
Grapevine, 94
"Guided Self-Change," 10, 315

H
health insurance, 9, 11, 12, 46, 341
heterosexism, 41, 144, 321, 325-26, 346
Higher Power, 29-30, 93-94, 110-11,
    202-4, 270, 275, 287, 311
homophobia, 19-21, 40-44, 219, 246,
    320-30
    unresolved, 326-27

I
identity development, 331-34

J
Jellinek's classification, 15-16, 316
    Alpha alcoholism, 15
    Beta alcoholism, 15
    Delta alcoholism, 15-16
    Epsilon alcoholism, 16
    Gamma alcoholism, 15
Jung, Carl, 94

K
Kinsey's scale, 323-24
Klein Sexual Orientation Grid, 324

L
legal issues, 38, 321-23
living-through, 63, 237, 240-41, 256, 289

M
Moderation Management, 10, 315

N
National Institute on Alcohol Abuse and
    Alcoholism, 14, 40
neurosis, 48
Niebuhr, Reinhold, 116

P
paradox, 88, 94-95, 272-73, 299
perfectionism, 111-12, 210, 257-59
Picucci, Michael, 53
"pink cloud," 168
Pride Institute, 13
problem drinking, 16-17, 310-11
Project Oasis, 110
psychopathology, 341
psychosis, 48
psychotherapists, 43-51, 52-57, 309-51
    certified addiction or alcoholism
        counselors, 48-49
    certified mental health counselors, 48
    clinical and counseling psychologists,
        47
    marital and family counselors, 48
    psychiatrists, 48
    psychologists, 47
    Psy.D.'s, 47
    social workers, 48

R
racial/ethnic issues, 327-29
relapse prevention, 7, 16, 312
religion, 9, 42, 92, 110, 112, 288
reorientation therapy, 32

S
"S & M," 327
self-esteem, 8, 39, 42, 147, 186, 197-99,
    201-3, 219, 223, 241, 275, 312, 313
social drinking, 16, 310-11
spiritual abuse, 9, 30, 92, 110, 272, 345
spiritual awakening 111, 289-90
sponsors, 114-16, 144, 150, 168-70, 188, 253
suffering, 42, 75, 90, 109, 162-64, 222
support group, 43, 90
survival tactics, 150, 164, 183, 211, 220

A father and daughter team, both Sheppard and Kathryn Kominars are active workshop and seminar facilitators. Sheppard Kominars is a writer and educator in San Francisco. Kathryn Kominars is a practicing therapist who also teaches in Fort Lauderdale, Florida. They have done seminars and workshops all over the United States for professionals and clients.

Sheppard Kominars received a B.A. from Kenyon College, an M.A. from Columbia University, and a Ph.D. from Boston University. He served as a consultant to the Episcopal Bishops of Pennsylvania and the California Special Subcommittee on Alcoholism and Substance Abuse. He has been Dean of City College in Chicago and vice president of several universities. Sheppard Kominars has a private practice in San Francisco.

Kathryn Kominars received a B.A. from St. John's College, a M.Ed. from Temple University, and a Ph.D. from Temple University. She is a certified addictions counselor and is finishing a post-doctoral residence in brief psychotherapy. As a therapist, Kathryn Kominars has done clinical work with diverse clients since 1985.